KING LEAR

William Shakespeare

The Tragedy of King Lear

With Classic and Contemporary Criticisms

Edited by Joseph Pearce

IGNATIUS PRESS SAN FRANCISCO

Cover art:
James Barry, *King Lear Weeping over the Body of Cordelia.*
Tate Gallery, London.

Photo Credit: Tate, London / Art Resource, N.Y.

Cover design by John Herreid

ISBN 978-1-58617-137-7
Library of Congress Control Number 2007927192
Printed in the United States of America ♾

Tradition is the extension of Democracy through time; it is the proxy of the dead and the enfranchisement of the unborn.

Tradition may be defined as the extension of the franchise. Tradition means giving votes to the most obscure of all classes, our ancestors. It is the democracy of the dead. Tradition refuses to submit to the small and arrogant oligarchy of those who merely happen to be walking about. All democrats object to men being disqualified by the accident of birth; tradition objects to their being disqualified by the accident of death. Democracy tells us not to neglect a good man's opinion, even if he is our groom; tradition asks us not to neglect a good man's opinion, even if he is our father. I, at any rate, cannot separate the two ideas of democracy and tradition.

—G. K. Chesterton

Ignatius Critical Editions—Tradition-Oriented Criticism for a new generation

CONTENTS

KING LEAR: AN INTRODUCTION

R. V. Young
North Carolina State University

For much of the twentieth century *King Lear* was widely regarded as Shakespeare's greatest play and possibly as the greatest tragic drama of all. Although nothing has occurred to alter this judgment, it is important to recall that numerous figures, some of them as distinguished as the great Russian novelist Leo Tolstoy, have found the play vulgar and absurd. More telling, it has often been considered impossible to act and stage successfully. In fact, in 1681 the Restoration hack Nahum Tate (1652–1715) rewrote *King Lear* so that Cordelia survives, marries Edgar, and lives happily ever after as Queen of England. Subsequently, this was the only version of *King Lear* known to have been produced in the theatre until 1838.[1] No less a critic than Dr. Samuel Johnson acquiesced in this preference for "the final triumph of persecuted virtue":

> In the present case the public has decided. Cordelia, from the time of Tate, has always retired with victory and felicity. And, if my sensations could add anything to the general suffrage, I might relate, I was many years ago so shocked by Cordelia's death that I know not whether I ever endured to read again the last scenes of the play till I undertook to revise them as an editor.[2]

In some respects, then, *King Lear* appears insufficiently tragic, tainted by unseemly comedy and the improbabilities of fairy

[1] For a lively account of these familiar matters, see the first chapter of Maynard Mack, *King Lear in Our Time* (Berkeley and Los Angeles: University of California Press, 1965), pp. 3–41.

[2] *Samuel Johnson on Shakespeare*, ed. W. K. Wimsatt, Jr. (New York: Hill and Wang, 1960), p. 98.

tale and romance; viewed from another perspective it seems *all too tragic*, even insupportable in the horror of its ending.

While several earlier generations of actors, directors, and audiences dealt with the terrible catastrophe of the play by romanticizing its dénouement and mitigating its terrors, in the twentieth century remorseless cruelty and violence were emphasized, and *King Lear* was treated as an anticipation of the existentialist nihilism of the Theatre of the Absurd. Productions in the 1950s and '60s stripped away every vestige of dignity and hope, reducing Lear and his allies to the semblance of Samuel Becket's alienated and disoriented characters. An age that had witnessed two devastating world wars and the horrors of Nazi death camps and Soviet show trials and contrived famines seemed to many critics and directors the first truly able to respond to the negation of all order and meaning they found implied in the text of *King Lear*.

Shakespeare wrote the play, however, for an audience that knew as well as modern men and women about the abominable deeds of the wicked and the terrible suffering created by human vice and folly. Yet the actual text of the play suggests that Shakespeare's society still retained the spiritual and moral resources—even if they were then threatened—to contemplate the representation of such evil with neither sentimental evasion nor the cynical despair. *King Lear* dramatizes grand themes: the crisis of natural law and the challenge to Christian belief, which marked the waning of the Renaissance; but it does so within a tale that is intimate and domestic as well as national and political. If, as Chesterton maintains, Saint Thomas Aquinas is the philosopher of common sense and the common man, Shakespeare may not unreasonably be termed playwright of common sense and the common man, for his vision of the human condition assumes that the health of society depends upon the character of the individual men and women it comprises. In *King Lear*, the destruction of a nation and a social order begins in the disordered relations of fathers and their children; lapses of personal virtue lead inexorably to terrifying political consequences.

Interpretation of this complex tragedy may well begin by noticing the obsessive repetition of the words "nature" and "natural" by many of its principal characters in incompatible, even contradictory, senses. In proclaiming to Cordelia's suitors, the King of France and the Duke of Burgundy, that he has just disinherited and disowned her, Lear calls her "a wretch whom nature is ashamed / Almost t'acknowledge hers" (I.i.213–14). The King of France, finding this turn of events "most strange", remarks, "Sure her offense / Must be of such unnatural degree / That monsters it [. . .]" (I.i.214, 219–21). When he quarrels with his eldest daughter, Goneril, he admits that Cordelia's "most small fault [. . .] / like an engine wrenched my frame of nature / From the fixed place, drew from my heart all love / And added to the gall" (I.iv.258–62). He invokes "Nature" as a "dear goddess" to curse his eldest daughter with sterility, so that her physical condition will mirror her moral corruption (I.iv.267ff.). Similarly, the Earl of Gloucester, convinced by his illegitimate son, Edmund, that Edgar, the eldest son and heir, has betrayed his father, calls him an "unnatural, detested, brutish villain" (I.ii.76) and subsequently lauds Edmund as a "loyal and natural boy" (II.i.84).

Calling Edmund "natural" is, however, ironically ambiguous, since a *natural child* could refer either to a legitimate child begotten "naturally" in the course of marriage or to an illegitimate child begotten through mere "natural" inclination—in other words, a bastard, as Edmund literally is.[3] In a powerful soliloquy the guileful Edmund invokes a "goddess" of very different character than the "Nature" upon whom Lear and his father call:

> Thou, Nature, art my goddess; to thy law
> My services are bound. Wherefore should I
> Stand in the plague of custom, and permit
> The curiosity of nations to deprive me?
> For that I am some twelve or fourteen moonshines

[3] *Oxford English Dictionary*, s.v. "natural", III.13.a, c.

Lag of a brother? Why bastard? Wherefore base?
When my dimensions are as well compact,
My mind as generous and my shape as true
As honest madam's issue? Why brand they us
With base? With baseness, bastardy? Base, base?
Who in the lusty stealth of nature take
More composition and fierce quality
Than doth within a dull stale tired bed
Go to the creating of a whole tribe of fops
Got 'tween a sleep and wake. Well, then,
Legitimate Edgar, I must have your land.
Our father's love is to the bastard Edmund
As to the legitmate. Fine word, "legitimate"!
Well, my legitimate, if this letter speed
And my invention thrive, Edmund the base
Shall top the legitimate. I grow, I prosper:
Now gods, stand up for bastards!

(I.ii.1–22)

The seductive vigor of Edmund's rhetoric and the sense that the ignominy and disadvantages of illegitimacy are—especially to a modern audience—unfair create a good deal of initial sympathy for him, despite the fact that he is engaged in a vicious scheme to deceive his father and deprive his brother and endanger his life. Moreover, Edmund's championing of an idea of the *natural* as what is opposed to the merely *conventional* or *traditional* will likewise seem very appealing to contemporary culture, with its bias in favor of the individual and against the rules and strictures of the community, especially whatever is inherited from the past.

Edmund and the characters allied with him may thus be regarded as representing a vision of nature and the law of nature that challenges and threatens what was in Shakespeare's day the more traditional conception of nature and natural law, associated with Lear and Gloucester and the characters who support them. As John F. Danby observes, "The universal playwright, without self-contradiction, can include Hooker and Hobbes in the same play [. . .]. There is a real sense in which *King Lear* incorporates the living parts of both *Ecclesiastical Polity* and *Leviathan*."[4] Danby is indulging in a paradoxical whimsy. Although Shakespeare would certainly have known about the first five books of Richard Hooker's *Of the Laws of Ecclesiastical Polity* (1593, 1597) and may well have read them, Thomas Hobbes's *Leviathan* (1651) did not appear until thirty-five years after the poet's death and nearly half a century after the composition of *King Lear*. Nevertheless, Danby makes a significant point: Hooker's treatise was in Shakespeare's day the most recent articulation of an ancient vision of the human condition that furnished the intellectual foundation for the moral attitudes of Lear and Gloucester, of Kent, Edgar, and Cordelia. It would only be decades later, in the aftermath of a decade of civil war and the beheading of a lawfully anointed king, that the contrary view could be fully and openly proclaimed in a work of serious political philosophy.

In the course of defending the governing hierarchy and liturgical worship of the Church of England from radical puritans, who demanded that every aspect of institutional religion be justified by reference to a specific, literally interpreted passage of Scripture, Hooker invoked the traditional idea that morality is intrinsic to human nature and apprehensible through reason:

> Law rational therefore, which men commonly use to call the law of Nature, meaning thereby the Law which human Nature knoweth itself in reason universally bound unto, which also for that cause may be termed most fitly the Law of Reason; this Law, I say, comprehendeth all those things which men by the light of their natural understanding evidently know, or at leastwise may know, to be beseeming or unbeseeming, virtuous or vicious, good or evil for them to do.
>
> (I.viii.9)

Hooker is elaborating the idea of moral absolutes emerging from the kind of creatures that human beings are in essence. This

[4] John F. Danby, *Shakespeare's Doctrine of Nature: A Study of* King Lear (London: Faber and Faber, 1948), p. 18.

idea can be found in classical thinkers like Plato, Aristotle, and Cicero as well as in the Bible when, for instance, Saint Paul maintains that even pagans, to whom the Law has not been revealed, "show the work of the law written in their hearts" (Rom 2:15, KJV).

Hooker's most important source, however, may have been Saint Thomas Aquinas, who distinguishes between the great generality of created beings, which follow the law of their natures necessarily and without reflection, and a rational creature, who actually "participates in the eternal reason, through which he has a natural inclination toward the fitting act and purpose. And such participation in the eternal law in a rational creature is called natural law."[5] We should bear in mind that this traditional conception of law differs greatly in tone from its modern counterpart, as Danby explains: "The law it [the Elizabethan community] observed was felt more as self-expression than as external restraint. It was a law, in any case, which the creature was most itself when it obeyed. And rebellion against this law was rebellion against one's self, loss of all nature, lapse into chaos."[6]

Little more than fifty years later, Thomas Hobbes was proclaiming a contradictory vision of human nature and the human condition in which law was conceived as a set of arbitrarily imposed rules aimed at controlling unbridled human nature and saving men from the anarchy of their own desires. The natural state of humanity, he insists in *Leviathan*, is "that condition which is called war, and such a war as is of every man against every man" (I.xiii.8–9). In this "state of nature" before the imposition of laws by a sovereign power, there is only "continual fear and danger of violent death, and the life of man, solitary, poor, nasty, brutish, and short".[7] Moreover, Hobbes does not see human nature as essentially rational with a definite purpose or end:

[5] *Summa Theologiae* I–II, 91, 3: "Unde et in ipsa participatur ratio aeterna, per quam habet naturalem inclinationem ad debitum actum et finem. Et talis participatio legis aeternae in rationali creatura lex naturalis dicitur."

[6] Danby, *Shakespeare's Doctrine of Nature*, p. 25.

[7] *Leviathan*, ed. Edwin Curley (Indianapolis/Cambridge: Hackett Publishing, 1994), p. 76.

> For there is no such *Finis ultimus* (utmost aim) nor *Summum Bonum* (greatest good) as is spoken of in the books of the old moral philosophers. Nor can a man any more live, whose desires are at an end, than he whose senses and imaginations are at a stand. Felicity is a continual progress of the desire, from one object to another, the attaining of the former being still but the way to the latter.[8]

Although Hobbes is writing long after the first performances of *King Lear*, the ideas he so forcibly articulates were already in the air during Shakespeare's lifetime. They are implicit in the amoral politics of Machiavelli; the French essayist Montaigne toys with such ideas; they are darkly expounded by Giordano Bruno; yet their influence in late Renaissance society is perhaps most visible in the numerous attacks by orthodox thinkers on what they perceived to be rampant atheism. Hobbes is simply the first to lay out in cold rationalistic prose the moral relativism associated with a thoroughly materialist view of human nature.

Shakespeare's outstanding achievement is to have dramatized the consequences of this philosophy, nearly fifty years before Hobbes so clearly expounded it, in the characters and actions of representative human beings. Edmund, Goneril, and Regan—and in a cruder way, Cornwall—are embodiments of a materialist interpretation of humanity that substitutes for natural law a Renaissance *naturalism*, which in many ways anticipates by more than two centuries Darwin's notion of natural selection and the survival of the fittest. Nevertheless, *King Lear* is neither an allegory nor a simple morality tale. Edmund, Goneril, and Regan are not mere personifications of vices like cruelty, ambition, and greed; and the philosophy that they in some sense embody was gaining adherents in Shakespeare's day and could claim the approval of much enlightened opinion in the modern world. While it is true that by the end of the tragedy, these three have unleashed an orgy of betrayal, brutality, and murder, for at least the first two acts they can claim to have

[8] I. xi. 1, in ibid., p. 57.

been intolerably provoked, and Lear's two daughters even maintain a semblance of respectability. By the same token the good characters are not altogether or unambiguously good. The brave and faithful Kent perhaps shows excess pride in his pugnacious dealings with Oswald and certainly imprudence, harming his master's cause more than he helps it. Kent even admits that he had "more man than wit" about him when he "drew" on Oswald (II.ii.40). Gloucester's loyal son Edgar seems hopelessly obtuse at first, and then he seems to trifle with his father's misery when he convinces him that he has miraculously survived a leap off the cliff at Dover. Looking down upon the illegitimate brother whom he has mortally wounded, he recalls their father:

> The gods are just and of our pleasant vices
> Make instruments to plague us:
> The dark and vicious place where thee he got
> Cost him his eyes.
>
> (V.iii.168–71)

Some critics find nothing in this but harsh self-righteousness, but it may with equal reason be reckoned grim moral realism. Even Cordelia, who becomes a figure of luminous charity, may with some show of plausibility be faulted for obstinacy in the first scene: Why not swallow her pride, tell her aged father what he wishes to hear, and spare everyone the horrors that follow?

At the center of the drama is of course King Lear himself, whose tragedy has an analogue in the subplot involving the Earl of Gloucester and his sons. In the play's opening scene, these two old men both behave selfishly and irresponsibly, completely oblivious to the effect of their words on their children and the other courtiers. Gloucester introduces his illegitimate son to Kent with a mixture of embarrassment and smirking pride in the sexual exploits of his youth. An evidently uncomfortable Kent handles the situation with delicate courtesy, but we can only guess the effect of this mortifying treatment on Edmund until his cynical disdain for his father and respectable society emerges at the beginning of the following scene.

King Lear's decision to divide up his kingdom between his three daughters and live among them as a king in name only would seem the height of imprudence to a Jacobean audience, his demand that his three daughters each "earn" their third of the realm by fulsome protestations of their love is plainly self-indulgent arrogance, and his disinheritance and banishment of Cordelia—and her defender Kent—for failing the "love test" manifests an unconscionable lack of self-control as well as deplorable wrath.

Lear and Gloucester have, in effect, taken their own privileged position in family and society for granted, while neglecting their obligation to maintain these naturally ordained hierarchies in their full integrity. After all, natural law entails the *participation* of the rational creature in the eternal reason; it is not, as Gloucester supposes, a magic formula by which "the gods" ensure the positions of the great by imposing constraints upon their inferiors. Both Lear and Gloucester have forgotten their responsibilities and failed to acknowledge that the actions of free, rational agents have consequences even in a providentially ordered universe. Neglect of their responsibilities and egotistical self-indulgence unleash a flood of horrors that neither man could have anticipated. Lear is by no means so wicked as his elder daughters, and Gloucester comes nowhere near the depravity of the bastard son who scorns him. Nevertheless, the heart-wrenching power of the tragedy comes precisely from the fact that unspeakable violence and cruelty are set loose by the vanity and petty vice of reasonably good men.

And Shakespeare is at pains to show that they both are good men. For all his adolescent smirking over a youthful sexual indiscretion and his obliviousness to the real nature of his sons, it is clear that Gloucester has acknowledged Edmund and sought to provide a decent, respectable life for him. More important, when the crisis comes, Gloucester proves a loyal and courageous subject to Lear and instinctively takes the side of justice—at a terrible personal cost. The case of King Lear himself is more complex, but not finally less decisive. To be sure, his conduct in the opening scene is simply unconscionable, and the audience is likely to take at face value Regan's observation: " 'Tis the infirmity of his age, yet he hath ever but slenderly known himself" (I.i.294–95). In addition, there are Goneril's complaints about the "riotous" behavior of his knights and her father's own "gross crime [. . .]/That sets us all at odds" (I.iii.7, 5–6). Merely contemplating the housing, feeding, and entertaining a rather demanding aged parent and one-hundred of his armed followers will generate some sympathy for Goneril.

But of course we forget that these are royal households (reflecting Shakespeare's own era rather than 800 B.C.), where huge retinues were the norm. Moreover, Shakespeare wisely refrains from actually showing us the bad behavior on the part of Lear and his knights, and anyone who has (foolishly!) attempted to mediate between an elderly parent living with a mature child with a family will recognize that there is no getting to the bottom of the complaints, recriminations, and hurt feelings. The single exception, of course, is Oswald's roughing up at the hands of Kent, with Lear's approval. It is essential, however, that we recognize that Oswald has offered the king an insufferable insult. When Lear demands that the Steward say who Lear is, the bland reply, "My lady's father" (I.iv.77), may sound inoffensive to modern ears, but it effectively denies Lear his royal identity and any independent existence. Whatever the old king's faults, it is Goneril who has deliberately provoked the confrontation: "Put on what weary negligence you please,/You and your fellows; I'd have it come to question" (I.iii.13–14). It would seem that Lear's grave error is less his conduct in his daughter's house than in making himself dependent upon her, so that he is vulnerable to slights from men such as Oswald.

In their conversation toward the close of the first scene, Goneril and Regan suggest that Lear has always been self-centered and irresponsible: "The best and soundest of his time hath been but rash" (I.i.296). We have, however, more reliable contrary evidence. First, there is the fact that Kent stands up and disputes the king's foolhardy decision in the first scene in very vigorous terms; it is hard to imagine him doing so if Lear had *never* listened to reason in the past. And Cordelia's refusal to profess her love in the fulsome terms of her sisters looks more like the response of someone who is surprised and dumbfounded than a calculated refusal to conform. Her aside, "What shall Cordelia speak? Love, and be silent" (I.i.62), suggests that she had no idea what was coming, and that she expected her father to respond reasonably to her exposition of the "bond" of filial love. Even after he has been banished, Kent returns in disguise to serve Lear in spite of the king's unjust sentence and tells his old master that he would serve because he finds in the king's countenance something worth serving, "Authority" (I.iv.30). Kent is no fool, and it is hard to imagine him showing such loyalty to a man whom he thought to be a fool. His loyalty is seconded by Gloucester, Edgar, eventually Albany, and—above all—Cordelia, who knows her father to be a better man than he shows himself in the first scene. Finally, and most important, there is Lear's moral growth in the course of his ordeal in the middle acts of the play: his recognition of the shortcomings of his reign in his neglect of the poor and in government corruption, his growing compassion, and his ability to humble himself and be reconciled with Cordelia.

A man who has thus grown morally and spiritually, a man who has truly called himself "more sinned against that sinning" (III.ii.60), a man who seems finally to have found the genuine love he craved in the first scene—King Lear dies with his beloved youngest daughter in his arms, in apparent despair, surrounded by the corpses of his enemies. Or is it despair? Lear's final words seem to suggest that he has, mistakenly, seen breath on Cordelia's lips and dies in joy believing that she lives: "Do you see this? Look on her: look, her lips,/Look there, look there!" (V.iii.309–10). Now a delusion would seem a frail basis on which to build a case that Lear dies hopeful and in some sense "redeemed", and this consideration leads to the issue of in what sense *King Lear* is a "Christian" play. Its setting eight-hundred years before the birth of Christ is not really a relevant consideration. As early as 1589, the Privy Council had warned against the treatment of "matters of Divinytie and of state" on the stage, and by 1606 the Statue of Oaths sharply curtailed the utterance of words associated with religion in stage plays. Moreover, the performance of plays required a license from the Master of Revels, who could order anything he deemed offensive or even questionable removed.[9] To set a play among ancient pagans provided a Jacobean dramatist with a prudent means of dealing with Christian themes by implication with less danger of censorship, and the wealth of scriptural language and allusion in *King Lear* makes it evident that Shakespeare expected his audience to interpret the work in Christian terms.

A multitude of Christian references does not, however, constitute a Christian play. It is possible to read the play as a titanic tragedy of existential despair, which finds "nature" either indifferent to human suffering or positively hostile—in league, as it were, with Edmund and the wicked sisters—and the "gods" absent or even more hostile. According to this view, Lear is transformed from a pious pagan into a defiant rebel against nature and divinity. He denies the reality of natural justice and authority: "There thou mightst behold the great image of authority: a dog's obeyed in office" (IV.vi.154–55); and the death of Cordelia leaves him raging against heaven and dying in delusion or despair:

> Howl, howl, howl, howl! O, you are men of stones!
> Had I your tongues and eyes, I'd use them so
> That heaven's vault should crack: she's gone for ever.
> I know when one is dead and when one lives;
> She's dead as earth.
>
> (V.3.255–59)

The Christian allusions in the play thus form an ironic comment on the pious illusions—now shattered—of the virtuous

[9] Park Honan, *Shakespeare: A Life* (Oxford/New York: Oxford University Press, 1998), 130; Gerald Eades Bentley, *The Profession of Dramatist in Shakespeare's Time* (Princeton, N.J.: Princeton University Press, 1971), p. 161.

characters. "The popular modern theory of Christian optimism" is thus exploded,[10] and the meaning of the play is summed up by the blinded, disillusioned Gloucester, as he wanders in search of the cliffs of Dover in order to cast himself down and take his own life: "As flies to wanton boys are we to the gods, / They kill us for their sport" (IV.i.38–39).

Such a reading manifests a certain plausibility from a modern secularist perspective, but it rests on a faulty understanding of Christianity. Neither the New Testament nor traditional Christian orthodoxy expounds a religion of "optimism". In the face of worldly optimism—the expectation that "good" men and women with good intentions will be rewarded in this life—Christianity offers hope, the conviction that amidst all the terror and misery wrought by sin human destiny is still controlled by divine Providence: "For we are saved by hope. But hope that is seen is not hope. For what a man seeth, why doth he hope for? But if we hope for that which we see not, we wait for it with patience" (Rom 8:24–25). The nihilistic reading of *King Lear* gains a good deal of traction from the contrast between Shakespeare's play and the anonymous *True Chronicle Historie of King Leir and his three daughters*,[11] which ends with the king and his daughter Cordella reconciled and safely restored to happiness, and which treats the ostensibly pagan

[10] The phrase is taken from William R. Elton, King Lear *and the Gods* (San Marino, Calif.: The Huntington Library, 1966/1968), 8. Elton's work stands as a sufficient epitome of the existentialist/materialist reading of *King Lear*. Previous authors who share his view never came close to the comprehensiveness of his account, and his successors seem to have taken his argument as definitive and added nothing of substance.

[11] First published in 1605, about the time Shakespeare was composing *King Lear*, the chronicle play was probably written ca. 1588–1594. It may have been revived and published in 1605 because of public interest over an actual incident in 1603 involving the effort of the two elder daughters of the aged courtier, Brian Annesley, to have him declared mentally incompetent and to seize control of his property. Annesley successfully resisted this effort with the help of his youngest daughter, Cordell. For information about the sources of *King Lear*, as well as the texts themselves, see Geoffrey Bullough, ed., *Narrative and Dramatic Sources of Shakespeare* (London: Routledge and Kegan Paul, and New York: Columbia University Press, 1973), vol. 7, pp. 269–420.

setting as if it were fully Christian. Shakespeare's elimination of the explicitly Christian assumptions of the old play, so the argument goes, his treatment of the characters as pre-Christian pagans, and—above all—his conversion of the happy ending into a tragic catastrophe must indicate that he is rejecting the Christian vision in favor of something very like the modern existentialist view that regards man as a fortuitous alien being in an absurd cosmos.

It is, to be sure, evident that Shakespeare radically alters the version of the story in the chronicle play, but it makes at least as much sense to infer that he is rejecting not Christianity, but rather a shallow, sentimental conception of Christianity as a gospel of earthly comfort and prosperity. His treatment of the other sources reinforces this view. The Lear story was first introduced into England by Geoffrey of Monmouth in his *Historia Anglicana* in the twelfth century and recounted numerous times in sixteenth-century histories and poems. The story is told, for example, in Raphael Holinshed's *Historie of England* (1587), the most important source for Shakespeare's English history plays, in *The Mirror for Magistrates* (1574), and in the second book of Edmund Spenser's *Faerie Queene* (1590, 1596). In all of these prominent sources, after a successful effort to restore her father, the Cordelia figure is again defeated and cast into prison, *where she commits suicide, usually by hanging herself*. A playwright who wished to suggest that the universe is a meaningless chaos affording no basis for human hope or value would have no reason to change this traditional conclusion. How better to emphasize the indifference of the "gods" than to allow the character who most persistently evokes Christian overtones to take her own life in despair—a mortal sin? After all, Shakespeare is content to follow Plutarch and other classical sources in depicting the suicides of Roman tragic figures, Brutus and Cassius and Antony and Cleopatra.

Disapproval of suicide, however, is a recurrent motif in Shakespearean drama. Hamlet broods on "self-slaughter" more than once, but rejects it for himself and expends his final dying breath in forestalling the impulse in Horatio. Even the elvish trickster

Puck improbably condemns suicide in a remark that seems utterly gratuitous in the plot of *A Midsummer Night's Dream* (III.ii.382–87). This preoccupation also provides an understanding of Edgar's elaborate ruse to wean his father away from suicidal intentions and his continual concern lest the old man again be thus tempted. If Gloucester's bitter condemnation of the "gods"—"they kill us for their sport"—were true, then suicide would be an unexceptionable choice. Edgar answers this complaint reasonably by insisting that "the gods are just": as dreadful as his father's suffering is, its ultimate cause is his own sin and folly. Edgar provides a far more profound rejoinder, however, when his father, having learned of the defeat of Cordelia's forces, wishes to give up and wait to be taken and slain by his enemies: "What, in ill thoughts again? Men must endure / Their going hence even as their coming hither. / Ripeness is all" (V.ii.9–11). This assertion that we are not autonomous agents, but rather subjects of a higher power, is not a passing fancy of Shakespeare's; it echoes a similar observation by Hamlet, stressing the force of Providence: "There is special providence in the fall of a sparrow. If it be now, 'tis not to come; if it be not to come, it will be now; if it be not now, yet it will come—the readiness is all" (V.ii.219–23).

Of course the most striking evidence of the play's Christian overtones is the luminous figure of Cordelia. Throughout the tragedy she is associated in general terms with Christian ideas and attitudes and not infrequently with Christ himself. When her father has cast her off, the king of France, enraptured by her virtue, describes her in paradoxical terms that call to mind the Beatitudes of the Sermon on the Mount: "Fairest Cordelia, that art most rich being poor, / Most choice forsaken and most loved despised" (I.i.252–53). When she invades England with her husband's French army, she justifies her action by claiming, "O dear father, / It is thy business that I go about" (IV.iv.23–24), echoing the twelve-year-old Jesus' words when Mary and Joseph find him disputing with the rabbis in the temple; and a nameless gentleman says to a raving Lear, "Thou hast one daughter / Who redeems nature from the general curse /

Which twain have brought her to" (IV.vi.201–3).The pagan character is undoubtedly thinking of Goneril and Regan, but a Christian audience will see an allusion to Adam and Eve, whose sin will be redeemed by the sacrificial death of Jesus Christ. Hence when Lear emerges at the very end of the play's last scene with the body of Cordelia in his arms and sinks to his knees, we are confronted with a powerful, reversed image of the *Pietà*—a father with his dead daughter in his arms, rather than a mother with her son. Most important, however, is the reconciliation scene, when Lear humbled with remorse says to Cordelia,

> If you have poison for me, I will drink it.
> I know you do not love me, for your sisters
> Have, as I do remember, done me wrong.
> You have some cause, they have not.
> (IV.vii.72–75)

It is difficult to think of a more poignant expression of Christian charity and forgiveness in all of English literature than her reply: "No cause, no cause."

Cordelia is of course not Jesus Christ; she is not the bearer of supernatural grace who saves nature "from the general curse / Which twain have brought her to." Nevertheless, she does provide an image, an analogue, of the grace that is missing from the pagan world of *King Lear*. Even if men like Lear and Gloucester were capable of adhering to the moral imperatives of natural law, which they rightly perceive lays obligations on parents and children, rulers and subjects, husbands and wives, and all men and women in all their social relations—even then, nature is not enough. It is too easily subverted by the selfish, amoral version of nature propounded by Edmund, and it finally fails, in any case, to satisfy the deepest needs of the human heart. Lear dimly and momentarily apprehends this as he tries to come to terms with the humiliation inflicted upon him by Goneril and Regan as they strip him of dignity by divesting him of "unneeded" followers:

O, reason not the need! Our basest beggars
Are in the poorest thing superfluous;
Allow not nature more than nature needs,
Man's life is cheap as beast's.
(II.ii.453–56)

One may contemplate the bleak, terrible close of *King Lear* and find a depiction of man as "a poor, bare, forked animal" unaccountably lost in a blind, meaningless swirl of matter and energy. This is the *Lear* of materialist skepticism and existential despair. Or one may find in the grief of its heart-rending catastrophe the vision of a world in which Cordelia and all that she represents cannot survive because Redemption has not yet come. "You were at that time", Saint Paul writes, "without Christ, being aliens from the conversation of Israel and strangers to the testament, having no hope of the promise and without God in the world" (Eph 2:12). By *not* being an explicitly Christian play, *King Lear* is thus a *very* Christian play indeed.

TEXTUAL NOTE

The earliest version of Shakespeare's *King Lear* is the First Quarto of 1608, of which twelve copies survive. The Second Quarto was published in 1619 and appears to be a copy of the earlier version with a number of amendments. Four years later *King Lear* was published again, in the first collection of Shakespeare's works, the First Folio of 1623.

The Folio and Quarto versions differ significantly, the Folio omitting 285 lines from the First Quarto and adding 115 lines that do not appear in the earlier version. Scholars have disputed the importance of these differences in the text. Some believe that the First Quarto is Shakespeare's initial version, and the version that would have been first performed, whereas the version that appears in the First Folio is the product of later revisions prior to Shakespeare's death in 1616. These scholars favor the later version as being the playwright's final word on his work, the definitive edition. Other scholars question whether we can be sure that the later revisions were the work of Shakespeare and therefore favor the First Quarto as being more certainly his original work. The present text relies chiefly on the Folio edition, whilst incorporating elements of the Quarto version.

The Tragedy of

KING LEAR

Existentialism
↳ Humans spend their lives in void plagued by angst & despaire in a world defined by alienation & absurdity

Authenticity
↳ Describes the attribute of taking responsibility of one's own action/exp instead of viewing your experience as defined by outside forces
An Authentic life is one in which you choose what matters to create your own meaning, an awareness of which leads to freedom.

Because King Lear was written during the Elizabethan Period, which was predominantly Christian, it is hard to believe that it would be an existential play; Shakespeare may have been subtly opposing the Christian Ideals of his time

Edmund
↳ Edmund's moral lacking & power thirst may derive from his illegitimate status
- Self-motivated decisions are made out of a desire to prove himself worthy & develop a status besides that of a bastard son (pg. 19-20)

Edgar
↳ Legitimate son of Gloucester, chooses to exist to keep his power & have the most influence over the events that occur in "King Lear" pg. 124

DRAMATIS PERSONAE

Lear, King of Britain
King of France
Duke of Burgundy
Duke of Cornwall, husband to Regan
Duke of Albany, husband to Goneril
Earl of Kent
Earl of Gloucester
Edgar, son to Gloucester
Edmund, bastard son to Gloucester
Curan, a courtier
Oswald, steward to Goneril
Old Man, tenant to Gloucester
Doctor
Lear's Fool
A Captain, subordinate to Edmund
Gentlemen, attending on Cordelia
A Herald
Servants to Cornwall
Goneril, Regan, Cordelia } daughters to Lear
Knights attending on Lear, Officers, Messengers, Soldiers, Attendants

Scene: Britain

The Tragedy of King Lear

ACT 1

Scene 1. [*King Lear's palace.*]

Enter Kent, Gloucester, and Edmund

Kent. I thought the King had more affected[1] the Duke of Albany[2] than Cornwall.

Gloucester. It did always seem so to us; but now, in the division of the kingdom, it appears not which of the dukes he values most, for qualities are so weighed that curiosity[3] in neither can make choice of either's moiety.[4]

Kent. Is not this your son, my lord?

Gloucester. His breeding,[5] sir, hath been at my charge. I have so often blushed to acknowledge him that now I am brazed[6] to't.

Kent. I cannot conceive[7] you.

Gloucester. Sir, this young fellow's mother could;[8] whereupon she grew round-wombed, and had indeed, sir, a son for her cradle ere she had a husband for her bed. Do you smell a fault?

[1] **affected** preferred

[2] **Albany** the kingdom of the Picts in Scotland, north of the river Firth; Scotland

[3–5] **for . . . moiety** Not even the most scrupulous examination of either share could lead either duke to prefer the other's share to his own.

[3] **curiosity** scrupulous examination

[4] **moiety** portion

[5] **breeding** education; conception

[6] **brazed** hardened; made brazen

[7] **conceive** understand

[8] punning on Kent's use of "conceive"

Kent. I cannot wish the fault undone, the issue[9] of it being so proper.[10]

Gloucester. But I have a son, sir, by order of law,[11] some year[12] elder than this, who yet is no dearer in my account:[13] though this knave[14] came something[15] saucily[16] to the world before he was sent for, yet was his mother fair, there was good sport at his making, and the whoreson[17] must be acknowledged. Do you know this noble gentleman, Edmund?

Edmund. No, my lord.

Gloucester. My Lord of Kent. Remember him hereafter as my honorable friend.

Edmund. My services to your lordship.

Kent. I must love you, and sue[18] to know you better.

Edmund. Sir, I shall study deserving.

Gloucester. He hath been out[19] nine years, and away he shall again. The King is coming.

Sound a sennet.[20] *Enter one bearing a coronet,*[21] *then King Lear, then the Dukes of Cornwall and Albany, next Goneril, Regan, Cordelia, and Attendants.*

[9] **issue** result; offspring
[10] **proper** of good quality; handsome
[11] **by order of law** legitimate
[12] **some year** about a year
[13] **account** estimation
[14] **knave** lad; rogue
[15] **something** somewhat
[16] **saucily** tastily; lasciviously
[17] **whoreson** bastard; scoundrel
[18] **sue** make it my task
[19] **out** away; abroad
[20] **sennet** flourish of trumpet announcing the entry or exit of a group
[21] **coronet** a small crown; a crown denoting a rank inferior to that of the sovereign

Lear. Attend[22] the lords of France and Burgundy,
Gloucester.

Gloucester. I shall, my lord. *Exit [with Edmund]*.

Lear. Meantime we[23] shall express our darker[24] purpose.
Give me the map there. Know that we have divided
In three our kingdom; and 'tis our fast[25] intent
To shake all cares and business from our age,
Conferring them on younger strengths, while we
Unburthened crawl[26] toward death. Our son of
Cornwall,
And you our no less loving son of Albany,
We have this hour a constant will[27] to publish[28]
Our daughters' several[29] dowers,[30] that future strife
May be prevented[31] now. The Princes, France and
Burgundy,
Great rivals in our youngest daughter's love,
Long in our court have made their amorous sojourn,
And here are to be answered. Tell me, my daughters
(Since now we will divest us[32] both of rule,
Interest[33] of territory, cares of state),
Which of you shall we say doth love us most,
That we our largest bounty may extend
Where nature doth with merit challenge.[34] Goneril,
Our eldest-born, speak first.

[22] **Attend** attend to; usher in
[23] **we** the royal we
[24] **darker** secret; hidden
[25] **fast** firm; fixed
[26] **crawl** move slowly
[27] **constant will** firm intention
[28] **publish** announce; make public
[29] **several** distinct
[30] **dowers** dowries
[31] **prevented** thwarted
[32] **divest us** strip myself of; legally put aside
[33] **Interest** possesion
[34] **Where . . . challenge** i.e., to the one whose affection competes with ordinary inheritance rights

Goneril. Sir, I love you more than word can wield[35] the matter;
Dearer than eyesight, space and liberty;
Beyond what can be valued, rich or rare;
No less than life, with grace, health, beauty, honor;
As much as child e'er loved, or father found;
A love that makes breath poor, and speech unable:
Beyond all manner of so much I love you.

Cordelia. [*Aside*] What shall Cordelia speak? Love, and be silent.

Lear. Of all these bounds, even from this line to this,
With shadowy forests, and with champains[36] riched,
With plenteous rivers, and wide-skirted meads,[37]
We make thee lady. To thine and Albany's issues[38]
Be this perpetual. What says our second daughter,
Our dearest Regan, wife of Cornwall? Speak.

Regan. I am made of that self[39] mettle[40] as my sister,
And prize me at her worth. In my true heart
I find she names my very deed of love;[41]
Only she comes too short, that[42] I profess
Myself an enemy to all other joys
Which the most precious[43] square[44] of sense professes,
And find I am alone felicitate[45]
In your dear Highness' love.

[35] **wield** express, skillfully handle; govern; suffer; tolerate
[36] **champains** fields
[37] **meads** meadows
[38] **issues** progeny; children
[39] **self** very same
[40] **mettle** disposition or temperament, with perhaps a pun on "metal"
[41] **names . . . love** describes exactly what my love is
[42] **that** in that
[43] **precious** delicate; refined
[44] **square** criterion
[45] **felicitate** made happy

Cordelia. [*Aside*] Then poor Cordelia!
And yet not so, since I am sure my love's
More ponderous[46] than my tongue.

Lear. To thee and thine hereditary ever
Remain this ample third of our fair kingdom,
No less in space, validity,[47] and pleasure
Than that conferred on Goneril. Now, our joy,
Although our last and least;[48] to whose young love
The vines of France and milk of Burgundy
Strive to be interest;[49] what can you say to draw
A third more opulent than your sisters? Speak.

Cordelia. Nothing, my lord.

Lear. Nothing?

Cordelia. Nothing.

Lear. Nothing will come of nothing. Speak again.

Cordelia. Unhappy that I am, I cannot heave
My heart into my mouth. I love your Majesty
According to my bond,[50] no more nor less.

Lear. How, how, Cordelia? Mend your speech a little,
Lest you may mar your fortunes.

Cordelia. Good my lord,
You have begot me, bred me, loved me. I
Return those duties back as are right fit,[51]
Obey you, love you, and most honor you.
Why have my sisters husbands, if they say
They love you all?[52] Haply,[53] when I shall wed,

[46] **ponderous** weighty
[47] **validity** value
[48] **least** youngest; smallest
[49] **to be interest** involved; connected
[50] **bond** her duty as his daughter
[51] **fit** fitting; appropriate
[52] **all** exclusively
[53] **Haply** by chance; fortuitously

That lord whose hand must take my plight[54] shall carry
Half my love with him, half my care and duty.
Sure I shall never marry like my sisters,
To love my father all.

Lear. But goes thy heart with this?

Cordelia. Ay, my good lord.

Lear. So young, and so untender?

Cordelia. So young, my lord, and true.

Lear. Let it be so, thy truth then be thy dower!
For, by the sacred radiance of the sun,
The mysteries[55] of Hecate[56] and the night,
By all the operation of the orbs[57]
From whom we do exist and cease to be,
Here I disclaim all my paternal care,
Propinquity[58] and property of blood,[59]
And as a stranger to my heart and me
Hold thee from this for ever. The barbarous Scythian,[60]
Or he that makes his generation[61] messes[62]
To gorge his appetite, shall to my bosom
Be as well neighbored, pitied, and relieved,
As thou my sometime[63] daughter.

[54] **plight** marriage pledge
[55] **mysteries** secret rites
[56] **Hecate** Greek goddess associated with the moon, witchcraft, and black magic; she is often referred to in Elizabethan and Jacobean drama as Queen of the Witches.
[57] **operation of the orbs** influence of the stars and planets
[58] **Propinquity** kinship; closeness
[59] **property of blood** blood relationship
[60] **Scythian** native of Scythia—a region north of the Black Sea; a savage
[61] **generation** children; offspring
[62] **messes** portions of food
[63] **sometime** former

Kent. Good my liege——

Lear. Peace, Kent!
Come not between the Dragon[64] and his wrath.
I loved her most, and thought to set my rest[65]
On her kind nursery.[66] Hence and avoid my sight!
So be my grave my peace, as here I give
Her father's heart from her! Call France. Who stirs?[67]
Call Burgundy. Cornwall and Albany,
With my two daughters' dowers digest[68] the third;
Let pride, which she calls plainness,[69] marry her.
I do invest you jointly with my power,
Pre-eminence, and all the large[70] effects[71]
That troop with[72] majesty. Ourself, by monthly
course,
With reservation of an hundred knights,[73]
By you to be sustained,[74] shall our abode
Make with you by due turn. Only we shall retain
The name, and all th' addition[75] to a king. The sway,[76]
Revènue, execution of the rest,
Belovèd sons, be yours; which to confirm,
This coronet part between you.

Kent. Royal Lear,
Whom I have ever honored as my king,

[64] **Dragon** possibly a reference to the dragon of Britain, which Lear would have had as part, at least, of his heraldic device. Shakespeare often uses the dragon as a symbol of savage ferocity.
[65] **to set my rest** to stake my all
[66] **nursery** tender care
[67] **Who stirs** quickly
[68] **digest** incorporate
[69] **plainness** frankness; honesty
[70] **large** ample; impressive
[71] **effects** outward signs; display
[72] **troop with** accompany
[73] **Ourself . . . knights** I shall set aside one hundred knights for my own use.
[74] **sustained** kept; supported
[75] **addition** honors
[76] **sway** power; authority

Loved as my father, as my master followed,
As my great patron thought on in my prayers——

Lear. The bow is bent and drawn; make from[77] the shaft.[78]

Kent. Let it fall[79] rather, though the fork[80] invade
The region of my heart. Be Kent unmannerly
When Lear is mad. What wouldst thou do, old man?
Think'st thou that duty shall have dread to speak
When power to flattery bows? To plainness honor's bound
When majesty falls to folly. Reserve thy state,[81]
And in thy best consideration[82] check[83]
This hideous rashness. Answer my life my judgment,
Thy youngest daughter does not love thee least,
Nor are those empty-hearted whose low sounds
Reverb[84] no hollowness.[85]

Lear. Kent, on thy life, no more!

Kent. My life I never held[86] but as a pawn[87]
To wage[88] against thine enemies; nor fear to lose it,
Thy safety being motive.[89]

Lear. Out of my sight!

[77] **make from** avoid
[78] **shaft** arrow
[79] **fall** befall
[80] **fork** the barbed head of an arrow
[81] **Reserve thy state** retain your position (as king)
[82] **consideration** judgment; reflection
[83] **check** halt
[84] **Reverb** reverberate
[85] **hollowness** insincerity
[86] **held** considered
[87] **pawn** stake
[88] **wage** wager; carry on (war, a contest)
[89] **motive** moving cause

Kent. See better, Lear, and let me still[90] remain
The true blank[91] of thine eye.[92]

Lear. Now by Apollo——

Kent. Now by Apollo, King,
Thou swear'st thy gods in vain.

Lear. O vassal![93] Miscreant![94]

[*Laying his hand on his sword.*]

Albany, Cornwall. Dear sir, forbear!

Kent. Kill thy physician, and the fee bestow
Upon the foul disease. Revoke thy gift,
Or, whilst I can vent[95] clamor from my throat,
I'll tell thee thou dost evil.

Lear. Hear me, recreant![96]
On thine allegiance,[97] hear me!
That[98] thou hast sought to make us break our vows,
Which we durst[99] never yet, and with strained[100] pride
To come betwixt our sentence and our power,
Which nor[101] our nature nor our place can bear,
Our potency made good, take thy reward.[102]
Five days we do allot thee for provision

[90] **still** always
[91] **blank** white; bull's-eye
[92] **let . . . eye** let me remain your truest counselor
[93] **vassal** in the feudal system, someone holding lands from a superior on condition of homage and allegiance; a base or abject person
[94] **Miscreant** unbeliever; villain
[95] **vent** give vent to
[96] **recreant** traitor
[97] **On thine allegiance** as you are faithful to your king
[98] **That** as
[99] **durst** dared
[100] **strained** excessive
[101] **nor** neither
[102] **Our . . . reward** I take back my power: to punish you.

To shield thee from diseases[103] of the world,
And on the sixth to turn thy hated back
Upon our kingdom. If, on the tenth day following,
Thy banished trunk[104] be found in our dominions,
The moment is thy death. Away! By Jupiter,
This shall not be revoked.

Kent. Fare thee well, King. Sith[105] thus thou wilt appear,
Freedom lives hence, and banishment is here.
[*To Cordelia*] The gods to their dear shelter take thee, maid,
That justly think'st, and hast most rightly said.
[*To Regan and Goneril*] And your large[106] speeches may your deeds approve,[107]
That good effects[108] may spring from words of love.
Thus Kent, O Princes, bids you all adieu;
He'll shape his old course[109] in a country new. *Exit.*

Flourish.[110] *Enter Gloucester, with France and Burgundy; Attendants.*

Gloucester. Here's France and Burgundy, my noble lord.

Lear. My Lord of Burgundy,
We first address toward you, who with this king
Hath rivaled for our daughter. What in the least
Will you require in present[111] dower with her,
Or cease your quest of love?

[103] **diseases** disasters; misfortunes
[104] **trunk** body
[105] **Sith** since
[106] **large** grand
[107] **approve** confirm
[108] **effects** deeds
[109] **old course** customary (i.e., honest) ways
[110] **Flourish** fanfare of trumpets
[111] **present** immediate

Burgundy. Most royal Majesty,
I crave no more than hath your Highness offered,
Nor will you tender less.

Lear. Right noble Burgundy,
When she was dear[112] to us, we did hold her so;
But now her price is fallen. Sir, there she stands.
If aught within that little seeming[113] substance,[114]
Or all of it, with our displeasure pieced,[115]
And nothing more, may fitly like[116] your Grace,[117]
She's there, and she is yours.

Burgundy. I know no answer.

Lear. Will you, with those infirmities she owes,[118]
Unfriended, new adopted to our hate,
Dow'red with our curse, and strangered with[119] our oath,
Take her, or leave her?

Burgundy. Pardon me, royal sir.
Election makes not up[120] on such conditions.

Lear. Then leave her, sir; for, by the pow'r that made me,
I tell you all her wealth. [*To France.*] For[121] you, great King,
I would not from your love make such a stray
To[122] match you where I hate; therefore beseech you[123]

[112] **dear** beloved; valuable
[113] **seeming** attractive; misleading
[114] **substance** being; something of value
[115] **pieced** added
[116] **fitly like** suitably please
[117] **your Grace** correct form of address to a duke
[118] **owes** owns
[119] **strangered with** disowned by
[120] **Election makes not up** no one can choose
[121] **For** as for
[122] **make such a stray/To** stray so far as to
[123] **beseech you** I beseech you

T' avert your liking a more worthier way
Than on a wretch whom nature is ashamed
Almost t' acknowledge hers.

France. This is most strange,
That she whom even but now was your best object,[124]
The argument[125] of your praise, balm of your age,
The best, the dearest, should in this trice of time
Commit a thing so monstrous to dismantle[126]
So many folds of favor. Sure her offense
Must be of such unnatural degree
That monsters it,[127] or your fore-vouched affection
Fall into taint;[128] which to believe of her
Must be a faith that reason without miracle
Should never plant in me.[129]

Cordelia. I yet beseech your Majesty,
If for[130] I want[131] that glib and oily art
To speak and purpose not,[132] since what I well intend
I'll do't before I speak, that you make known
It is no vicious blot, murder, or foulness,
No unchaste action or dishonored step,
That hath deprived me of your grace and favor;
But even for want of that for which I am richer,
A still-soliciting[133] eye, and such a tongue
That I am glad I have not, though not to have it
Hath lost[134] me in your liking.

[124] **best object** i.e., of love

[125] **argument** subject; theme

[126] **dismantle** divest; strip

[127] **monsters it** makes it a monster

[128] **Fall into taint** must have fallen into corruption

[129] **Must . . . me** is something so unlikely that reason unaided by revelation could never believe it

[130] **for** because

[131] **want** lack

[132] **To speak . . . not** to say or promise what I do not intend to do

[133] **still-soliciting** always begging

[134] **lost** ruined

Lear. Better thou
Hadst not been born than not t' have pleased me better.

France. Is it but this? A tardiness in nature[135]
Which often leaves the history[136] unspoke
That it intends to do. My Lord of Burgundy,
What say you to[137] the lady? Love's not love
When it is mingled with regards[138] that stands
Aloof from th' entire[139] point.[140] Will you have her?
She is herself a dowry.

Burgundy. Royal King,
Give but that portion which yourself proposed,
And here I take Cordelia by the hand,
Duchess of Burgundy.

Lear. Nothing. I have sworn. I am firm.

Burgundy. I am sorry then you have so lost a father
That you must lose a husband.

Cordelia. Peace be with Burgundy.
Since that[141] respects of[142] fortune are his love,
I shall not be his wife.

France. Fairest Cordelia, that art most rich being poor,
Most choice[143] forsaken, and most loved despised,
Thee and thy virtues here I seize upon.
Be it lawful I take up what's cast away.

[135] **tardiness in nature** natural reticence
[136] **history** account
[137] **What say you to** will you have
[138] **regards** considerations; motives
[139] **entire** essential
[140] **entire point** i.e., love
[141] **Since that** since
[142] **respects of** considerations of; attention to; regard for; deferential esteem for
[143] **choice** well chosen; worthy of being chosen; of special excellence

Gods, gods! 'Tis strange that from their cold'st neglect
My love should kindle to inflamed respect.[144]
Thy dow'rless daughter, King, thrown to my chance,[145]
Is Queen of us, of ours, and our fair France.
Not all the dukes of wat'rish[146] Burgundy
Can buy this unprized precious[147] maid of me.
Bid them farewell, Cordelia, though unkind.
Thou losest here, a better where[148] to find.

Lear. Thou hast her, France; let her be thine, for we
Have no such daughter, nor shall ever see
That face of hers again. Therefore be gone,
Without our grace, our love, our benison.[149]
Come, noble Burgundy.

Flourish. Exeunt [Lear, Burgundy, Cornwall, Albany, Gloucester, and Attendants].

France. Bid farewell to your sisters.

Cordelia. The jewels of our father,[150] with washed Eyes[151]
Cordelia leaves you. I know you what you are,
And, like a sister, am most loath[152] to call
Your faults as they are named.[153] Love well our father.
To your professèd bosoms I commit him.[154]

[144] **respect** partiality; esteem
[145] **chance** lot
[146] **wat'rish** watery or diluted; also a reference to the many rivers in Burgundy
[147] **unprized precious** precious, though unappreciated by others
[148] **where** place
[149] **benison** blessing
[150] **The jewels of our father** i.e., her sisters
[151] **washed Eyes** eyes washed, and made clear, with tears
[152] **loath** unwilling
[153] **as they are named** by their true names
[154] **To . . . him** That is, I commit him to the love you have professed, rather than what you really feel.

But yet, alas, stood I within his grace,
I would prefer[155] him to a better place.
So farewell to you both.

Regan. Prescribe not us[156] our duty.

Goneril. Let your study
Be to content your lord, who hath received you
At Fortune's alms.[157] You have obedience scanted,[158]
And well are worth the want that you have wanted.[159]

Cordelia. Time shall unfold what plighted[160] cunning hides,
Who[161] covers faults, at last shame them derides.[162]
Well may you prosper.[163]

France. Come, my fair Cordelia.

Exit France and Cordelia.

Goneril. Sister, it is not little I have to say of what most nearly appertains to us both. I think our father will hence tonight.

Regan. That's most certain, and with you; next month with us.

Goneril. You see how full of changes his age is. The observation we have made of it hath not been little. He always loved our sister most, and with what

[155] **prefer** recommend

[156] **Prescribe not us** Do not presume to tell us

[157] **At Fortune's alms** when Fortune was handing out petty charities

[158] **scanted** stinted

[159] **And . . . wanted** And you well deserve to lose your share; and you well deserve to be neglected by your husband.

[160] **plighted** pleated; concealed; dissembling

[161] **Who** Those who

[162] **at . . . derides** shame eventually derides those who conceal their faults

[163] **Well . . . prosper** Cordelia is being sarcastic here, as the preceding line paraphrases Proverbs 28:13: "He that hideth his sins, shall not prosper."

poor judgment he hath now cast her off appears too grossly.[164]

Regan. 'Tis the infirmity of his age; yet he hath ever but slenderly known himself.

Goneril. The best and soundest of his time hath been but rash;[165] then must we look from his age to receive not alone[166] the imperfections of long-ingrafted[167] condition,[168] but therewithal[169] the unruly waywardness that infirm and choleric[170] years bring with them.

Regan. Such unconstant starts[171] are we like to have from him as this of Kent's banishment.

Goneril. There is further compliment[172] of leave-taking between France and him. Pray you, let's hit together;[173] if our father carry authority with such disposition as he bears,[174] this last surrender[175] of his will but offend[176] us.

Regan. We shall further think of it.

Goneril. We must do something, and i' th' heat.[177]

Exeunt.

[164] **grossly** obviously
[165] **The best . . . rash** Even in his best years he was given to hot-headedness.
[166] **alone** only
[167] **ingrafted** implanted; set firmly in
[168] **condition** disposition
[169] **therewithal** in addition to that
[170] **choleric** one of the four humors, characterized by anger and passion
[171] **unconstant starts** sudden whims
[172] **compliment** formality
[173] **hit together** agree
[174] **carry . . . bears** continues to wield his authority in the way we have just seen
[175] **last surrender** recent resignation of royal authority
[176] **offend** be a nuisance to
[177] **i' th' heat** i.e., strike while the iron is hot

Scene 2. [*The Earl of Gloucester's castle.*]

Enter Edmund [with a letter].

Edmund. Thou, Nature, art my goddess;[178] to thy law
My services are bound. Wherefore should I
Stand in[179] the plague of custom,[180] and permit
The curiosity[181] of nations to deprive me,
For that[182] I am some twelve or fourteen moonshines[183]
Lag of[184] a brother? Why bastard? Wherefore[185] base?[186]
When my dimensions[187] are as well compact,[188]
My mind as generous,[189] and my shape as true,
As honest[190] madam's issue? Why brand they us
With base? With baseness? Bastardy? Base? Base?
Who, in the lusty[191] stealth of nature, take
More composition[192] and fierce[193] quality
Than doth, within a dull, stale, tired bed,
Go to th' creating a whole tribe of fops[194]
Got[195] 'tween a sleep and wake? Well then,
Legitimate Edgar, I must have your land.

[178] **Thou ... goddess** i.e., as opposed to the authority of either established religion or the state. Edmund is, after all, a "natural child".

[179] **Stand in** be dependent on

[180] **the plague of custom** pestilential custom

[181] **curiosity** excessive delicacy

[182] **For that** because

[183] **moonshines** months

[184] **Lag of** behind

[185] **Wherefore** why; on account of what

[186] **base** low; degraded; counterfeit

[187] **dimensions** proportions; bodily parts

[188] **compact** put together; made

[189] **generous** gallant; courageous

[190] **honest** chaste

[191] **lusty** full of sexual desire; full of healthy vigor

[192] **More composition** a fuller mixture

[193] **fierce** more energetic

[194] **fops** fools

[195] **Got** begotten

Our father's love is to the bastard Edmund
As to th' legitimate. Fine word, "legitimate."
Well, my legitimate, if this letter speed,[196]
And my invention[197] thrive, Edmund the base
Shall top th' legitimate. I grow, I prosper.
Now, gods, stand up for bastards.

Enter Gloucester.

Gloucester. Kent banished thus? and France in choler parted?
And the King gone tonight? Prescribed[198] his pow'r?
Confined to exhibition?[199] All this done
Upon the gad?[200] Edmund, how now? What news?

Edmund. So please your lordship, none.

Gloucester. Why so earnestly[201] seek you to put up[202] that letter?

Edmund. I know no news, my lord.

Gloucester. What paper were you reading?

Edmund. Nothing, my lord.

Gloucester. No? What needed then that terrible dispatch[203] of it into your pocket? The quality of nothing hath not such need to hide itself. Let's see. Come, if it be nothing, I shall not need spectacles.

Edmund. I beseech you, sir, pardon me. It is a letter from my brother that I have not all o'er-read; and

[196] **speed** prospers
[197] **invention** plan
[198] **Prescribed** restricted; limited
[199] **Confined to exhibition** restricted to an allowance
[200] **Upon the gad** on the spur of the moment; suddenly
[201] **earnestly** eagerly
[202] **put up** put away
[203] **terrible dispatch** fearful hast

for so much as I have perused, I find it not fit for your o'erlooking.[204]

Gloucester. Give me the letter, sir.

Edmund. I shall offend, either to detain[205] or give it. The contents, as in part I understand them, are to blame.[206]

Gloucester. Let's see, let's see.

Edmund. I hope, for my brother's justification, he wrote this but as an essay or taste[207] of my virtue.

Gloucester. (*Reads*) "This policy and reverence of Age[208] makes the world bitter to the best of our times;[209] keeps our fortunes from us till our oldness cannot relish[210] them. I begin to find an idle and fond[211] bondage in the oppression of aged tyranny, who sways,[212] not as it hath power,[213] but as it is suffered.[214] Come to me, that of this I may speak more. If our father would sleep till I waked him, you should enjoy half his revenue for ever, and live the beloved of your brother, EDGAR." Hum! Conspiracy? "Sleep till I waked him, you should enjoy half his revenue." My son Edgar! Had he a hand to write this? A heart and brain to breed it in? When came you to this? Who brought it?

[204] **o'erlooking** perusal
[205] **detain** withhold
[206] **to blame** blameworthy
[207] **essay or taste** trial or test
[208] **This . . . Age** This policy of reverencing age
[209] **best of our times** the best years of our lives
[210] **relish** appreciate
[211] **fond** foolish
[212] **sways** rules
[213] **not as it hath power** not by its strength
[214] **but as it is suffered** but insofar as we put up with it

Edmund. It was not brought me, my lord; there's the cunning of it. I found it thrown in at the casement[215] of my closet.[216]

Gloucester. You know the character[217] to be your brother's?

Edmund. If the matter were good, my lord, I durst[218] swear it were his; but in respect of[219] that, I would fain[220] think it were not.

Gloucester. It is his.

Edmund. It is his hand, my lord; but I hope his heart is not in the contents.

Gloucester. Has he never before sounded you[221] in this business?

Edmund. Never, my lord. But I have heard him oft maintain it to be fit that, sons at perfect age,[222] and fathers declined,[223] the father should be as ward to the son, and the son manage his revenue.

Gloucester. O villain, villain! His very opinion in the letter. Abhorred villain, unnatural, detested,[224] brutish villain; worse than brutish! Go, sirrah,[225] seek him. I'll apprehend him. Abominable villain! Where is he?

[215] **casement** window
[216] **closet** private room
[217] **character** handwriting
[218] **I durst** I would dare to
[219] **in respect of** with respect to
[220] **fain** like to; willingly
[221] **sounded you** sounded you out
[222] **at perfect age** arrived at maturity
[223] **declined** past their prime
[224] **detested** detestable
[225] **sirrah** sir: form of address to a man or boy expressing contempt, reprimand, or (as here) authoritativeness

Edmund. I do not well know, my lord. If it shall please you to suspend your indignation against my brother till you can derive from him better testimony of his intent, you should run a certain course;[226] where, if you violently proceed against him, mistaking his purpose, it would make a great gap[227] in your own honor and shake in[228] pieces the heart of his obedience. I dare pawn down[229] my life for him that he hath writ this to feel[230] my affection to your honor, and to no other pretense of danger.[231]

Gloucester. Think you so?

Edmund. If your honor judge it meet,[232] I will place you where you shall hear us confer of this, and by an auricular assurance[233] have your satisfaction, and that without any further delay than this very evening.

Gloucester. He cannot be such a monster.

Edmund. Nor is not, sure.

Gloucester. To his father, that so tenderly and entirely loves him. Heaven and earth! Edmund, seek him out; wind me into him,[234] I pray you; frame[235] the business after[236] your own wisdom. I would unstate myself[237] to be in a due resolution.[238]

[226] **run a certain course** adopt a safe course of action
[227] **gap** breach
[228] **shake in** shake to
[229] **pawn down** wager
[230] **feel** test
[231] **pretense of danger** dangerous intention
[232] **meet** fitting
[233] **auricular assurance** i.e., by the evidence of your ears
[234] **wind me into him** insinuate yourself into his confidence for me
[235] **frame** fashion; manage
[236] **after** according to
[237] **I would unstate myself** I would give up my rank and fortune.
[238] **to be in a due resolution** to know for sure

Edmund. I will seek him, sir, presently;[239] convey[240] the business as I shall find means, and acquaint you withal.[241]

Gloucester. These late[242] eclipses in the sun and moon portend no good to us. Though the wisdom of Nature[243] can reason[244] it thus and thus, yet Nature[245] finds itself scourged by the sequent effects.[246] Love cools, friendship falls off,[247] brothers divide. In cities, mutinies;[248] in countries, discord; in palaces, treason; and the bond cracked 'twixt son and father. This villain of mine[249] comes under the prediction,[250] there's son against father; the King falls from bias of nature,[251] there's father against child. We have seen the best of our time.[252] Machinations,[253] hollowness,[254] treachery, and all ruinous disorders follow us disquietly[255] to our graves. Find out this villain, Edmund; it shall lose thee nothing. Do it carefully. And the noble and true-hearted Kent banished; his offense, honesty. 'Tis strange.

Exit.

[239] **presently** at once
[240] **convey** manage
[241] **withal** with the results
[242] **late** recent
[243] **wisdom of Nature** scientific knowledge
[244] **reason** explain
[245] **Nature** the natural world
[246] **sequent effects** disasters that follow
[247] **falls off** becomes estranged
[248] **mutinies** riots
[249] **villain of mine** i.e., Edgar
[250] **This villain ... prediction** This villainous behavior of Edgar's would be consistent with the events that are said to follow these signs.
[251] **the King ... nature** The King goes against natural instincts (from the game of bowls, the bowls being weighted on one side).
[252] **We have seen the best of our time** Our best days are behind us.
[253] **Machinations** plottings
[254] **hollowness** insincerity
[255] **disquietly** unquietly

Edmund. This is the excellent foppery[256] of the world, that when we are sick in fortune, often the surfeits[257] of our own behavior, we make guilty of our disasters the sun, the moon, and stars;[258] as if we were villains on[259] necessity; fools by heavenly compulsion; knaves, thieves, and treachers by spherical predominance;[260] drunkards, liars, and adulterers by an enforced obedience of planetary influence; and all that we are evil in, by a divine thrusting on.[261] An admirable evasion of whoremaster[262] man, to lay his goatish[263] disposition on the charge of a star.[264] My father compounded[265] with my mother under the Dragon's Tail,[266] and my nativity was under Ursa Major,[267] so that it follows I am rough and lecherous. Fut![268] I should have been that[269] I am, had the maidenliest star in the firmament twinkled on my bastardizing.[270] Edgar——

Enter Edgar.

[256] **foppery** foolishness; stupidity

[257] **often the surfeits** often owing to the excesses

[258] **we make guilty . . . stars** We blame the influence of the heavenly bodies for our problems.

[259] **on** of

[260] **spherical predominance** astrological reference to the influence of the ascendant star or planet at one's birth

[261] **a divine thrusting on** supernatural coercion or impelling. There are sexual overtones to Edmund's language throughout this passage.

[262] **whoremaster** sexually promiscuous; lecherous

[263] **goatish** lascivious

[264] **to lay . . . star** to blame his lascivious condition on the influence of a star

[265] **compounded** combined; made up a composite product (i.e., Edmund)

[266] **Dragon's Tail** the descending node of the moon's orbit with the elliptic

[267] **Ursa Major** the Great Bear or Big Dipper, associated with lechery and impetuosity

[268] **Fut** God's foot (an oath)

[269] **that** what

[270] **bastardizing** extramarital conception

And pat[271] he comes, like the catastrophe[272] of the old comedy. My cue is villainous melancholy,[273] with a sigh like Tom o' Bedlam.[274]—O, these eclipses do portend these divisions.[275] Fa, sol, la, mi.[276]

Edgar. How now, brother Edmund; what serious contemplation are you in?

Edmund. I am thinking, brother, of a prediction I read this other day, what should follow these eclipses.

Edgar. Do you busy yourself with that?

Edmund. I promise you, the effects he writes of succeed[277] unhappily: as of unnaturalness between the child and the parent, death, dearth, dissolutions of ancient amities,[278] divisions in state, menaces and maledictions[279] against King and nobles, needless diffidences,[280] banishment of friends, dissipation[281] of cohorts, nuptial breaches, and I know not what.

Edgar. How long have you been a sectary astronomical?[282]

[271] **pat** appositely

[272] **catastrophe** dénouement: the change that produces the final event of a play

[273] **My . . . melancholy** This is my cue to act (villainously) as though I were melancholy.

[274] **Tom o' Bedlam** "Poor Tom" was the name generally assumed by beggars pretending to be mad. Bedlam was London's madhouse. "Poor Tom" is also identified with the "Abraham man", one of a class of pretended lunatics who wandered over England seeking alms after the dissolution of the religious houses.

[275] **divisions** conflicts; musical modulations

[276] **Fa, sol, la, mi** the notes of an augmented fourth—what was known as "the diabolical progression"

[277] **succeed** come to pass; turn out

[278] **amities** friendships; alliances

[279] **maledictions** curses; slanders

[280] **diffidences** suspicions; mutual distrust

[281] **dissipation** melting away

[282] **sectary astronomical** believer in, or student of, astrology

Edmund. Come, come, when saw you my father last?

Edgar. Why, the night gone by.

Edmund. Spake you with him?

Edgar. Ay, two hours together.

Edmund. Parted you in good terms? Found you no displeasure in him by word nor countenance?[283]

Edgar. None at all.

Edmund. Bethink yourself wherein you may have offended him; and at my entreaty forbear[284] his presence until some little time hath qualified[285] the heat of his displeasure, which at this instant so rageth in him that with the mischief of your person it would scarcely allay.[286]

Edgar. Some villain hath done me wrong.

Edmund. That's my fear, brother I pray you have a continent forbearance[287] till the speed of his rage goes slower; and, as I say, retire with me to my lodging, from whence I will fitly[288] bring you to hear my lord speak. Pray ye, go; there's my key. If you do stir abroad, go armed.

Edgar. Armed, brother?

Edmund. Brother, I advise you to the best. Go armed. I am no honest man if there be any good meaning[289] toward you. I have told you what I have seen and

[283] **countenance** facial expression
[284] **forbear** withhold yourself from; avoid
[285] **qualified** mitigated
[286] **with . . . allay** Even were you to come to harm, it would not be enough to appease it.
[287] **have a continent forbearance** Restrain your feelings and keep away.
[288] **fitly** when the time is right
[289] **meaning** intention

heard; but faintly, nothing like the image and horror of it.[290] Pray you, away.

Edgar. Shall I hear from you anon?[291]

Edmund. I do serve you in this business.

Exit Edgar.

A credulous father, and a brother noble,
Whose nature is so far from doing harms
That he suspects none; on whose foolish honesty
My practices[292] ride easy. I see the business.
Let me, if not by birth, have lands by wit.
All with me's meet[293] that I can fashion fit.[294,295] *Exit*

Scene 3. [*The Duke of Albany's palace.*]

Enter Goneril, and [Oswald, her] Steward.

Goneril. Did my father strike my gentleman for chiding of his Fool?

Oswald. Ay, madam.

Goneril. By day and night he wrongs me. Every hour
He flashes into one gross crime[296] or other
That sets us all at odds. I'll not endure it.
His knights grow riotous, and himself upbraids us
On every trifle. When he returns from hunting,
I will not speak with him. Say I am sick.

[290] **image and horror of it** the horror of it as it truly was
[291] **anon** soon
[292] **practices** intrigues
[293] **meet** fitting
[294] **fashion fit** use for any purposes
[295] **All . . . fit** I'll gladly do anything that will further my designs.
[296] **gross crime** outrageous offense

If you come slack of former services,[297]
You shall do well; the fault of it I'll answer.[298]

[*Horns within.*]

Oswald. He's coming, madam; I hear him.

Goneril. Put on what weary negligence you please,
You and your fellows. I'd have it come to question.[299]
If he distaste[300] it, let him to my sister,
Whose mind and mine I know in that are one,
Not to be overruled. Idle[301] old man,
That still would manage those authorities
That he hath given away. Now, by my life,
Old fools are babes again, and must be used[302]
With checks as flatteries,[303] when they are seen abused.[304]
Remember what I have said.

Oswald. Well, madam.

Goneril. And let his knights have colder looks among you.
What grows of it, no matter; advise your fellows so.
I would breed from hence occasions, and I shall,
That I may speak. I'll write straight[305] to my sister
To hold my course.[306] Go, prepare for dinner.

Exeunt.

[297] **come . . . services** allow your former standard of service to him to deteriorate
[298] **I'll answer** I'll be answerable for
[299] **come to question** come to a head
[300] **distaste** dislike
[301] **Idle** foolish
[302] **used** treated
[303] **With checks as flatteries** with rebukes as well as flatteries
[304] **seen abused** seen to be mistaken
[305] **straight** straightaway
[306] **To hold my course** to follow my example/course of action

Scene 4. [*A hall in the same.*]

Enter Kent [disguised].

Kent. If but as well I other accents borrow
That can my speech defuse,[307] my good intent
May carry through itself to that full issue[308]
For which I razed my likeness.[309] Now, banished Kent,
If thou canst serve where thou dost stand condemned,
So may it come,[310] thy master whom thou lov'st
Shall find thee full of labors.

Horns within. Enter Lear, [Knights] and Attendants.

Lear. Let me not stay[311] a jot[312] for dinner; go, get it ready. [*Exit an Attendant.*] How now, what art thou?

Kent. A man, sir.

Lear. What dost thou profess?[313] What wouldst thou with us?

Kent. I do profess[314] to be no less than I seem, to serve him truly that will put me in trust, to love him that is honest, to converse[315] with him that is wise

[307] **defuse** disguise; disorder
[308] **full issue** successful result
[309] **razed my likeness** erased my true appearance (i.e., disguised myself)
[310] **So may it come** It may happen that; or, So may it transpire!
[311] **stay** wait
[312] **jot** moment
[313] **What dost thou profess** What is your job?
[314] **profess** claim
[315] **converse** consort

and says little, to fear judgment,[316] to fight when I cannot choose, and to eat no fish.[317]

Lear. What art thou?

Kent. A very honest-hearted fellow, and as poor as the King.

Lear. If thou be'st as poor for a subject as he's for a king, thou art poor enough. What wouldst thou?

Kent. Service.

Lear. Who wouldst thou serve?

Kent. You.

Lear. Dost thou know me, fellow?

Kent. No, sir, but you have that in your countenance[318] which I would fain[319] call master.

Lear. What's that?

Kent. Authority.

Lear. What services canst thou do?

Kent. I can keep honest counsel,[320] ride, run, mar a Curious[321] tale in telling it, and deliver a plain message bluntly. That which ordinary men are fit for, I am qualified in, and the best of me is diligence.

[316] **fear judgment** respect authority, divine and human

[317] **eat no fish** This might be meant as a symbol of his loyalty: Protestants showed their loyalty in Elizabethan times by **not** eating fish, especially on Fridays, to distinguish themselves from Catholics, who, fasting from meat on Fridays, often had fish instead. It may also imply that he is a man's man (meat-eater), and/or that he refrained from using the services of pimps, who were called "fishmongers".

[318] **countenance** face; bearing

[319] **fain** gladly

[320] **I can keep honest counsel** I will not reveal secret matters that are honorable.

[321] **curious** complicated; exquisite

Lear. How old art thou?

Kent. Not so young, sir, to love a woman for singing, nor so old to dote on her for anything. I have years on my back forty-eight.

Lear. Follow me; thou shalt serve me. If I like thee no worse after dinner, I will not part from thee yet. Dinner, ho, dinner! Where's my knave?[322] my Fool? Go you and call my Fool hither.

[*Exit an Attendant.*]

Enter Oswald.

You, you, sirrah, where's my daughter?

Oswald. So please you—— *Exit.*

Lear. What says the fellow there? Call the clotpoll[323] back. [*Exit a Knight.*] Where's my Fool? Ho, I think the world's asleep.

[*Re-enter Knight.*]

How now? Where's that mongrel?

Knight. He says, my lord, your daughter is not well.

Lear. Why came not the slave back to me when I called him?

Knight. Sir, he answered me in the roundest[324] manner, he would not.

Lear. He would not?

Knight. My lord, I know not what the matter is; but to my judgment your Highness is not entertained[325] with that ceremonious affection as you were wont.[326] There's a great abatement of kindness

[322] **knave** boy; servant
[323] **clotpoll** blockhead
[324] **roundest** bluntest; rudest
[324] **entertained** treated
[326] **wont** accustomed to

appears as well in the general dependants[327] as in the Duke himself also and your daughter.

Lear. Ha? Say'st thou so?

Knight. I beseech you pardon me, my lord, if I be mistaken; for my duty cannot be silent when I think your Highness wronged.

Lear. Thou but remembʼrest[328] me of mine own conception.[329] I have perceived a most faint[330] neglect of late, which I have rather blamed as mine own jealous curiosity[331] than as a very pretense[332] and purpose of unkindness. I will look further into 't. But where's my Fool? I have not seen him this two days.

Knight. Since my young lady's going into France, sir, the Fool hath much pined away.

Lear. No more of that; I have noted it well. Go you and tell my daughter I would speak with her. Go you, call hither my Fool. [*Exit an Attendant*]

Enter Oswald.

O, you, sir, you! Come you hither, sir. Who am I, sir?

Oswald. My lady's father.

Lear. "My lady's father"? My lord's knave, you whoreson dog, you slave, you cur!

Oswald. I am none of these, my lord; I beseech your pardon.

[327] **general dependants** servants
[328] **rememb'rest** remind
[329] **conception** idea; impression
[330] **most faint** barely perceptible; cold
[331] **jealous curiosity** scrupulous attentiveness to what is owed to my dignity
[332] **very pretense** actual intention

Lear. Do you bandy[333] looks with me, you rascal?

[*Striking him.*]

Oswald. I'll not be strucken, my lord.

Kent. Nor tripped neither, you base football[334] player.

[*Tripping up his heels.*]

Lear. I thank thee, fellow. Thou serv'st me, and I'll love thee.

Kent. Come, sir, arise, away. I'll teach you differences.[335] Away, away. If you will measure your lubber's[336] length[337] again, tarry; but away. Go to![338] Have you wisdom?[339] So.[340] [*Pushes Oswald out.*]

Lear. Now, my friendly knave, I thank thee. There's Earnest[341] of thy service. [*Giving Kent money.*]

Enter Fool.

Fool. Let me hire him too. Here's my coxcomb.[342]

[*Offering Kent his cap.*]

Lear. How now, my pretty knave? How dost thou?

Fool. Sirrah, you were best[343] take my coxcomb.

[333] **bandy** exchange as an equal (from "bandying" the ball back and forth in tennis)

[334] **football** football (soccer) was regarded as a vulgar game in Shakespeare's day

[335] **differences** differences of station (i.e., between you and the King)

[336] **lubber** lout

[337] **If . . . length** if you would like me to knock you to the ground again

[338] **Go to** Set to work! Go on!

[339] **Have you wisdom** Don't you know what's good for you?

[340] **So** That's right.

[341] **earnest** money in part payment for the purpose of sealing a bargain

[342] **coxcomb** cap worn by a jester, like a cock's comb in shape and color; a conceited fool

[343] **you were best** you had better

Kent. Why, Fool?

Fool. Why? For taking one's part that's out of favor. Nay, an[344] thou canst not smile as the wind sits,[345] thou'lt catch cold[346] shortly. There, take my coxcomb. Why, this fellow has banished[347] two on's[348] daughters, and did the third a blessing against his will. If thou follow him, thou must needs wear my coxcomb. —How now, Nuncle?[349] Would I had two coxcombs and two daughters.

Lear. Why, my boy?

Fool. If I gave them all my living,[350] I'd keep my coxcombs myself. There's mine; beg another of thy daughters.

Lear. Take heed, sirrah—the whip.[351]

Fool. Truth's a dog must to kennel; he must be whipped out, when Lady the Brach[352] may stand by th' fire and stink.

Lear. A pestilent gall[353] to me.

Fool. Sirrah, I'll teach thee a speech.

Lear. Do.

Fool. Mark it, Nuncle.

[344] **an** if
[345] **smile . . . sits** back the stronger side
[346] **thou'lt catch cold** You'll be turned out of doors; so much the worse for you.
[347] **banished** alienated
[348] **on's** of his
[349] **Nuncle** contraction of "mine uncle"—the customary term of address of the court jester to his superior
[350] **living** property
[351] **the whip** Jesters could be whipped for going too far.
[352] **Brach** a hunting bitch
[353] **gall** irritation; sore; bile

Have more than thou showest,
Speak less than thou knowest,
Lend less than thou owest,[354]
Ride more than thou goest,[355]
Learn more than thou trowest,[356]
Set less than thou throwest,[357]
Leave thy drink and thy whore,
And keep in-a-door,[358]
And thou shalt have more
Than two tens to a score.[359]

Kent. This is nothing, Fool.

Fool. Then 'tis like the breath of an unfeed[360] lawyer[361] —you gave me nothing for't. Can you make no use of nothing, Nuncle?

Lear. Why, no, boy. Nothing can be made out of nothing.

Fool. [*To Kent*] Prithee tell him, so much the rent of his land comes to; he will not believe a Fool.

Lear. A bitter[362] Fool.

Fool. Dost thou know the difference, my boy, between a bitter Fool and a sweet one?

Lear. No, lad; teach me.

[354] **owest** own

[355] **goest** walk

[356] **trowest** guess

[357] **Set . . . throwest** Don't stake everything on a single throw of the dice.

[358] **in-a-door** indoors

[359] **And . . . score** And you will have more than twenty shillings for each pound (there were twenty shillings in the pound)—i.e., you will come away a richer man.

[360] **unfeed** unpaid

[361] **breath . . . lawyer** nothing. (No lawyer would breathe—that is, speak—unless he were paid.)

[362] **bitter** sarcastic; caustic

Fool.

That lord that counseled thee
To give away thy land,
Come place him here by me,
Do thou for him stand.
The sweet and bitter fool
Will presently appear;
The one in motley[363] here,
The other found out[364] there.[365]

Lear. Dost thou call me fool, boy?

Fool. All thy other titles thou hast given away; that thou wast born with.

Kent. This is not altogether fool, my lord.

Fool. No, faith; lords and great men will not let me. If I had a monopoly out, they would have part on't. And ladies too, they will not let me have all the fool to myself; they'll be snatching. Nuncle, give me an egg, and I'll give thee two crowns.

Lear. What two crowns shall they be?

Fool. Why, after I have cut the egg i' th' middle and eat up the meat, the two crowns of the egg. When thou clovest thy crown i' th' middle and gav'st away both parts, thou bor'st thine ass on thy back o'er the dirt.[366] Thou hadst little wit in thy bald crown when thou gav'st thy golden one away. If I speak like myself[367] in this, let him be whipped that first finds it so.

[363] **motley** the multicolored costume of the court jester

[364] **found out** revealed; exposed

[365] **there** i.e., in Lear

[366] **bor'st . . . dirt** (as the farmer did in Aesop's fable of the man, his two sons and the ass)

[367] **like myself** i.e., like a fool

[*Singing*] Fools had ne'er less grace[368] in a year,
For wise men are grown foppish,[369]
And know not how their wits to wear,[370]
Their manners are so apish.[371]

Lear. When were you wont to be so full of songs, sirrah?

Fool. I have used it,[372] Nuncle, e'er since thou mad'st thy daughters thy mothers; for when thou gav'st them the rod, and put'st down thine own breeches,

[*Singing*] Then they for sudden joy did weep,
And I for sorrow sung,
That such a king should play bo-peep[373]
And go the fools among.

Prithee, Nuncle, keep a schoolmaster that can teach thy Fool to lie. I would fain learn to lie.

Lear. And[374] you lie, sirrah, we'll have you whipped.

Fool. I marvel what kin thou and thy daughters are. They'll have me whipped for speaking true; thou'lt have me whipped for lying; and sometimes I am whipped for holding my peace. I had rather be any kind o' thing than a Fool, and yet I would not be thee, Nuncle: thou hast pared thy wit[375] o' both sides and left nothing i' th' middle. Here comes one o' the parings.

Enter Goneril

[368] **grace** favor
[369] **foppish** foolish
[370] **wear** i.e., use
[371] **apish** to ape is to mimic
[372] **used it** made a habit of it
[373] **play bo-peep** play hide-and-seek; play silly games
[374] **And** if
[375] **wit** mind; intellectual powers; sanity

Lear. How now, daughter? What makes[376] that frontlet[377]
on?[378] Methinks you are too much of late i' th'
frown.

Fool. Thou wast a pretty[379] fellow when thou hadst no
need to care for her frowning. Now thou art an O
without a figure.[380] I am better than thou art now: I
am a Fool, thou art nothing. [*To Goneril*.] Yes,
forsooth,[381] I will hold my tongue. So your face bids
me, though you say nothing. Mum,[382] mum,
He that keeps nor crust nor crum,[383]
Weary of all, shall want[384] some.
[*Pointing to Lear*] That's a shealed peascod.[385]

Goneril. Not only, sir, this your all-licensed[386] Fool,
But other[387] of your insolent retinue
Do hourly carp and quarrel, breaking forth
In rank[388] and not-to-be-endurèd riots. Sir,
I had thought by making this well known unto you
To have found a safe[389] redress,[390] but now grow
fearful,
By what yourself too late[391] have spoke and done,

[376] **makes** is . . . doing. (That is, What is that frontlet doing on?)
[377] **frontlet** coronet (implying a wrinkled brow)
[378] **What . . . on** Why are you wearing a frown?
[379] **pretty** fine
[380] **O. . . figure** a mere cipher, without a number to the left of it to give it value
[381] **forsooth** truly
[382] **Mum** silence
[383] **crum** small particle; the soft part of bread
[384] **want** need; lack
[385] **shealed peascod** shelled peapod (i.e., an empty thing)
[386] **all-licensed** to whom anything is permitted
[387] **other** others
[388] **rank** excessive; coarse
[389] **safe** sure
[390] **redress** remedy; reparation
[391] **too late** very recently

That you protect this course, and put it on[392]
By your allowance;[393] which if you should, the fault
Would not 'scape censure, nor the redresses sleep,[394]
Which,[395] in the tender of[396] a wholesome[397] weal,[398]
Might in their working do you that offense,
Which else were shame, that then necessity
Will call discreet proceeding.[399]

Fool. For you know, Nuncle,
The hedge-sparrow fed the cuckoo[400] so long
That it had it head bit off by it[401] young.
So out went the candle, and we were left darkling.[402]

Lear. Are you our daughter?

Goneril. Come, sir,
I would you would make use of your good wisdom
Whereof I know you are fraught[403] and put away
These dispositions[404] which of late transport you
From what you rightly are.

[392] **put it on** instigate it

[393] **allowance** approbation

[394] **which ... sleep** If you do this, it will not go without rebuke, and the response will be swift in coming.

[395] **Which** i.e., the measures Goneril will take in response

[396] **tender of** solicitude for; strong desire for

[397] **wholesome** healthy

[398] **weal** state

[399] **Might ... proceeding** These measures might offend you, and would, in other circumstances, be to my discredit. Here, however, being necessary, they will be recognized as the prudent thing to do.

[400] **cuckoo** (The cuckoo is called a "brood parasite" because it lays its eggs in the nests of birds of another species. The young cuckoo often quickly outgrows its foster-parents.)

[401] **it ... it** its ... its

[402] **darkling** in the dark

[403] **fraught** well-stocked/stored

[404] **dispositions** temperamental fits

Fool. May not an ass[405] know when the cart draws the horse?[406] Whoop, Jug,[407] I love thee![408]

Lear. Does any here know me? This is not Lear.
Does Lear walk thus? Speak thus? Where are his
eyes?
Either his notion[409] weakens, or his discernings[410]
Are lethargied[411]—Ha! Waking?[412] 'Tis not so.
Who is it that can tell me who I am?

Fool. Lear's shadow.

Lear. I would learn that; for, by the marks of sovereignty, knowledge, and reason, I should be false[413] persuaded I had daughters.

Fool. Which[414] they will make an obedient father.

Lear. Your name, fair gentlewoman?

Goneril. This admiration,[415] sir, is much o' th' savor[416]
Of other your[417] new pranks. I do beseech you
To understand my purposes aright.
As you are old and reverend, should be wise.
Here do you keep a hundred knights and squires,
Men so disordered,[418] so deboshed,[419] and bold,
That this our court, infected with their manners,

[405] **ass** i.e., even a fool
[406] **when . . . horse** i.e., when a daughter tells her father and king what to do
[407] **Jug** nickname for Joan
[408] **Whoop . . . thee** possibly a refrain from a popular song
[409] **notion** mental power
[410] **discernings** faculties of perception
[411] **lethargied** dulled
[412] **Waking** Am I awake?
[413] **false** falsely
[414] **Which** whom
[415] **admiration** affected astonishment
[416] **o' th' savor** of the same flavor or type
[417] **other your** some of your other
[418] **disordered** disorderly
[419] **deboshed** debauched

Shows[420] like a riotous inn. Epicurism[421] and lust
Makes it more like a tavern or a brothel
Than a graced[422] palace. The shame itself doth speak
For instant remedy. Be then desired[423]
By her, that else will take the thing she begs,
A little to disquantity[424] your train,[425]
And the remainders[426] that shall still depend,[427]
To be such men as may besort[428] your age,
Which know themselves, and you.

Lear. Darkness and devils!
Saddle my horses; call my train together.
Degenerate bastard, I'll not trouble thee:
Yet have I left a daughter.

Goneril. You strike my people, and your disordered rabble
Make servants of their betters.

Enter Albany.

Lear. Woe, that[429] too late repents. O, sir, are you come?
Is it your will? Speak, sir. Prepare my horses.
Ingratitude! thou marble-hearted fiend,
More hideous when thou show'st thee in a child
Than the sea-monster.

Albany. Pray,[430] sir, be patient.

[420] **Shows** looks; seems
[421] **Epicurism** gluttony; riotous living
[422] **graced** honorable; stately
[423] **desired** requested
[424] **disquantity** reduce the size of
[425] **train** retinue
[426] **remainders** those who remain
[427] **depend** attend you as dependents
[428] **besort** befit
[429] **Woe, that** woe to him that
[430] **Pray** please

Lear. Detested kite,[431] thou liest.
My train are men of choice and rarest[432] parts,[433]
That all particulars of duty know,
And, in the most exact regard,[434] support[435]
The worships[436] of their name.[437] O most small fault,
How ugly didst thou in Cordelia show!
Which, like an engine,[438] wrenched my frame of nature
From the fixed place;[439] drew from my heart all love,
And added to the gall.[440] O Lear, Lear, Lear!
Beat at this gate that let thy folly in [*Striking his head.*]
And thy dear judgment out. Go, go, my people.

Albany. My lord, I am guiltless, as I am ignorant
Of what hath moved you.

Lear. It may be so, my lord.
Hear, Nature, hear; dear Goddess, hear:
Suspend thy purpose if thou didst intend
To make this creature fruitful.
Into her womb convey sterility,
Dry up in her the organs of increase,[441]
And from her derogate[442] body never spring

[431] **kite** a bird of prey; one who preys upon others; a term of detestation (Lear is addressing Goneril.)

[432] **rarest** finest

[433] **parts** qualities

[434] **in . . . regard** with the most scrupulous attention

[435] **support** live up to

[436] **worships** honor

[437] **The . . . name** the honorable reputation they have earned

[438] **engine** a machine of some kind

[439] **Which . . . place** The image is either one of a machine moving a building off its foundations, or of a lever introduced into Lear's frame and prising it apart.

[440] **gall** bitterness

[441] **increase** fertility

[442] **derogate** debased

A babe to honor her. If she must teem,[443]
Create her child of spleen,[444] that it may live
And be a thwart[445] disnatured[446] torment to her.
Let it stamp wrinkles in her brow of youth,
With cadent[447] tears fret[448] channels in her cheeks,
Turn all her mother's pains[449] and benefits[450]
To laughter and contempt, that she may feel
How sharper than a serpent's tooth it is
To have a thankless child. Away, away! *Exit.*

Albany. Now, gods that we adore, whereof comes this?

Goneril. Never afflict yourself to know the cause,
But let his disposition[451] have that scope
As[452] dotage[453] gives it.

Enter Lear.

Lear. What, fifty of my followers at a clap?[454]
Within a fortnight?[455]

Albany. What's the matter, sir?

Lear. I'll tell thee. [*To Goneril*] Life and death, I am ashamed

[443] **teem** bear offspring
[444] **spleen** spite; violent ill-temper
[445] **thwart** contrary; perverse
[446] **disnatured** without natural affection
[447] **cadent** falling
[448] **fret** erode; gnaw; carve
[449] **pains** cares
[450] **benefits** good deeds; kindnesses
[451] **disposition** humor; mood
[452] **As** that
[453] **dotage** senility
[454] **at a clap** all at once
[455] **a fortnight** two weeks

That thou hast power to shake my manhood[456]
thus!
That these hot tears, which break from me
perforce,[457]
Should make thee worth them. Blasts[458] and fogs
upon thee!
Th' untented woundings[459] of a father's curse
Pierce every sense about thee! Old fond[460] eyes,
Beweep[461] this cause again, I'll pluck ye out
And cast you, with the waters that you loose,[462]
To temper[463] clay. Yea, is it come to this?
Ha! Let it be so. I have another daughter,
Who I am sure is kind and comfortable.[464]
When she shall hear this of thee, with her nails
She'll flay thy wolvish visage. Thou shalt find
That I'll resume the shape[465] which thou dost think
I have cast off for ever.

Exit [Lear with Kent and Attendants].

Goneril. Do you mark that?

Albany. I cannot be so partial, Goneril,
To the great love I bear you——

Goneril. Pray you, content. What, Oswald, ho!
[*To the Fool*] You, sir, more knave than fool,
after your master!

[456] **shake my manhood** i.e., by bringing him to tears
[457] **perforce** forcibly; by violence
[458] **Blasts** lightning bolts; strong gusts of wind; curses
[459] **untented woundings** wounds too deep for a tent (a roll of lint used to cleanse wounds)
[460] **fond** foolish
[461] **Beweep** if you weep for
[462] **loose** emit; waste
[463] **temper** mix with; soften
[464] **comfortable** able to give comfort
[465] **shape** outward appearance; role

Fool. Nuncle Lear, Nuncle Lear, tarry.[466] Take the Fool with thee.[467]

A fox, when one has caught her,
And such a daughter,
Should sure[468] to the slaughter,
If my cap would buy a halter.[469]
So the Fool follows after.[470] *Exit.*

Goneril. This man hath had good counsel. A hundred knights!
'Tis politic[471] and safe to let him keep
At point[472] a hundred knights: yes, that on every dream,
Each buzz,[473] each fancy, each complaint, dislike,
He may enguard[474] his dotage with their pow'rs
And hold our lives in mercy.[475] Oswald, I say!

Albany. Well, you may fear too far.

Goneril. Safer than trust too far.
Let me still take away the harms I fear,
Not fear still[476] to be taken.[477] I know his heart.
What he hath uttered I have writ my sister.
If she sustain him and his hundred knights,
When I have showed th' unfitness——

Enter Oswald.

[466] **tarry** wait

[467] **Take . . . thee** Take me with you; take the epithet "fool" with you.

[468] **Should sure** should certainly be sent

[469] **halter** rope with a noose by which horses or cattle are led or fastened; rope with a noose for hanging criminals

[470] **halter, after** both rhymed with "slaughter" in Shakespeare's day

[471] **politic** shrewd; prudent

[472] **At point** armed and ready

[473] **buzz** rumor

[474] **enguard** protect

[475] **in mercy** in jeopardy

[476] **still** always

[477] **taken** overtaken by harm

How now, Oswald?
What, have you writ that letter to my sister?

Oswald. Ay, madam.

Goneril. Take you some company,[478] and away to horse.
Inform her full of my particular[479] fear,
And thereto add such reasons of your own
As may compact[480] it more. Get you gone,
And hasten your return. [*Exit Oswald.*] No, no, my lord,
This milky gentleness and course[481] of yours,
Though I condemn not,[482] yet under pardon,[483]
You are much more attasked[484] for want[485] of wisdom
Than praised for harmful mildness.[486]

Albany. How far your eyes may pierce I cannot tell;
Striving to better, oft we mar what's well,

Goneril. Nay then——

Albany. Well, well, th' event.[487] *Exeunt.*

Scene 5. [*Court before the same.*]

Enter Lear, Kent, and Fool.

Lear. Go you before to Gloucester with these letters.
Acquaint my daughter no further with anything

[478] **company** body of soldiers
[479] **particular** personal
[480] **compact** confirm; strengthen
[481] **milky . . . course** mild and gentle course of action
[482] **condemn not** condemn it not
[483] **under pardon** with respect
[484] **attasked** to be reproved
[485] **want** lack
[486] **harmful mildness** dangerous leniency
[487] **th' event** let us see how it turns out

you know than comes from her demand out of[488] the letter.[489] If your diligence be not speedy, I shall be there afore you.

Kent. I will not sleep, my lord, till I have delivered your letter. *Exit.*

Fool. If a man's brains were in's heels, were't[490] not in danger of kibes?[491]

Lear. Ay, boy.

Fool. Then I prithee be merry. Thy wit shall not go slipshod.[492, 493]

Lear. Ha, ha, ha.

Fool. Shalt[494] see thy other daughter will use thee kindly;[495] for though she's[496] as like[497] this[498] as a crab's[499] like an apple, yet I can tell what I can tell.

Lear. Why, what canst thou tell, my boy?

Fool. She will taste as like this as a crab does to a crab. Thou canst tell why one's nose stands i' th' middle on's[500] face?

[488] **out of** suggested by

[489] **than . . . letter** than what she asks after reading the letter

[490] **were't** were it (i.e., a man's brain)

[491] **kibes** chapped chilblains (inflammatory swelling produced by exposure to cold, affecting the hands and feet, accompanied with heat, itching, and occasionally ulceration)

[492] **slipshod** slippered

[493] **Thy . . . slipshod** that is, you have no brains in your heels either, as this journey to Regan makes plain.

[494] **Shalt** thou shalt

[495] **kindly** a play on two senses of "kindly": tenderly; according to her kind or nature

[496] **she** Regan

[497] **like** i.e., in appearance

[498] **this** Goneril

[499] **crab** crab apple (which is sour and harsh-tasting)

[500] **on's** of his

Lear. No.

Fool. Why, to keep one's eyes of[501] either side's[502] nose, that what a man cannot smell out, he may spy into.

Lear. I did her wrong.

Fool. Canst tell how an oyster makes his shell?

Lear. No.

Fool. Nor I neither; but I can tell why a snail has a house.

Lear. Why?

Fool. Why, to put 's[503] head in; not to give it away to his daughters, and leave his horns[504] without a case.

Lear. I will forget my nature.[505] So kind a father! Be my horses ready?

Fool. Thy asses[506] are gone about 'em. The reason why the seven stars[507] are no moe[508] than seven is a pretty[509] reason.

Lear. Because they are not eight.

Fool. Yes indeed. Thou wouldst make a good Fool.

Lear. To take't again[510] perforce![511] Monster ingratitude!

[501] **of** on
[502] **side's** side of his
[503] **put 's** put his
[504] **horns** the symbol of the cuckold
[505] **nature** natural affection (i.e., of a father)
[506] **Thy asses** Lear's servants
[507] **the seven stars** the Pleiades
[508] **moe** more
[509] **pretty** ingenious
[510] **To take't again** i.e., his royal authority
[511] **perforce** by force; by constraint of necessity

Fool. If thou wert my Fool, Nuncle, I'd have thee beaten for being old before thy time.

Lear. How's that?

Fool. Thou shouldst not have been old till thou hadst been wise.

Lear. O, let me not be mad,[512] not mad, sweet heaven!
Keep me in temper;[513] I would not be mad!

[*Enter Gentleman.*]

How now, are the horses ready?

Gentleman. Ready, my lord.

Lear. Come, boy.

Fool. She that's a maid now, and laughs at my departure,
Shall not be a maid long, unless things[514] be cut shorter.[515] *Exeunt*

[512] **let me not be mad** the first premonition
[513] **in temper** sane
[514] **things** penises
[515] **She . . . shorter** The maid who laughs at this point in the play is too naïve to remain a virgin for long.

ACT 2

Scene 1. [*The Earl of Gloucester's castle.*]

Enter Edmund and Curan, severally.[1]

Edmund. Save thee[2], Curan.

Curan. And you, sir. I have been with your father, and given him notice that the Duke of Cornwall and Regan his duchess will be here with him this night.

Edmund. How comes that?

Curan. Nay, I know not. You have heard of the news abroad? I mean the whispered ones, for they are yet but ear-kissing[3] arguments.[4]

Edmund. Not I. Pray you, what are they?

Curan. Have you heard of no likely wars toward,[5] 'twixt the Dukes of Cornwall and Albany?

Edmund. Not a word.

Curan. You may do, then, in time. Fare you well, sir. *Exit.*

Edmund. The Duke be here tonight? The better![6] best!
This weaves itself perforce[7] into my business.
My father hath set guard to take my brother,

[1] **severally** from different places
[2] **Save thee** God save thee
[3] **ear-kissing** (Some editions read "ear-bussing", which essentially means the same thing, with a pun on "bussing" [kissing] and buzzing [whispering].)
[4] **arguments** subject-matter
[5] **toward** imminently threatening
[6] **The better** so much the better
[7] **perforce** of necessity; forcibly

And I have one thing of a queasy[8] question[9]
Which I must act.[10] Briefness[11] and Fortune, work!
Brother, a word; descend. Brother, I say!

Enter Edgar.

My father watches. O sir, fly this place.
Intelligence[12] is given where you are hid.
You have now the good advantage of the night.
Have you not spoken 'gainst the Duke of Cornwall?
He's coming hither, now i' th' night, i' th' haste,[13]
And Regan with him. Have you nothing said
Upon[14] his party[15] 'gainst the Duke of Albany?
Advise yourself.[16]

Edgar. I am sure on't,[17] not a word.

Edmund. I hear my father coming. Pardon me:
In cunning I must draw my sword upon you.
Draw, seem to defend yourself; now quit you well.[18]
Yield! Come before my father! Light ho, here!
Fly, brother. Torches, torches!—So farewell.

Exit Edgar.

Some blood drawn on me would beget opinion

[*Wounds his arm*]

[8] **queasy** hazardous; delicate; affected with nausea
[9] **of . . . question** that requires delicate handling
[10] **act** put into action
[11] **Briefness** promptitude; swiftness
[12] **Intelligence** information
[13] **i' th' haste** in great haste
[14] **said / Upon** spoken against
[15] **party** side; faction
[16] **Advise yourself** consider
[17] **on't** of it
[18] **quit you well** acquit yourself well (i.e., fight well; make it look realistic)

Of my more fierce endeavor.[19] I have seen drunkards
Do more than this in sport. Father, father!
Stop, stop! No help?

Enter Gloucester, and Servants with torches.

Gloucester. Now, Edmund, where's the villain?

Edmund. Here stood he in the dark, his sharp sword out,
Mumbling of wicked charms, conjuring the moon[20]
To stand auspicious mistress.[21]

Gloucester. But where is he?

Edmund. Look, sir, I bleed.

Gloucester. Where is the villain, Edmund?

Edmund. Fled this way, sir, when by no means he could——

Gloucester. Pursue him, ho! Go after.

[*Exeunt some Servants*.]

By no means what?

Edmund. Persuade me to the murder of your lordship;
But that I told him the revenging gods
'Gainst parricides[22] did all the thunder bend;[23]
Spoke with how manifold and strong a bond
The child was bound to th' father. Sir, in fine,[24]
Seeing how loathly opposite[25] I stood

[19] **beget . . . endeavor** persuade people that I have been in a fierce fight

[20] **moon** and thus Hecate

[21] **To . . . mistress** to favor him with success as her votary

[22] **parricides** those who kill a near relative, especially either parent; those who kill the ruler of, or commit treason against, their country

[23] **bend** aim

[24] **in fine** to conclude; in short

[25] **loathly opposite** bitterly opposed

To his unnatural purpose, in fell[26] motion[27]
With his preparèd[28] sword he charges home
My unprovided[29] body, latched[30] mine arm;
But when he saw my best alarumed[31] spirits[32]
Bold in[33] the quarrel's right,[34] roused to th'
encounter,
Or whether gasted[35] by the noise I made,
Full suddenly he fled.

Gloucester. Let him fly far.
Not in this land shall he remain uncaught;
And found—dispatch.[36] The noble Duke my master,
My worthy arch[37] and patron, comes tonight.
By his authority I will proclaim it,
That he which finds him shall deserve our thanks,
Bringing the murderous coward to the stake.
He that conceals him, death.[38]

Edmund. When I dissuaded him from his intent,
And found him pight[39] to do it, with curst[40] speech
I threatened to discover[41] him. He replied,
"Thou unpossessing[42] bastard, dost thou think,
If I would stand against thee, would the reposal[43]

[26] **fell** fierce; deadly
[27] **motion** thrust (from fencing)
[28] **preparèd** drawn
[29] **unprovided** unprotected
[30] **latched** caught
[31] **alarumed** roused to action (as by a trumpet call)
[32] **spirits** energies
[33] **Bold in** made bold by
[34] **the quarrel's right** the justice of my cause
[35] **gasted** frightened
[36] **dispatch** kill him
[37] **arch** chief
[38] **death** i.e., shall deserve death
[39] **pight** resolved
[40] **curst** savage; vicious; malignant
[41] **discover** expose
[42] **unpossessing** landless; beggarly
[43] **reposal** placing

Of any trust, virtue, or worth in thee
Make thy words faithed?[44] No. What I should
deny—
As this I would, ay, though thou didst produce
My very character[45]—I'd turn it all
To thy suggestion,[46] plot, and damnèd practice.[47]
And thou must make a dullard of the world,[48]
If they not thought[49] the profits of my death
Were very pregnant[50] and potential[51] spirits[52]
To make thee seek it."

Gloucester. O strange and fastened[53] villain!
Would he deny his letter, said he? I never got[54] him.

Tucket[55] within.

Hark, the Duke's trumpets. I know not why he
comes.
All ports[56] I'll bar; the villain shall not 'scape;
The Duke must grant me that. Besides, his picture I
will send far and near, that all the kingdom
May have due note of him; and of my land,
Loyal and natural[57] boy, I'll work the means
To make thee capable.[58]

[44] **faithed** believed
[45] **character** handwriting
[46] **suggestion** crafty dealing
[47] **practice** intrigue
[48] **make . . . world** imagine the whole world to be stupid
[49] **If . . . thought** i.e., if they had not thought
[50] **pregnant** obvious; full of incentives
[51] **potential** potent; powerful
[52] **spirits** evil spirits; incitements
[53] **fastened** hardened
[54] **got** begot
[55] **Tucket** trumpet-call (Cornwall's special trumpet-call)
[56] **ports** seaports; gates
[57] **natural** Gloucester is quibbling on the two meanings of "natural"—"illegitimate" and "feeling natural affection"; "natural" could mean "legitimate" as well as "illegitimate".
[58] **capable** i.e., of inheriting

Enter Cornwall, Regan, and Attendants.

Cornwall. How now, my noble friend! Since I came hither,
Which I can call but now, I have heard strange news.

Regan. If it be true, all vengeance comes too short
Which can pursue th' offender. How dost, my lord?

Gloucester. O madam, my old heart is cracked, it's cracked.

Regan. What, did my father's godson seek your life?
He whom my father named, your Edgar?

Gloucester. O lady, lady, shame would have it hid.

Regan. Was he not companion with the riotous knights
That tended upon my father?

Gloucester. I know not, madam. 'Tis too bad, too bad.

Edmund. Yes, madam, he was of that consort.[59]

Regan. No marvel then, though he were ill affected.[60]
'Tis they have put him on[61] the old man's death,
To have th' expense and waste[62] of his revenues.
I have this present evening from my sister
Been well informed of them, and with such cautions
That, if they come to sojourn at my house,
I'll not be there.

Cornwall. Nor I, assure thee, Regan.
Edmund, I hear that you have shown your father
A childlike[63] office.[64]

[59] **consort** company
[60] **ill affected** disloyal
[61] **put him on** urged him to
[62] **expense and waste** squandering
[63] **childlike** filial; befitting a son
[64] **office** service

Edmund. It was my duty, sir.

Gloucester. He did bewray[65] his practice,[66] and received
This hurt you see, striving to apprehend him.

Cornwall. Is he pursued?

Gloucester. Ay, my good lord.

Cornwall. If he be taken, he shall never more
Be feared of doing[67] harm. Make your own purpose,
How in my strength you please.[68] For you, Edmund,
Whose virtue and obedience[69] doth this instant
So much commend itself, you shall be ours.[70]
Natures of such deep[71] trust we shall much need;
You we first seize on.

Edmund. I shall serve you, sir,
Truly, however else.

Gloucester. For him I thank your Grace.

Cornwall. You know not why we came to visit you?

Regan. Thus out of season,[72] threading dark-eyed night.[73]
Occasions, noble Gloucester, of some prize,[74]
Wherein we must have use of your advice.
Our father he hath writ, so hath our sister,
Of differences,[75] which[76] I best thought it fit

[65] **bewray** expose; disclose

[66] **practice** intrigue

[67] **of doing** lest he should do

[68] **Make . . . please** You may make what use of my power and authority as you please in apprehending him.

[69] **virtue and obedience** virtuous obedience

[70] **you shall be ours** I will take you in my service.

[71] **deep** ("deep" also has the connotation of "cunning" and "crafty")

[72] **Thus . . . season** at such an unusual or unsuitable time

[73] **threading . . . night** (A metaphor—based on threading the eye of a needle—for the difficulties of traveling roads in the dark.)

[74] **prize** importance

[75] **differences** quarrels

[76] **which** (referring to Lear's letter, not to "differences")

To answer from[77] our home. The several
messengers
From hence attend dispatch.[78] Our good old friend,
Lay comforts to your bosom,[79] and bestow
Your needful counsel to our businesses,
Which craves the instant use.[80]

Gloucester. I serve you, madam.
Your Graces are right welcome.

Exeunt. Flourish.

Scene 2. [*Before Gloucester's castle.*]

Enter Kent and Oswald, severally.

Oswald. Good dawning[81] to thee, friend. Art of this house?[82]

Kent. Ay.

Oswald. Where may we set our horses?

Kent. I' th' mire.

Oswald. Prithee, if thou lov'st me,[83] tell me.

Kent. I love thee not.

Oswald. Why then, I care not for thee.

Kent. If I had thee in Lipsbury[84] Pinfold,[85] I would make thee care for me.

[77] **from** away from, so that Lear cannot come to her before he has consulted Goneril

[78] **attend dispatch** are awaiting orders to be sent with all speed

[79] **Lay . . . bosom** take heart (addressed to Edgar)

[80] **Which . . . use** which require immediate attention

[81] **dawning** (the sun has not yet risen)

[82] **of this house** a servant here

[83] **if thou lov'st me** as an act of kindness

[84] **Lipsbury** literally, "Liptown"—thought to mean "between my teeth", i.e., "in my clutches"

[85] **Pinfold** a pen for stray cattle

Oswald. Why dost thou use me thus? I know thee not.

Kent. Fellow, I know thee.

Oswald. What dost thou know me for?

Kent. A knave,[86] a rascal, an eater of broken meats;[87] a base, proud, shallow, beggarly, three-suited,[88] hundred-pound,[89] filthy worsted-stocking[90] knave; a lily-livered,[91] action-taking,[92] whoreson, glass-gazing,[93] superserviceable,[94] finical[95] rogue; one-trunk-inheriting[96] slave; one that wouldst be a bawd[97] in way of good service,[98] and art nothing but the composition[99] of a knave, beggar, coward, pander, and the son and heir[100] of a mongrel bitch; one whom I will beat into clamorous whining if thou deniest the least syllable of thy addition.[101]

Oswald. Why, what a monstrous fellow art thou, thus to rail on one that is neither known of thee nor knows thee!

[86] **A knave** a servant; a menial; a base and crafty rogue (significantly the first epithet in Kent's litany of abuse, of which it is the theme)

[87] **broken meats** leftovers

[88] **three-suited** servants were given three suits a year

[89] **hundred-pound** (probably a contemptuous reference to James I's profuse creation of peerages for money)

[90] **worsted-stocking** (woolen stockings worn by servants [as opposed to silk stockings worn by gentlemen], so-called after the village of Worsted in Norfolk famous for the manufacture of cloth)

[91] **lily-livered** white-livered, bloodless. The liver was thought to be the seat of courage, thus, "cowardly".

[92] **action-taking** litigious because too cowardly to fight

[93] **glass** mirror

[94] **superserviceable** only too serviceable: someone who fawns upon his superiors for his own advancement

[95] **finical** excessively concerned with his clothes

[96] **one-trunk-inheriting** owning no more than would fill one trunk

[97] **bawd** pimp

[98] **wouldst . . . service** would prostitute yourself or others to earn the gratitude of your superiors

[99] **composition** compound

[100] **heir** inheritor of her characteristics

[101] **addition** list of titles just described

Kent. What a brazen-faced varlet art thou to deny thou knowest me! Is it two days since I tripped up thy heels and beat thee before the King? [*Drawing his sword*] Draw, you rogue, for though it be night, yet the moon shines. I'll make a sop o' th' moonshine[102] of you. You whoreson cullionly[103] barbermonger,[104] draw!

Oswald. Away, I have nothing to do with thee.

Kent. Draw, you rascal. You come with letters against the King, and take Vanity the puppet's[105] part against the royalty of her father. Draw, you rogue, or I'll so carbonado[106] your shanks. Draw, you rascal. Come your ways![107]

Oswald. Help, ho! Murder! Help!

Kent. Strike, you slave! Stand, rogue! Stand, you neat[108] slave! Strike! [*Beating him*]

Oswald. Help, ho! Murder, murder!

Enter Edmund, with his rapier drawn, Cornwall, Regan, Gloucester, Servants.

Edmund. How now? What's the matter?[109] Part!

[102] **sop o' th' moonshine** A sop was a wafer or piece of bread floating in a drink: Kent is threatening to pierce him full of holes and leave him to soak up the moonshine.

[103] **cullionly** cullion: testicle; despicable fellow; rascal

[104] **barbermonger** habitué of the barber shop: a dandy

[105] **Vanity the puppet's** a reference to morality plays, which were sometimes put on as puppet shows. The characters in such plays were allegorical, many of them being personifications of virtues and vices; Kent is identifying Goneril with vanity.

[106] **carbonado** slash and grill

[107] **Come your ways!** Come on!

[108] **neat** elegant; foppish; pure; unadulterated

[109] **the matter** the subject of the quarrel

Kent. With you,[110] goodman[111] boy, if you please! Come, I'll flesh[112] ye, come on, young master.

Gloucester. Weapons? Arms? What's the matter here?

Cornwall. Keep peace, upon your lives.
He dies that strikes again. What is the matter?

Regan. The messengers from our sister and the King.

Cornwall. What is your difference?[113] Speak.

Oswald. I am scarce in breath, my lord.

Kent. No marvel, you have so bestirred your valor. You cowardly rascal, nature disclaims in thee.[114] A tailor made thee.[115]

Cornwall. Thou art a strange fellow. A tailor make a man?

Kent. A tailor, sir. A stonecutter or a painter could not have made him so ill, though they had been but two years o' th' trade.

Cornwall. Speak yet, how grew your quarrel?

Oswald. This ancient ruffian, sir, whose life I have spared at suit of[116] his gray beard———

[110] **With you** i.e., The quarrel is with you (addressed to Edmund as is what follows).

[111] **goodman** A man of substance, not of gentle birth; prefixed to designations of occupation: Kent is addressing Edmund with mock respect, playing upon the latter's youth, humble birth, and pretended claim to respect.

[112] **flesh** initiate in bloodshed or warfare (originally a hunting term); plunge a weapon into someone

[113] **difference** quarrel

[114] **disclaims in thee** renounces any claim to have made you

[115] **A tailor made thee** (proverbial. "The tailor makes the man", suggesting that Oswald a mere fop—all display and no substance.)

[116] **suit** entreaty; supplication

Kent. Thou whoreson zed,[117] thou unnecessary letter!
My lord, if you will give me leave, I will tread this
unbolted[118] villain into mortar and daub the wall of
a jakes[119] with him. Spare my gray beard, you
wagtail![120]

Cornwall. Peace, sirrah!
You beastly knave, know you no reverence?

Kent. Yes, sir, but anger hath a privilege.

Cornwall. Why art thou angry?

Kent. That such a slave as this should wear a sword,
Who wears no honesty. Such smiling rogues as
these,
Like rats, oft bite the holy cords[121] atwain
Which are too intrince[122] t' unloose; smooth[123]
every passion
That in the natures of their lords rebel,
Being oil to fire, snow to the colder moods;
Renege,[124] affirm, and turn their halcyon[125] beaks
With every gale and vary[126] of their masters,
Knowing naught, like dogs, but following.

[117] **zed** worthless symbol. The letter "z" was considered superfluous by many in Shakespeare's day: "s" was often used in its stead; it was generally ignored in the dictionaries of the time; and it wasn't used in Latin.

[118] **unbolted** unsifted. Unbolted mortar is made of unsifted lime; in order to break up its lumps, it was the practice to trample on it with wooden shoes. Also, possibly, without a "bolt", i.e., impotent or effeminate.

[119] **jakes** latrine

[120] **wagtail** The wagtail's tail jerks up and down spasmodically: either a reference to Oswald's agitated state or to his obsequiousness.

[121] **holy cords** sacred family bonds. Oswald is the rat gnawing through the bonds between Lear and his daughter, and/or Goneril and her husband.

[122] **intrince** entangled; intricate; tightly drawn

[123] **smooth** flatter

[124] **Renege** deny

[125] **halcyon** Dried halcyon birds were hung up to serve as a sort of weathervane, turning with the wind; the halcyon (a type of kingfisher) was associated with calm and quietude.

[126] **gale and vary** varying gale

A plague upon your epileptic[127] visage!
Smile you[128] my speeches, as I were a fool?
Goose,[129] if I had you upon Sarum Plain,[130]
I'd drive ye cackling home to Camelot.[131]

Cornwall. What, art thou mad, old fellow?

Gloucester. How fell you out?[132] Say that.

Kent. No contraries[133] hold more antipathy
Than I and such a knave.

Cornwall. Why dost thou call him knave? What is his fault?

Kent. His countenance likes[134] me not.

Cornwall. No more perchance does mine, nor his, nor hers.

Kent. Sir, 'tis my occupation to be plain:
I have seen better faces in my time
Than stands on any shoulder that I see
Before me at this instant.

Cornwall. This is some fellow
Who, having been praised for bluntness, doth affect

[127] **epileptic** Pale and shaking like an epileptic, Oswald is nonetheless trying to put on a brave face.

[128] **Smile you** do you smile at

[129] **Goose** simpleton. Oswald may be cackling with laughter. In Shakespeare, the goose is often associated with disease and bitterness.

[130] **Sarum Plain** Salisbury Plain

[131] **Camelot** the residence of King Arthur. Shakespeare's allusion here is not clear: It has been suggested that he is referring to Winchester, one of the sites traditionally identified with Camelot. This would tie in with Kent's calling Oswald a goose, as "Winchester goose" was a term for both a venereal disorder and a prostitute. Camelot was also traditionally located in Somerset. Salisbury is in Somerset, and flocks of geese were said to gather on the moors there.

[132] **How . . . out?** How did you come to quarrel?

[133] **contraries** opposites

[134] **likes** pleases

A saucy roughness, and constrains the garb[135]
Quite from his[136] nature.[137] He cannot flatter, he;
An honest mind and plain, he must speak truth.
And[138] they will take it, so; if not, he's plain.
These kind of knaves I know, which in this
plainness
Harbor more craft and more corrupter ends
Than twenty silly-ducking[139] observants[140]
That stretch their duties nicely.[141]

Kent. Sir, in good faith, in sincere verity,
Under th' allowance[142] of your great aspect,[143]
Whose influence,[144] like the wreath of radiant fire
On flick'ring Phoebus'[145] front[146]——

Cornwall. What mean'st by this?

Kent. To go out of my dialect,[147] which you discommend so much. I know, sir, I am no flatterer. He that beguiled you in a plain accent[148] was a plain knave, which, for my part, I will not be, though I should win your displeasure to entreat me to't.[149]

Cornwall. What was th' offense you gave him?

[135] **garb** style; fashion (of speech)
[136] **his** its
[137] **constrains . . . nature** i.e., turns plain speech into a cloak for his meaning
[138] **And** if
[139] **silly-ducking** ridiculously obsequious (recalling the wagtail above)
[140] **observants** obsequious servants
[141] **stretch . . . nicely** strain to the utmost to fulfill their duties punctiliously
[142] **allowance** approval
[143] **aspect** look, appearance; positions and influence of the heavenly bodies. Kent is ironically comparing Cornwall to a star.
[144] **influence** astrological power
[145] **Phoebus** the god of the sun
[146] **front** forehead
[147] **dialect** usual manner of speaking
[148] **He . . . accent** i.e., the kind of man Cornwall has been describing
[149] **though . . . to't** meaning unclear; perhaps, "if you were to persuade me to flatter you, you would not be pleased with my performance"

Oswald. I never gave him any.
It pleased the King his master very late[150]
To strike at me, upon his misconstruction;[151]
When he, compact,[152] and flattering his displeasure,
Tripped me behind; being down, insulted, railed,
And put upon him such a deal of man[153]
That worthied him,[154] got praises of the King
For him attempting[155] who was self-subdued;
And, in the fleshment[156] of this dread exploit,
Drew on me here again.

Kent. None of these rogues and cowards
But Ajax is their fool.[157]

Cornwall. Fetch forth the stocks!
You stubborn[158] ancient knave, you reverent[159]
braggart,
We'll teach you.

Kent. Sir, I am too old to learn.
Call not your stocks for me, I serve the King,
On whose employment I was sent to you.
You shall do small respect, show too bold malice
Against the grace and person[160] of my master,
Stocking his messenger.

[150] **very late** very recently
[151] **misconstruction** misinterpretation
[152] **compact** in league with the king
[153] **put ... man** cut such a heroic figure
[154] **That ... him** that he won honor for himself
[155] **For him attempting** for attacking one
[156] **fleshment** excited by his first success
[157] **None ... fool** That is, Kent is likening Cornwall to Ajax, in being played for a fool by Oswald (as Ajax is by the rogue and coward Thersites in *Troilus and Cressida*).
[158] **stubborn** rude; fierce
[159] **reverent** old
[160] **grace and person** i.e., against Lear both as a man and as king

Cornwall. Fetch forth the stocks. As I have life and honor,
There shall he sit till noon.

Regan. Till noon? Till night, my lord, and all night too.

Kent. Why, madam, if I were your father's dog,
You should not use me so.

Regan. Sir, being his knave, I will.

Cornwall. This is a fellow of the selfsame color[161]
Our sister speaks of. Come, bring away[162] the stocks.

Stocks brought out.

Gloucester. Let me beseech your Grace not to do so.
His fault is much, and the good King his master
Will check[163] him for't. Your purposed[164] low correction
Is such as basest and contemnèd'st[165] wretches
For pilf' rings and most common trespasses
Are punished with.
The King his master needs must take it ill
That he, so slightly valued[166] in his messenger,
Should have him thus restrained.

Cornwall. I'll answer[167] that.

Regan. My sister may receive it much more worse,
To have her gentleman abused, assaulted,
For following her affairs. Put in his legs.

[161] **color** kind; complexion
[162] **away** here
[163] **check** rebuke
[164] **purposed** intended
[165] **contemnèd'st** most despised
[166] **valued** esteemed
[167] **answer** answer for

[*Kent is put in the stocks.*]

Come, my good lord, away!

[*Exeunt all but Gloucester and Kent.*]

Gloucester. I am sorry for thee, friend. 'Tis the Duke's
pleasure,
Whose disposition[168] all the world well knows
Will not be rubbed[169] nor stopped. I'll entreat for
thee.

Kent. Pray do not, sir. I have watched[170] and traveled
hard.
Some time I shall sleep out, the rest I'll whistle.
A good man's fortune may grow out at heels.[171]
Give[172] you good morrow.

Gloucester. The Duke's to blame in this. 'Twill be
ill taken. *Exit.*

Kent. Good King, that must approve[173] the common
saw,[174]
Thou out of Heaven's benediction com'st
To the warm sun.[175]
Approach, thou beacon[176] to this under globe,[177]
That by thy comfortable[178] beams I may
Peruse this letter. Nothing almost[179] sees miracles

[168] **disposition** temperament
[169] **rubbed** deflected (A "rub" is an obstacle in the game of bowls.)
[170] **watched** not slept
[171] **A . . . heels** even a good man's good fortune may wear thin
[172] **Give** God give
[173] **approve** confirm
[174] **saw** saying
[175] **out . . . sun** proverb: those who leave the shade to go into the hot sun, and thus from better to worse
[176] **beacon** the sun
[177] **under globe** earth
[178] **comfortable** comforting
[179] **Nothing almost** almost nothing/no one

But misery.[180] I know 'tis from Cordelia,
Who hath most fortunately been informed
Of my obscurèd[181] course. And shall find time
From this enormous[182] state,[183] seeking to give
Losses their remedies. All weary and o'erwatched,
Take vantage,[184] heavy eyes, not to behold
This shameful lodging. Fortune, good night;
Smile once more, turn thy wheel.[185]

Sleeps.

[Scene 3. *A wood.*]

Enter Edgar.

Edgar. I heard myself proclaimed,[186]
And by the happy[187] hollow of a tree
Escaped the hunt. No port is free, no place
That guard and most unusual vigilance
Does not attend my taking.[188] Whiles I may 'scape,
I will preserve myself; and am bethought[189]
To take the basest and most poorest shape
That ever penury,[190] in contempt of man,
Brought near to beast;[191] my face I'll grime with filth,

[180] **misery** the miserable
[181] **obscurèd** disguised
[182] **enormous** lawless; abnormal
[183] **state** state of affairs
[184] **vantage** advantage
[185] **turn thy wheel** People's lives were thought to be governed by the Wheel of Fortune. Kent sees himself at the bottom, thus a turning of the Wheel can only improve his lot.
[186] **proclaimed** declared a traitor or outlaw
[187] **happy** lucky; opportune
[188] **attend my taking** wait to capture me
[189] **am bethought** am of a mind
[190] **penury** destitution
[191] **Brought . . . beast** reduced to the level of an animal

Blanket my loins,[192] elf all my hairs in knots,[193]
And with presented[194] nakedness outface[195]
The winds and persecutions of the sky.
The country gives me proof[196] and precedent
Of Bedlam beggars,[197] who, with roaring voices,
Strike[198] in their numbed and mortified[199] bare arms
Pins, wooden pricks,[200] nails, sprigs of rosemary;
And with this horrible object,[201] from low[202] farms,
Poor pelting[203] villages, sheepcotes, and mills,
Sometimes with lunatic bans,[204] sometime with prayers,
Enforce their charity. Poor Turlygod,[205] Poor Tom,[206]
That's something yet: Edgar I nothing am.[207] *Exit.*

[Scene 4. *Before Gloucester's castle. Kent in the stocks.]*

Enter Lear, Fool, and Gentleman.

Lear. 'Tis strange that they should so depart from home,
And not send back my messenger.

[192] **Blanket my loins** wrap my loins in a blanket

[193] **elf . . . knots** tangle my hair (The elves were thought to tangle hair in one's sleep, hence "elf-locks".)

[194] **presented** exhibited; exposed

[195] **outface** brave; defy

[196] **proof** example

[197] **Bedlam beggars** (See note at 1.2.147.)

[198] **Strike** stick

[199] **mortified** deadened to pain

[200] **pricks** skewers

[201] **object** spectacle; person or thing of pitiable or ridiculous appearance

[202] **low** lowly; humble

[203] **pelting** petty; contemptible

[204] **bans** curses

[205] **Poor Turlygod** unclear—possibly a corruption of Turlupin, a sect of crazed Parisian beggars

[206] **Poor Tom** (See note at 1.2.147.)

[207] **That's . . . am** At least Poor Tom is something, whereas "Edgar" is nothing any more.

Gentleman. As I learned,
The night before there was no purpose[208] in them
Of this remove.[209]

Kent. Hail to thee, noble master.

Lear. Ha!
Mak'st thou this shame thy pastime?

Kent. No, my lord.

Fool. Ha, ha, he wears cruel[210] garters. Horses are tied by the heads, dogs and bears by th' neck, monkeys by th' loins, and men by th' legs. When a man's overlusty at legs,[211] then he wears wooden netherstocks.[212]

Lear. What's he that hath so much thy place mistook
To[213] set thee here?

Kent. It is both he and she,
Your son and daughter.

Lear. No.

Kent. Yes.

Lear. No, I say.

Kent. I say yea.

Lear. No, no, they would not.

Kent. Yes, they have.

Lear. By Jupiter, I swear no!

[208] **purpose** intention

[209] **remove** departure; change of residence

[210] **cruel** a pun on "crewel", the thin worsted yarn used to make garters

[211] **overlusty at legs** too much of a vagabond; too eager to use his legs; sexually promiscuous

[212] **netherstocks** stockings. Breeches were then known as "upper-stocks".

[213] **To** as to

Kent. By Juno, I swear ay!

Lear. They durst not do't;
They could not, would not do't. 'Tis worse than murder
To do upon respect such violent outrage.[214]
Resolve[215] me with all modest[216] haste which way
Thou mightst[217] deserve or they impose this usage,
Coming from us.[218]

Kent. My lord, when at their home
I did commend[219] your Highness' letters to them,
Ere I was risen from the place that showed
My duty kneeling, came there a reeking post,[220]
Stewed[221] in his haste, half breathless, panting forth
From Goneril his mistress salutations,
Delivered letters, spite of intermission,[222]
Which presently[223] they read; on[224] whose contents
They summoned up their meiny,[225] straight took horse,
Commanded me to follow and attend
The leisure of their answer, gave me cold looks,
And meeting here the other messenger,
Whose welcome I perceived had poisoned mine,
Being the very fellow which of late

[214] **To ... outrage** to commit such an outrage upon the respect due to the king's messenger

[215] **Resolve** inform; answer

[216] **modest** sober; becoming

[217] **mightst** couldst

[218] **Coming from us** as one sent by me. This is the last time Lear will use the royal we.

[219] **commend** deliver

[220] **reeking post** steaming messenger

[221] **Stewed** sweating, but also suggestive of having visited a "stew" or brothel

[222] **spite of intermission** even though it interrupted the business I had with them

[223] **presently** immediately

[224] **on** upon the reading of

[225] **meiny** retinue; servants

Displayed[226] so saucily[227] against your Highness,
Having more man than wit[228] about me, drew;[229]
He raised the house,[230] with loud and coward cries.
Your son and daughter found this trespass worth
The shame which here it suffers.

Fool. Winter's not gone yet, if the wild geese fly that way.[231]

Fathers that wear rags
 Do make their children blind,[232]
But fathers that bear bags[233]
 Shall see their children kind.
Fortune, that arrant whore,
 Ne'er turns the key[234] to th' poor.

But for all this, thou shalt have as many dolors[235] for thy daughters as thou canst tell[236] in a year.

Lear. O, how this mother swells up toward my heart!
Hysterica passio,[237] down, thou climbing sorrow,
Thy element's[238] below. Where is this daughter?

Kent. With the Earl, sir, here within.

[226] **Displayed** behaved

[227] **saucily** insolently

[228] **Having . . . wit** having more courage than good sense

[229] **drew** i.e., my sword

[230] **raised the house** awakened the servants

[231] **Winter's . . . way** Judging by these signs, more trouble is sure to follow (for "geese", see note at 2.2.85 and 86).

[232] **blind** to their filial responsibilities

[233] **bags** money-bags

[234] **turns the key** i.e., opens the door

[235] **dolors** sorrows, with a pun on "dollar" (the English name for the German coin, "thaler")

[236] **tell** meaning both "count" and "speak about"

[237] **mother . . . Hysterica passio** disease, known by various names, including "Passio Hysterica" and "the Mother", the latter because it affected mostly women and its feelings of suffocation or choking were thought to arise from the womb or bottom of the belly

[238] **element** proper sphere

Lear. Follow me not;
Stay here. *Exit.*

Gentleman. Made you no more offense but what you speak of?

Kent. None.
How chance[239] the King comes with so small a number?

Fool. And[240] thou hadst been set i' th' stocks for that question, thou'dst well deserved it.

Kent. Why, Fool?

Fool. We'll set thee to school to an ant, to teach thee there's no laboring i' th' winter.[241] All that follow their noses are led by their eyes but blind men, and there's not a nose among twenty but can smell him that's stinking.[242] Let go thy hold when a great wheel runs down a hill, lest it break thy neck with following. But the great one that goes upward, let him draw thee after.[243] When a wise man gives thee better counsel, give me mine again. I would

[239] **How chance** how does it chance, or come about, that

[240] **And** if

[241] **We'll . . . winter** from the fable in which the ant, unlike the grasshopper (or, in some versions, the fly), labored all summer long to lay up provisions for the winter to come. Lear now finds himself, like the grasshopper, bereft of the provisions (men, support, and money) he will need to sustain him in the "winter" of his fortunes. See also Proverbs 6:6–11: "Go to the ant, O sluggard, and consider her ways, and learn wisdom: / Which, although she hath no guide, nor master, nor captain, / Provideth her meat for herself in the summer, and gathereth her food in the harvest. / How long wilt thou sleep, O sluggard? when wilt thou rise out of thy sleep? / Thou wilt sleep a little, thou wilt slumber a little, thou wilt fold thy hands a little to sleep: / And want shall come upon thee, as a traveller, and poverty as a man armed."

[242] **him that's stinking** That is, even a blind man would be able to tell that Lear has fallen, from the stench of Fortune's displeasure. Compare with *All's Well That Ends Well*: "I am now, sir, muddied in Fortune's mood, and smell somewhat strong of her strong displeasure" (V.ii.406).

[243] **wheel . . . after** Fortune's wheel is also implied.

have none but knaves follow it since a Fool gives it.[244]

That sir,[245] which serves and seeks for gain,
And follows but for form,[246]
Will pack,[247] when it begins to rain,
And leave thee in the storm.
But I will tarry; the Fool will stay,
And let the wise[248] man fly.
The knave turns Fool that runs away,
The Fool no knave,[249] perdy.[250]

Kent. Where learned you this, Fool?

Fool. Not i' th' stocks, fool.

Enter Lear and Gloucester.

Lear. Deny[251] to speak with me? They are sick, they are weary,
They have traveled all the night? Mere fetches,[252]
The images of revolt and flying off![253]
Fetch me a better answer.

Gloucester. My dear lord,
You know the fiery quality[254] of the Duke,

[244] **I . . . follow . . . it** I only wish knaves (rogues) to follow my advice (leave the king).

[245] **sir** man; knight

[246] **form** outward show, with no inner loyalty

[247] **pack** i.e., his bags: depart

[248] **wise** sensible; prudent

[249] **the Fool . . . knave** Ultimately, the knave (servant) who forsakes his master will be exposed as a fool (for where there is no fidelity, there can be no wisdom), whereas this "fool" will remain true and so, by God, is no knave (rogue). Cf. 1 Corinthians 3:19: "If any one among you thinks that he is wise in this age, let him become a fool that he may become wise. For the wisdom of this world is folly with God."

[250] **perdy** *par Dieu*, French for "by God"

[251] **Deny** refuse

[252] **fetches** tricks; dodges (nautical terminology, from a sailboat tacking)

[253] **images . . . off** the very images or symbols of rebellion and desertion

[254] **quality** nature; disposition

How unremovable and fixed he is
In his own course.

Lear. Vengeance, plague, death, confusion!
Fiery? What quality? Why, Gloucester, Gloucester,
I'd speak with the Duke of Cornwall and his wife.

Gloucester. Well, my good lord, I have informed them so.

Lear. Informed them? Dost thou understand me, man?

Gloucester. Ay, my good lord.

Lear. The King would speak with Cornwall. The dear father
Would with his daughter speak, commands—tends[255] —service.
Are they informed of this? My breath and blood!
Fiery? The fiery Duke, tell the hot Duke that—
No, but not yet. May be he is not well.
Infirmity doth still neglect all office
Whereto our health is bound.[256] We are not ourselves
When nature, being oppressed, commands the mind
To suffer with the body. I'll forbear;
And am fallen out[257] with my more headier[258] will[259]
To take[260] the indisposed and sickly fit

[255] **commands—tends** perhaps a conciliatory gesture, shifting from his role as king to father; alternatively, Lear commands Regan's service and tenders his own; "tends" meaning "offers" or "awaits"

[256] **Infirmity . . . bound** When we are ill, we always neglect the duties we are bound to perform when we are in good health.

[257] **am fallen out** quarrel

[258] **headier** headstrong; impetuous

[259] **will** impulse

[260] **To take** for taking

For the sound man. [*Looking on Kent*] Death on my state![261] Wherefore
Should he sit here? This act persuades me
That this remotion[262] of the Duke and her
Is practice[263] only. Give me my servant forth.[264]
Go tell the Duke and's wife I'd speak with them!
Now, presently![265] Bid them come forth and hear me,
Or at their chamber door I'll beat the drum
Till it cry sleep to death.[266]

Gloucester. I would have all well betwixt you.

Exit.

Lear. O me, my heart, my rising heart! But down!

Fool. Cry to it, Nuncle, as the cockney did to the eels when she put 'em i' th' paste[267] alive. She knapped[268] em o' th' coxcombs[269] with a stick and cried, "Down, wantons,[270] down!"[271,272] 'Twas her brother[273] that, in pure kindness to his horse, buttered his hay.[274]

[261] **Death on my state** an oath, significantly referring both to his condition or situation and to his royal authority

[262] **remotion** remoteness, and also, perhaps, their removal to Gloucester's castle

[263] **practice** a device; trickery

[264] **forth** i.e., from the stocks

[265] **presently** at once

[266] **beat . . . death** beat sleep to death with noise

[267] **paste** pastry pie

[268] **knapped** rapped

[269] **coxcombs** Eels have a long fin running the length of their backs resembling a coxcomb; heads; also, by association, fools (See note at 1.4.97.)

[270] **wantons** roguish, ungovernable creatures, with a sexual implication

[271] **down** recalling Lear's words, like hers, uttered too late

[272] **cockney . . . down!** "Cockney" could mean a townsman (especially a Londoner; the reference is pejorative), a milksop, or a pampered child. The foolish "cockney" (however one construes the word) should have knocked the eels on the head before putting the ungovernable creatures into the pastry.

[273] **her brother** (the sense is figurative as well as literal)

[274] **kindness . . . hay** not a kindness in the view of the horses, who won't eat greasy hay: a second example of foolish tender-heartedness, like Lear's

Enter Cornwall, Regan, Gloucester, Servants.

Lear. Good morrow[275] to you both.

Cornwall. Hail to your Grace.

Kent here set at liberty.

Regan. I am glad to see your Highness.

Lear. Regan, I think you are. I know what reason
I have to think so. If thou[276] shouldst not be glad,
I would divorce me from thy mother's tomb,
Sepulchring an adultress.[277] [*To Kent*] O, are you free?
Some other time for that. Beloved Regan,
Thy sister's naught.[278] O Regan, she hath tied
Sharp-toothed unkindness, like a vulture,[279] here.

[*Points to his heart.*]

I can scarce speak to thee. Thou'lt not believe
With how depraved a quality[280]—O Regan!

Regan. I pray you, sir, take patience. I have hope
You less know how to value her desert
Than she to scant her duty.[281]

[275] **Good morrow** It is evening: Lear is being sarcastic.

[276] **thou** Lear's addressing Regan with the more intimate "thou" suggests his expectation of a tender reception; when it becomes clear that she means to abuse him, he reverts to "you" (152).

[277] **adultress** There is nothing in the play to substantiate the illegitimacy of Goneril and Regan, other than Lear's calling Goneril a "degenerate bastard" (1.4.260), and most critics have interpreted these remarks as references to the unnatural behavior of Lear's first two daughters, as well as, possibly, an attempt to dissociate himself from them and responsibility for their character. It also links Goneril and Regan to Edmund.

[278] **naught** wicked; worthless

[279] **vulture** This is an illusion to the Greek myth of Prometheus: he stole fire from the gods to give it to men and was punished by being chained to a rock where a vulture came each day to gnaw at his immortal liver.

[280] **quality** manner; nature; character; disposition

[281] **You less . . . duty** that you are less capable of appreciating her worth than she is of neglecting her duty

Lear. Say? how is that?

Regan. I cannot think my sister in the least
Would fail her obligation. If, sir, perchance
She have restrained the riots of your followers,
'Tis on such ground, and to such wholesome end,
As clears her from all blame.

Lear. My curses on her!

Regan. O, sir, you are old,
Nature in you stands on the very verge
Of his confine.[282] You should be ruled, and led
By some discretion that discerns your state
Better than you yourself. Therefore I pray you
That to our sister you do make return,
Say you have wronged her.

Lear. Ask her forgiveness?
Do you but mark how this becomes the house:[283]
"Dear daughter, I confess that I am old.

[*Kneeling.*]

Age is unnecessary.[284] On my knees I beg
That you'll vouchsafe me raiment, bed, and food."

Regan. Good sir, no more. These are unsightly tricks.
Return you to my sister.

Lear. [*Rising*] Never, Regan.
She hath abated[285] me of half my train,
Looked black upon me, struck me with her tongue,
Most serpentlike, upon the very heart.
All the stored vengeances of heaven fall

[282] **Nature . . . confine** Life in you is at the very edge of its assigned limit.

[283] **becomes . . . house** befits the family, or royal house

[284] **Age is unnecessary** Old people are unnecessary, or useless. Dr. Johnson suggests: "Old age has few wants."

[285] **abated** deprived

On her ingrateful top![286] Strike her young bones,[287]
You taking airs,[288] with lameness.

Cornwall. Fie, sir, fie!

Lear. You nimble lightnings, dart your blinding flames
Into her scornful eyes! Infect her beauty,
You fen-sucked[289] fogs, drawn by the pow'rful sun,
To fall and blister[290] her pride.

Regan. O the blest gods!
So will you wish on me when the rash mood is on.

Lear. No, Regan, thou shalt never have my curse.
Thy tender-hefted[291] nature shall not give
Thee o'er to harshness. Her eyes are fierce, but thine
Do comfort, and not burn. 'Tis not in thee
To grudge my pleasures, to cut off my train,
To bandy[292] hasty words, to scant my sizes,[293]
And, in conclusion, to oppose the bolt[294]
Against my coming in. Thou better know'st
The offices[295] of nature, bond of childhood,[296]
Effects[297] of courtesy, dues of gratitude.
Thy half o' th' kingdom hast thou not forgot,
Wherein I thee endowed.

Regan. Good sir, to th' purpose.[298]

[286] **top** head
[287] **young bones** Goneril herself or the children she may conceive
[288] **taking airs** infecting vapors
[289] **fen-sucked** drawn from the marshes. (Infectious air was thought to be drawn out of marshes by the heat of the sun.)
[290] **blister** raise blisters on
[291] **tender-hefted** set in a delicately framed body, hence gentle
[292] **bandy** (See note at 1.4.86.)
[293] **scant my sizes** reduce my allowances
[294] **oppose the bolt** lock the door. (It is Regan who later orders the doors to be shut against him.)
[295] **offices** duties; obligations
[296] **bond of childhood** the child's duty to her parent. (See note at 1.1.95.)
[297] **Effects** gestures; outward signs
[298] **to th' purpose** come to the point

Tucket within.

Lear. Who put my man i' th' stocks?

Cornwall. What trumpet's that?

Regan. I know't—my sister's. This approves[299] her letter,
That she would soon be here.

Enter Oswald.

Is your lady come?

Lear. This is a slave, whose easy borrowed pride[300]
Dwells in the fickle grace[301] of her he follows.
Out, varlet,[302] from my sight.

Cornwall. What means your Grace?

Lear. Who stocked my servant? Regan, I have good hope
Thou didst not know on't.

Enter Goneril.

Who comes here? O heavens!
If you do love old men, if your sweet sway
Allow[303] obedience, if you yourselves are old,
Make it[304] your cause. Send down, and take my part.
[*To Goneril*] Art not ashamed to look upon this beard?
O Regan, will you take her by the hand?

[299] **approves** confirms

[300] **easy borrowed pride** whose smug pride derives not from any native strength, but from the favor of his superiors (i.e., borrowed without security)

[301] **grace** favor

[302] **varlet** rascal; minion

[303] **Allow** approves of

[304] **it** the respect due to elders

Goneril. Why not by th' hand, sir? How have I offended?
All's not offense that indiscretion finds[305]
And dotage terms so.

Lear. O sides,[306] you are too tough!
Will you yet hold? How came my man i' th' stocks?

Cornwall. I set him there, sir; but his own disorders
Deserved much less advancement.[307]

Lear. You? Did you?

Regan. I pray you, father, being weak, seem so.[308]
If till the expiration of your month
You will return and sojourn with my sister,
Dismissing half your train, come then to me.
I am now from home, and out of that provision
Which shall be needful for your entertainment.[309]

Lear. Return to her, and fifty men dismissed?
No, rather I abjure all roofs, and choose
To wage[310] against the enmity o' th' air,
To be a comrade with the wolf and owl,
Necessity's[311] sharp pinch. Return with her?
Why, the hot-blooded[312] France, that dowerless took
Our youngest born, I could as well be brought
To knee[313] his throne, and, squirelike,[314] pension beg
To keep base life afoot. Return with her?

[305] **finds** deems
[306] **sides** i.e., of his bodily frame, holding down his rising heart
[307] **advancement** honor; promotion
[308] **seem so** act like it
[309] **entertainment** upkeep; maintenance
[310] **wage** contend
[311] **Necessity** fate; poverty
[312] **hot-blooded** ardent; passionate
[313] **knee** kneel before
[314] **squirelike** like a vassal

Persuade me rather to be slave and sumpter[315]
To this detested groom.[316] [*Pointing at Oswald.*]

Goneril. At your choice, sir.

Lear. I prithee, daughter, do not make me mad.
I will not trouble thee, my child; farewell.
We'll no more meet, no more see one another.
But yet thou art my flesh, my blood, my daughter,
Or rather a disease that's in my flesh,
Which I must needs call mine. Thou art a boil,
A plague-sore, or embossèd[317] carbuncle[318]
In my corrupted blood. But I'll not chide thee.
Let shame come when it will, I do not call it.
I do not bid the Thunder-bearer[319] shoot,
Nor tell tales of thee to high-judging[320] Jove.
Mend when thou canst, be better at thy leisure,
I can be patient, I can stay with Regan,
I and my hundred knights.

Regan. Not altogether so.
I looked not for you yet, nor am provided
For your fit welcome. Give ear, sir, to my sister,
For those that mingle reason with your passion[321]
Must be content to think you old, and so—
But she knows what she does.

Lear. Is this well spoken?

Regan. I dare avouch[322] it, sir. What, fifty followers?
Is it not well? What should you need of more?

[315] **sumpter** pack horse; pack animal
[316] **groom** servant; person employed to take care of horses
[317] **embossèd** swollen, bulging
[318] **carbuncle** tumor; boil; severe abscess
[319] **Thunder-bearer** i.e., Jupiter (Jove), the king of the gods, who threw thunderbolts down upon the wicked
[320] **high-judging** judging from on high; supreme judge
[321] **mingle . . . passion** apply reason to your passionate outbursts
[322] **avouch** guarantee; affirm

Yea, or so many, sith that both charge[323] and
danger
Speak 'gainst so great a number? How in one house
Should many people, under two commands,
Hold[324] amity? 'Tis hard, almost impossible.

Goneril. Why might not you, my lord, receive
attendance
From those that she calls servants, or from mine?

Regan. Why not, my lord? If then they chanced to
Slack[325] ye,
We could control them.[326] If you will come to me
(For now I spy a danger), I entreat you
To bring but five-and-twenty. To no more
Will I give place or notice.[327]

Lear. I gave you all.

Regan. And in good time you gave it.

Lear. Made you my guardians, my depositaries,[328]
But kept a reservation[329] to be followed
With such a number. What, must I come to you
With five-and-twenty? Regan, said you so?

Regan. And speak't again, my lord. No more with me.

Lear. Those wicked creatures yet do look well-
Favored[330]
When others are more wicked; not being the worst

[323] **charge** expense

[324] **Hold** maintain

[325] **Slack** be negligent in serving or respecting

[326] **If ... them** a doubtful assurance, given Oswald's behavior and, particularly, Goneril's instructions to the contrary (1.3.13)

[327] **To ... notice** I will neither house nor recognize any more than that.

[328] **depositaries** trustees

[329] **kept a reservation** reserved the right

[330] **well-favored** good-looking

Stands in some rank of praise.[331] [*To Goneril*] I'll
go with thee.
Thy fifty yet doth double five-and-twenty,
And thou art twice her love.[332]

Goneril. Hear me, my lord.
What need you five-and-twenty? ten? or five?
To follow[333] in a house where twice so many
Have a command to tend you?

Regan. What need one?

Lear. O reason not the need![334] Our basest beggars
Are in the poorest thing superfluous.[335]
Allow not nature more than nature needs,
Man's life is cheap as beast's.[336] Thou art a lady:
If only to go warm were gorgeous,
Why, nature needs not what thou gorgeous wear'st,
Which scarcely keeps thee warm.[337] But, for true
need—
You heavens, give me that patience, patience I
need.
You see me here, you gods, a poor old man,
As full of grief as age, wretched in both.
If it be you that stirs these daughters' hearts
Against their father, fool me not so much
To bear[338] it tamely; touch me with noble anger,
And let not women's weapons, water drops,

[331] **Stands . . . praise** is worth some praise

[332] **twice her love** Lear still speaks of love as something that can be quantified.

[333] **follow** be your followers

[334] **reason not the need** do not hold the need up to the scrutiny of reason, or try to quantify it

[335] **Are . . . superfluous** have something, however little, above what they need to survive

[336] **Allow . . . beast's** If you were to allow a man no more than he needs for bare survival, he would be reduced to the level of an animal.

[337] **If . . . warm** If it were gorgeous merely to be warm, you would not need the very clothes you are wearing, which are hardly enough to keep you warm.

[338] **fool . . . bear** do not make me such a fool as to tolerate patiently

Stain my man's cheeks. No, you unnatural hags!
I will have such revenges on you both
That all the world shall—I will do such things—
What they are, yet I know not; but they shall be
The terrors of the earth. You think I'll weep.
No, I'll not weep.

Storm and tempest.[339]

I have full cause of weeping, but this heart
Shall break into a hundred thousand flaws[340]
Or ere[341] I'll weep. O Fool, I shall go mad!

Exeunt Lear, Gloucester, Kent, and Fool.

Cornwall. Let us withdraw, 'twill be a storm.

Regan. This house is little; the old man and's people
Cannot be well bestowed.[342]

Goneril. 'Tis his own blame; hath[343] put himself from
Rest[344]
And must needs taste his folly.

Regan. For his particular,[345] I'll receive him gladly,
But not one follower.

Goneril. So am I purposed.[346]
Where is my Lord of Gloucester?

Cornwall. Followed the old man forth.

Enter Gloucester.

He is returned.

[339] **Storm and tempest** (It is as though the heavens break out instead.)
[340] **flaws** "fragments"; "defects"; "gusts of passion"; "sudden squalls"
[341] **Or ere** before
[342] **bestowed** housed
[343] **hath** he hath
[344] **Rest** a place to rest (reside); peace of mind
[345] **For his particular** as for him personally
[346] **purposed** resolved

Gloucester. The King is in high rage.

Cornwall. Whither is he going?

Gloucester. He calls to horse, but will I know not whither.

Cornwall. 'Tis best to give him way,[347] he leads himself.

Goneril. My lord, entreat him by no means to stay.

Gloucester. Alack, the night comes on, and the high winds
Do sorely ruffle.[348] For many miles about
There's scarce a bush.

Regan. O, sir, to willful men
The injuries that they themselves procure
Must be their schoolmasters. Shut up your doors.
He is attended with a desperate train,
And what they may incense[349] him to, being apt
To have his ear abused,[350] wisdom bids fear.

Cornwall. Shut up your doors, my lord; 'tis a wild night.
My Regan counsels well. Come out o' th' storm.

Exeunt.

[347] **give him way** give way (yield) to him; let him have his own way
[348] **ruffle** bluster; rage
[349] **incense** incite
[350] **have . . . abused** be misled by poor advice

ACT 3

Scene 1. [A *heath*.]

Storm still[1] *Enter Kent and a Gentleman severally.*

Kent. Who's there besides foul weather?

Gentleman. One minded like the weather most unquietly.[2]

Kent. I know you. Where's the King?

Gentleman. Contending with the fretful elements;
Bids the wind blow the earth into the sea,
Or swell the curlèd waters 'bove the main,[3]
That things might change, or cease; tears his white hair,
Which the impetuous blasts, with eyeless[4] rage,
Catch in their fury, and make nothing of;
Strives in his little world of man[5] to outscorn
The to-and-fro-conflicting wind and rain.
This night, wherein the cub-drawn[6] bear would couch,[7]
The lion, and the belly-pinchèd[8] wolf
Keep their fur dry, unbonneted[9] he runs,
And bids what will take all.[10]

Kent. But who is with him?

[1] **still** continually

[2] **minded . . . unquietly** one, the condition of whose mind is, like the weather, disturbed

[3] **main** mainland

[4] **eyeless** blind

[5] **little world of man** (the microcosm, as opposed to the universe or macrocosm, which it copies in little)

[6] **cub-drawn** fiercely hungry after having suckled her cubs

[7] **couch** lie in its lair

[8] **belly-pinchèd** starving

[9] **unbonneted** without a head-covering; reckless

[10] **bids . . . all** gambles everything he has on a final throw of the dice

Gentleman. None but the Fool, who labors to outjest
His heart-struck injuries.[11]

Kent. Sir, I do know you,
And dare upon the warrant of my note[12]
Commend a dear thing[13] to you. There is division,
Although as yet the face of it is covered
With mutual cunning, 'twixt Albany and Cornwall;
Who have—as who have not, that their great stars
Throned[14] and set high?[15]—servants, who seem no less,[16]
Which are to France the spies and speculations
Intelligent[17] of our state. What hath been seen,
Either in snuffs[18] and packings[19] of the Dukes,
Or the hard rein[20] which both of them hath borne
Against the old kind King,[21] or something deeper,
Whereof, perchance, these are but furnishings[22]—
But, true it is, from France there comes a power[23]
Into this scattered[24] kingdom, who already,
Wise in our negligence, have secret feet
In some of our best ports, and are at point[25]
To show their open banner. Now to you:

[11] **labors . . . injuries** tries to drive away his sorrows by jesting

[12] **upon . . . note** to take assurance in my observation of you

[13] **Commend . . . thing** entrust important information

[14] **that . . . Throned** who owe their high station to the influence of the stars

[15] **As . . . high?** And who, among the powerful, do not?

[16] **seem no less** i.e., seem to be servants (and not spies)

[17] **speculations/Intelligent** observers giving intelligence

[18] **snuffs** huffs; resentments

[19] **packings** plots

[20] **hard rein** "tight rein", metaphor from strictly (even harshly) restraining a horse; as well as a possible pun on "reign"

[21] **both . . . King** Kent is not aware of Albany's apparent lack of complicity in Goneril's actions toward her father.

[22] **furnishings** window dressing; trimmings; pretexts

[23] **power** army

[24] **scattered** unsettled; divided

[25] **at point** ready

If on my credit you dare build so far
To[26] make your speed to Dover, you shall find
Some that will thank you, making[27] just[28] report
Of how unnatural and bemadding[29] sorrow
The King hath cause to plain.[30]
I am a gentleman of blood and breeding,[31]
And from some knowledge and assurance[32] offer
This office[33] to you.

Gentleman. I will talk further with you.

Kent. No, do not.
For confirmation that I am much more
Than my out-wall,[34] open this purse and take
What it contains. If you shall see Cordelia,
As fear not but you shall, show her this ring,
And she will tell you who that fellow[35] is
That yet you do not know. Fie on this storm!
I will go seek the King.

Gentleman. Give me your hand. Have you no more to say?

Kent. Few words, but, to effect,[36] more than all yet:
That when we have found the King—in which your pain[37]
That way, I'll this—he that first lights on him,
Holla the other. *Exeunt [severally].*

[26] **If . . . To** if you trust me far enough to
[27] **making** for making
[28] **just** accurate (perhaps also suggesting the justice of the action)
[29] **bemadding** maddening
[30] **plain** complain
[31] **blood and breeding** noble birth and upbringing
[32] **assurance** reliable information
[33] **office** responsibility (bringing information to Dover)
[34] **out-wall** exterior; outward appearance
[35] **fellow** companion
[36] **to effect** in importance
[37] **pain** effort

Scene 2. [*Another part of the heath.*]

Storm still.

Enter Lear and Fool.

Lear. Blow, winds, and crack your cheeks. Rage, blow!
You cataracts[38] and hurricanoes,[39] spout
Till you have drenched our steeples, drowned the cocks.[40]
You sulph'rous and thought-executing fires,[41]
Vaunt-couriers[42] of oak-cleaving thunderbolts,
Singe my white head. And thou, all-shaking thunder,
Strike flat the thick rotundity o' th' world,[43]
Crack Nature's molds,[44] all germains[45] spill[46] at once,
That makes ingrateful man.[47]

Fool. O Nuncle, court holy-water[48] in a dry house is better than this rain water out o' door. Good Nuncle, in; ask thy daughters blessing. Here's a night pities neither wise man nor fools.

[38] **cataracts** torrential downpours

[39] **hurricanoes** waterspouts arising from the seas

[40] **cocks** weathercocks. (The cock was also often planted on top of church steeples as a symbol of faith, watchfulness, and the Resurrection.)

[41] **thought-executing fires** lightning bolts. Critics are divided as to Lear's meaning here: Dr. Johnson suggests "doing execution with rapidity equal to thought"; while some contend that Lear is commanding the lightning to execute (carry out) his thought (wishes); and others that Lear is entreating it to kill thought itself.

[42] **Vaunt-couriers** forerunners; heralds (the flash precedes the sound of thunder)

[43] **thick ... world** (perhaps imaging the world as pregnant. The following line's imagery suggests a fertile Mother Earth.)

[44] **Nature's molds** the molds in which Nature forms creatures. (A cracked mold cannot be used again.)

[45] **all germains** the germs or seeds of all life

[46] **spill** destroy

[47] **Strike ... man** apocalyptic images of worldwide destruction. The unnatural behavior of Lear's daughters has suggested to him the overturning of the entire natural order in the vengeance of heaven.

[48] **court holy-water** fair but empty words; flattery

Lear. Rumble thy bellyful.[49] Spit, fire. Spout, rain!
Nor rain, wind, thunder, fire are my daughters.
I tax[50] not you, you elements, with unkindness.
I never gave you kingdom, called you children,
You owe me no subscription.[51] Then let fall
Your horrible pleasure.[52] Here I stand your slave,[53]
A poor, infirm, weak, and despised old man.
But yet I call you servile ministers,[54]
That will with two pernicious daughters join
Your high-engendered[55] battles 'gainst a head
So old and white as this. O, ho! 'tis foul.

Fool. He that has a house to put 's head in has a good headpiece.[56]
The codpiece[57] that will house[58]
Before the head has any,[59]
The head and he[60] shall louse:
So beggars marry many.[61,62]
The man that makes his toe
What he his heart should make
Shall of a corn cry woe,

[49] **thy bellyful** to your satisfaction
[50] **tax** accuse
[51] **subscription** submission, obedience
[52] **pleasure** will; pleasure
[53] **slave** helpless victim
[54] **ministers** agents carrying out the will of their superiors
[55] **high-engendered** provoked from on high; produced in the heavens
[56] **headpiece** helmet or covering for the head; head or brain
[57] **codpiece** part of a man's attire that covered (but also emphasized) the male sexual organs; euphemism for phallus
[58] **house** have sexual intercourse
[59] **head has any** man has a house (i.e., before he is married). The implicit suggestion is that it is foolish to allow the imprudence of the loins to take precedence over the prudence of the head.
[60] **he** it
[61] **marry many** i.e., lice; have a series of sexual companions to support
[62] **The . . . many** The Fool is rebuking Lear for putting his passions (pride and anger) before prudence, which has led him to squalid destitution.

And turn his sleep to wake.[63]
For there was never yet fair woman but she made mouths in a glass.[64]

Enter Kent.

Lear. No, I will be the pattern of all patience,
I will say nothing.

Kent. Who's there?

Fool. Marry,[65] here's grace and a codpiece;[66] that's a wise man and a fool.

Kent Alas, sir, are you here? Things that love night
Love not such nights as these. The wrathful skies
Gallow[67] the very wanderers of the dark
And make them keep[68] their caves. Since I was man
Such sheets of fire, such bursts of horrid thunder,
Such groans of roaring wind and rain, I never
Remember to have heard. Man's nature cannot carry[69]
Th' affliction nor the fear.

Lear. Let the great gods
That keep this dreadful pudder[70] o'er our heads

[63] **The ... wake** The man who exalts a low part of himself (Goneril and Regan) and neglects a higher part (Cordelia, who was "Lear's heart") will suffer as a result, with the lower part causing the pain. Since the toe is here employed as a euphemism for a phallus, the corn is a euphemism for sexually transmitted disease, possibly syphilis, which proves fatal, turning sleep to a wake, i.e., a funeral.

[64] **made mouths in a glass** practiced smiling in the mirror, suggesting the vanity and hypocrisy of Goneril and Regan

[65] **Marry** interjection, "by the Virgin Mary"

[66] **grace and a codpiece** the king and a Fool (Fools often wore exaggerated codpieces). The juxtaposition reinforces the comparison between virtue (grace) and vice (codpiece), which has been the subject of the Fool's "wise" and "foolish" discourse.

[67] **Gallow** terrify

[68] **keep** keep to

[69] **carry** bear; endure

[70] **pudder** "pother" or disturbance; uproar

Find out their enemies now.[71] Tremble, thou wretch,
That hast within thee undivulgèd crimes
Unwhipped of justice. Hide thee, thou bloody hand,[72]
Thou perjured,[73] and thou simular[74] of virtue.[75]
That art incestuous. Caitiff,[76] to pieces shake,
That under covert and convenient[77] seeming[78]
Has practiced on[79] man's life. Close[80] pent-up guilts,
Rive[81] your concealing continents[82] and cry
These dreadful summoners[83] grace.[84] I am a man
More sinned against than sinning.

Kent. Alack, bareheaded?
Gracious my lord,[85] hard by here is a hovel;
Some friendship will it lend you 'gainst the
tempest.
Repose you there, while I to this hard[86] house
(More harder than the stones whereof 'tis raised,
Which even but now, demanding after[87] you,
Denied me to come in) return, and force
Their scanted[88] courtesy.

[71] **Find . . . now** (by the terror, the storm—the fury of the heavens—will inspire in sinners)
[72] **bloody hand** murderer
[73] **perjured** perjurer
[74] **simular** counterfeiter
[75] **virtue** any virtue, but especially chastity
[76] **Caitiff** wretch; villain
[77] **convenient** suited to the purpose
[78] **seeming** deception; hypocrisy
[79] **practiced on** plotted against
[80] **Close** secret
[81] **Rive** cleave open; burst
[82] **your concealing continents** that in which you are kept hidden and contained
[83] **summoners** It was the summoner's office to summon people before an ecclesiastical court.
[84] **cry . . . grace** cry for mercy from the dreadful ministers of justice
[85] **Gracious my lord** my gracious lord
[86] **hard** cruel
[87] **demanding after** asking for
[88] **scanted** withheld

Lear. My wits begin to turn.[89]
Come on, my boy. How dost, my boy? Art cold?
I am cold myself. Where is this straw, my fellow?
The art[90] of our necessities is strange,
That can make vile things precious. Come, your hovel.
Poor Fool and knave, I have one part in my heart
That's sorry yet for thee.

Fool. [*Singing*]
He that has and a little tiny wit,
With heigh-ho, the wind and the rain,
Must make content with his fortunes fit,[91]
Though the rain it raineth every day.[92]

Lear. True, my good boy. Come, bring us to this hovel.

Exit [*with Kent*].

Fool. This is a brave[93] night[94] to cool[95] a courtesan. I'll speak a prophecy ere I go:
When priests are more in word than matter;
When brewers mar their malt with water;
When nobles are their tailors' tutors,[96]
No heretics burned,[97] but wenches' suitors;[98,99]

[89] **turn** also the moment when his thoughts first turn to others

[90] **art** magical art, likening the effect of their sorrows to the art of alchemy, the endeavor to transform common metals into precious metals

[91] **make . . . fit** must make his happiness fit his fortunes

[92] **He . . . day** An adaptation of the song sung by Feste, the Fool, in *Twelfth Night* (which was written a few years earlier; the same actor, Robert Armin, probably sang both): "When that I was and a little tiny boy,/With hey, ho, the wind and the rain,/'Gainst knaves and thieves men shut their gate,/For the rain it raineth every day."

[93] **brave** suitable; fine

[94] **brave night** also, pun on "brave knight"

[95] **cool** i.e., to cool the lust of

[96] **When . . . tutors** when noblemen are excessively concerned with fashion

[97] **burned** at the stake

[98] **No . . . suitors** Men are burned, not as heretics, but with venereal disease.

[99] **When . . . suitors** These lines describe a world turned upside down. It is also a thinly disguised attack on the corruption of Shakespeare's England.

When every case in law is right,
No squire in debt nor no poor knight;
When slanders do not live in tongues;
Nor cutpurses come not to throngs;[100]
When usurers[101] tell[102] their gold i' th' field,[103]
And bawds and whores do churches build,[104]
Then shall the realm of Albion[105]
Come to great confusion.
Then comes the time, who lives to see't,
That going shall be used with feet.[106]
This prophecy Merlin[107] shall make, for I live before his time. *Exit.*

Scene 3. [*Gloucester's castle.*]

Enter Gloucester and Edmund.

Gloucester. Alack, alack, Edmund, I like not this unnatural dealing. When I desired their leave that I might pity[108] him, they took from me the use of mine own house, charged me on pain of perpetual displeasure neither to speak of him, entreat for him, or any way sustain[109] him.

[100] **throngs** crowded places (where it is easier to pick pockets)

[101] **usurers** moneylenders (inclined to secrecy)

[102] **tell** count

[103] **i' th' field** openly

[104] **When . . . build** These lines, in contrast, describe a perfect or utopian world; thus they are meant ironically: they will never be fulfilled.

[105] **Albion** England

[106] **going . . . feet** feet will be used for walking

[107] **Merlin** Besides his well-known role as wizard and counselor to King Arthur, Merlin was a legendary prophet. According to Holinshed, he lived in the sixth century A.D., while Lear lived in the eighth century B.C.

[108] **pity** show pity to, relieve

[109] **sustain** care for; assist; nourish. With these instructions, which can have no reasonable rationale, Goneril, Regan, and Cornwall seem to drop all pretense of dealing justly with Lear.

Edmund. Most savage and unnatural.

Gloucester. Go to; say you nothing. There is division between the Dukes, and a worse[110] matter than that. I have received a letter this night—'tis dangerous to be spoken[111]—I have locked the letter in my closet.[112] These injuries the King now bears will be revenged home;[113] there is part of a power[114] already footed;[115] we must incline to[116] the King. I will look[117] him and privily[118] relieve him. Go you and maintain talk with the Duke, that my charity be not of[119] him perceived. If he ask for me, I am ill and gone to bed. If I die for it, as no less is threatened me, the King my old master must be relieved. There is strange things toward,[120] Edmund; pray you be careful. *Exit.*

Edmund. This courtesy forbid thee[121] shall the Duke
Instantly know, and of that letter too.
This seems a fair deserving,[122] and must draw me
That which my father loses—no less than all.
The younger rises when the old doth fall.

Exit.

[110] **worse** i.e., the French invasion
[111] **be spoken** speak of it
[112] **closet** (See note at 1.2.65.)
[113] **home** (See note at 3.3.13.)
[114] **power** army
[115] **footed** landed
[116] **incline to** side with
[117] **look** look for
[118] **privily** secretly
[119] **of** by
[120] **toward** impending; being planned
[121] **forbid thee** you have been forbidden to give
[122] **fair deserving** a deed deserving of a fair reward

Scene 4. [*The heath. Before a hovel.*]

Enter Lear, Kent, and Fool.

Kent. Here is the place, my lord. Good my lord, enter.
The tyranny of the open night's too rough
For nature to endure.

Storm still.

Lear. Let me alone.

Kent. Good my lord, enter here.

Lear. Wilt break my heart?[123]

Kent. I had rather break mine own. Good my lord, enter.

Lear. Thou think'st 'tis much that this contentious storm
Invades us to the skin: so 'tis to thee;
But where the greater malady is fixed,[124]
The lesser is scarce felt. Thou'dst shun a bear;
But if thy flight lay toward the roaring sea,
Thou'dst meet the bear i' th' mouth.[125] When the mind's free,[126]
The body's delicate. The tempest in my mind
Doth from my senses take all feeling else,
Save what beats there. Filial ingratitude,
Is it not as[127] this mouth should tear this hand
For lifting food to't? But I will punish home.[128]
No, I will weep no more. In such a night

[123] **Wilt . . . heart?** Lear would rather brave the storm than face the ingratitude of his daughters, which he fears will break his heart.
[124] **fixed** lodged (in the mind)
[125] **meet . . . mouth** turn and confront the bear face to face
[126] **free** i.e., from trials
[127] **as** as if
[128] **home** (See note at 3.3.13.)

To shut me out! Pour on, I will endure.
In such a night as this! O Regan, Goneril,
Your old kind father, whose frank[129] heart gave all—
O, that way madness lies; let me shun that.
No more of that.

Kent. Good my lord, enter here,

Lear. Prithee go in thyself; seek thine own ease.
This tempest will not give me leave to ponder
On things would hurt me more, but I'll go in.
[*To the Fool*] In, boy; go first. You houseless poverty[130]—
Nay, get thee in. I'll pray, and then I'll sleep.

Exit [*Fool*].

Poor naked wretches, wheresoe'er you are,
That bide[131] the pelting of this pitiless storm,
How shall your houseless heads and unfed sides,
Your looped and windowed[132] raggedness, defend you
From seasons such as these? O, I have ta'en
Too little care of this! Take physic,[133] pomp;[134]
Expose thyself to feel what wretches feel,
That thou mayst shake the superflux[135] to them,
And show the heavens more just.

Edgar. [*Within*] Fathom and half, fathom and half![136]
Poor Tom!

[129] **frank** generous
[130] **poverty** the "Poor naked wretches" of lines 28ff.
[131] **bide** endure
[132] **looped and windowed** full of holes
[133] **physic** medicine
[134] **pomp** splendid display; glory (perhaps addressing himself)
[135] **superflux** superfluity; surplus
[136] **Fathom and half** (Edgar, feigning insanity, calls out—inspired, perhaps, by the floods of rain—as though a sailor sounding the depth of water [a fathom is six feet].)

Enter Fool.

Fool. Come not in here, Nuncle, here's a spirit. Help me, help me!

Kent. Give me thy hand. Who's there?

Fool. A spirit, a spirit. He says his name's Poor Tom.

Kent. What art thou that dost grumble there i' th' straw?
Come forth.

Enter Edgar [disguised as a madman].

Edgar. Away! the foul fiend follows me.[137] Through the sharp hawthorn blows the cold wind.[138] Humh! Go to thy cold bed, and warm thee.[139]

Lear. Didst thou give all to thy daughters? And art thou come to this?

Edgar. Who gives anything to Poor Tom? Whom the foul fiend hath led through fire and through flame, through ford and whirlpool, o'er bog and quagmire; that hath laid knives under his pillow and halters in his pew,[140] set ratsbane[141, 142] by his porridge,[143] made him proud of heart, to ride on a bay trotting horse[144] over four-inched

[137] **He . . . me** In his portrayal of Edgar as Poor Tom, Shakespeare will draw heavily on Samuel Harsnett's *Declaration of Egregious Popish Impostures* (1603), a sardonic attack, by the chaplain to the (Anglican) Bishop of London, upon the Catholic exorcisms of Fr. Edmunds and his circle.

[138] **Through . . . wind** (from a ballad, "The Friar of Orders Gray")

[139] **Go . . . thee** (This line, which also appears in *The Taming of the Shrew* [Induction, 1.10], echoes passages in Kyd's *Spanish Tragedy* [2.5.1; 3.12.31].)

[140] **pew** balcony; gallery

[141] **ratsbane** rat poison

[142] **knives . . . halters . . . ratsbane** various temptations to suicide, by which the fiend hopes to get him damned to hell

[143] **porridge** soup

[144] **trotting horse** a horse trained to trot in stately fashion

bridges,[145] to course[146] his own shadow for[147] a traitor. Bless thy five wits,[148] Tom's a-cold. O, do, de, do, de, do, de.[149] Bless thee from whirlwinds, star-blasting,[150] and taking.[151] Do Poor Tom some charity, whom the foul fiend vexes. There could I have him now—and there—and there again—and there.

Storm still.

Lear. What, has his daughters brought him to this pass?
Couldst thou save nothing? Wouldst thou give 'em all?[152]

Fool. Nay, he reserved a blanket, else we had been all shamed.

Lear. Now all the plagues that in the pendulous[153] air[154]
Hang fated o'er[155] men's faults light on thy daughters!

Kent. He hath no daughters, sir.

Lear. Death, traitor; nothing could have subdued
Nature[156]

[145] **ride . . . bridges** An impossible endeavor, which, if attempted, would probably end in a fatal accident.

[146] **course** chase

[147] **for** as

[148] **five wits** (not the five senses, but rather common wit, imagination, fantasy, estimation, memory)

[149] **O . . . de** unclear. Some critics have suggested that Edgar is shivering with cold.

[150] **star-blasting** evil influence of unfavorable stars

[151] **taking** infection; disease

[152] **What . . . all** (Perhaps the first indication of Lear's madness)

[153] **pendulous** overhanging

[154] **plagues . . . air** plagues were thought to infect the air

[155] **fated o'er** Infection was thought to be inflicted as a punishment by the powers above.

[156] **subdued Nature** reduced his powers

To such a lowness but his unkind daughters.
Is it the fashion that discarded fathers
Should have thus little mercy on their flesh?
Judicious punishment—'twas this flesh begot
Those pelican[157] daughters.

Edgar. Pillicock[158] sat on Pillicock Hill.[159,160] Alow, alow, loo, loo![161]

Fool. This cold night will turn us all to fools and mad-men.

Edgar. Take heed o' th' foul fiend; obey thy parents; keep thy word's justice;[162] swear not; commit not with man's sworn spouse; set not thy sweet heart on proud array.[163,164] Tom's a-cold.

Lear. What hast thou been?

Edgar. A servingman, proud in heart and mind; that curled my hair, wore gloves in my cap;[165] served the lust of my mistress' heart, and did the act of darkness with her; swore as many oaths as I spake words, and broke them in the sweet face of

[157] **pelican** The "pious" pelican was thought either to feed or revive its young with its own blood; alternately, it was sometimes said that the chicks attacked their parents.

[158] **Pillicock** a term of endearment; slang for the phallus

[159] **Pillicock Hill** (perhaps the female genitals: the *mons Veneris*)

[160] **Pillicock ... Hill** (probably brought to mind by "pelican"; possibly from the nursery rhyme: "Pillycock, Pillycock sat on a hill;/If he's not gone, he sits there still.")

[161] **Alow ... loo** various possibilities. "Halloo" and "loo" were hunting calls to excite the dogs; similarly "halloo" was a call to a hawk; imitation of cockcrow; the sound of Bedlam's horn; perhaps the refrain from a song, or merely the refrain of this song.

[162] **justice** ("justly" in some editions)

[163] **proud array** sumptuous clothes

[164] **obey ... array** echoing five of the Ten Commandments: one must obey one's parents but must not bear false witness, take the Lord's name in vain ("swear not"), commit adultery, or covet others' goods (sumptuous clothes)

[165] **gloves in my cap** (a sign of favor from his mistress)

heaven. One that slept in the contriving of lust, and waked to do it. Wine loved I deeply, dice dearly; and in woman out-paramoured the Turk.[166] False of heart, light of ear,[167] bloody of hand; hog in sloth, fox in stealth, wolf in greediness, dog in madness, lion in prey.[168] Let not the creaking of shoes[169] nor the rustling of silks[170] betray thy poor heart to woman. Keep thy foot out of brothels, thy hand out of plackets,[171] thy pen from lenders' books,[172] and defy the foul fiend. Still through the hawthorn blows the cold wind; says suum, mun, nonny.[173] Dolphin[174] my boy, boy,[175] sessa![176] let him trot by.

Storm still.

Lear. Thou wert better in a grave than to answer[177] with thy uncovered body this extremity[178] of the skies. Is man no more than this? Consider him well. Thou ow'st[179] the worm no silk, the beast no

[166] **out-paramoured the Turk** had more mistresses than a Sultan's harem

[167] **light of ear** listened eagerly to vicious gossip ("light" here meaning "unchaste")

[168] **hog . . . prey** (The seven deadly sins [some of which are listed here] were often represented by animals.)

[169] **creaking of shoes** (Creaking shoes were fashionable at the time.)

[170] **silks** a woman's dress

[171] **plackets** slits in petticoats

[172] **lenders' books** money lenders' account books (i.e., don't borrow from money lenders)

[173] **suum, mun, nonny** unclear: perhaps imitating the wind, or nonsense. "Nonny" was a common refrain for a song.

[174] **Dolphin** Dauphin (heir to the French throne, and in one play equated with the Devil). Dolphin is also a possible name for a horse.

[175] **Dolphin my boy, boy** probably from a ballad

[176] **sessa** perhaps an interjection, "Off you go!" or possibly derived from the French *cessez*, meaning "stop" or "be quiet"

[177] **answer** encounter; face

[178] **extremity** ruthlessness

[179] **ow'st** owe to

hide, the sheep no wool, the cat[180] no perfume. Ha! here's three on's[181] are sophisticated.[182] Thou art the thing itself; unaccommodated[183] man is no more but such a poor, bare, forked[184] animal as thou art. Off, off, you lendings![185] Come, unbutton here.

[*Tearing off his clothes.*]

Fool. Prithee, Nuncle, be contented, 'tis a naughty[186] night to swim in. Now a little fire in a wild field were like an old lecher's heart—a small spark, all the rest on's[187] body, cold. Look, here comes a walking fire.[188]

Enter Gloucester, with a torch.

Edgar. This is the foul fiend Flibbertigibbet.[189] He begins at curfew,[190] and walks till the first cock.[191] He gives the web and the pin,[192] squints the eye, and makes the harelip; mildews the white[193] wheat, and hurts the poor creature of earth.

[180] **cat** civet cat, whose glands were used in the making of perfume

[181] **on's** of us

[182] **sophisticated** adulterated

[183] **unaccommodated** uncivilized

[184] **forked** two-legged

[185] **lendings** garments ("lent" by the worm, sheep, etc., but also, within the wider moral context of the play, "lent" by God, our life and possessions being "lent" us until we are parted from them at death)

[186] **naughty** wicked

[187] **on's** of his

[188] **walking fire** (not only referring to Gloucester's carrying a torch, but to Gloucester himself, who is an "old lecher")

[189] **Flibbertigibbet** demon in Harsnett—where he is called Flibberdigibbet; associated with grimacing and making faces

[190] **curfew** nightfall

[191] **first cock** midnight

[192] **web and the pin** cataract in the eye

[193] **white** nearly ripe

Swithold[194] footed thrice[195] the old;[196]
He met the nightmare,[197] and her nine fold;[198]
Bid her alight[199]
And her troth plight,[200]
And aroint[201] thee, witch, aroint thee![202]

Kent. How fares your Grace?

Lear. What's he?

Kent. Who's there? What is't you seek?

Gloucester. What are you there? Your names?

Edgar. Poor Tom, that eats the swimming frog, the toad, the todpole,[203] the wall-newt[204] and the water;[205] that in the fury of his heart, when the foul fiend rages, eats cow-dung for sallets,[206] swallows the old rat and the ditch-dog,[207] drinks the green mantle[208] of the standing[209] pool; who is whipped from tithing[210] to tithing, and stocked, punished, and imprisoned;

[194] **Swithold** St. Withold

[195] **thrice** Three was a virtuous number; "nine", below, is a multiple of three.

[196] **old** wold (piece of open uncultivated country)

[197] **nightmare** incubus/succubus: demon adopting male/female sexual identity for the purpose of copulating with the victim at night

[198] **fold** offspring, imps or familiars; or, possibly, the nine coils of its serpentine form

[199] **alight** get off

[200] **her troth plight** pledge her word

[201] **aroint** begone

[202] **Swithold ... thee!** This jingle appears to be a charm against evil spirits: The saint binds the demon to do him no harm and then rives it away.

[203] **todpole** tadpole

[204] **wall-newt** lizard

[205] **water** (i.e., water-newt; newt)

[206] **sallets** salads; something tasty

[207] **ditch-dog** dead dog thrown in a ditch

[208] **mantle** covering (i.e., the film on the pool)

[209] **standing** stagnant

[210] **tithing** parish or district of ten households. (Under the statute of 1597, a vagabond could be whipped and sent from parish to parish until reaching his native parish.)

who hath had three suits[211] to his back, six shirts to his body,
Horse to ride, and weapon to wear,
But mice and rats, and such small deer,[212]
Have been Tom's food for seven long year.[213]
Beware my follower![214] Peace, Smulkin,[215] peace, thou fiend!

Gloucester. What, hath your Grace no better company?

Edgar. The Prince of Darkness is a gentleman.[216]
Modo[217] he's called, and Mahu.[218]

Gloucester. Our flesh and blood, my Lord, is grown so vile
That it doth hate what gets[219] it.

Edgar. Poor Tom's a-cold.

Gloucester. Go in with me. My duty cannot suffer[220]
T' obey in all your daughters' hard commands.
Though their injunction be to bar my doors
And let this tyrannous night take hold upon you,

[211] **three suits** (See note at 2.2.15.)

[212] **deer** game

[213] **But . . . year** (adapted from the romance "Bevis of Hampton": "Ratons and myce and soche small dere/That was hys mete that seven yere")

[214] **follower** familiar; fiend

[215] **Smulkin** (in Harsnett, a minor devil that took the shape of a mouse. Harsnett calls him Smolkin.)

[216] **The Prince of Darknes is a gentleman** Edgar's demonic company is high-ranking; Satan is of "noble" blood and is at home in the company of nobility.

[217] **Modo** (in Harsnett, a fiend associated with murder. Harsnett calls him Modu and describes him as the commander over the captains of the seven deadly sins.)

[218] **Mahu** (in Harsnett, a demon associated with stealing. Harsnett calls him Maho and describes him as the "generall Dictator of hell".)

[219] **gets** begets

[220] **suffer** allow; bear

Yet have I ventured to come seek you out
And bring you where both fire and food is ready.

Lear. First let me talk with this philosopher.[221]
What is the cause of thunder?[222]

Kent. Good my lord, take his offer; go into th' house.

Lear. I'll talk a word with this same learnèd Theban.[223]
What is your study?[224]

Edgar. How to prevent[225] the fiend, and to kill vermin.

Lear. Let me ask you one word in private.

Kent. Importune him once more to go, my lord.
His wits begin t' unsettle.

Gloucester. Canst thou blame him?

Storm still.

His daughters seek his death. Ah, that good Kent,
He said it would be thus, poor banished man!
Thou say'st the King grows mad—I'll tell thee,
friend,
I am almost mad myself. I had a son,

[221] **philosopher** "natural scientist", "wise man", or "magician". (Kings sometimes kept philosophers at their courts.)

[222] **What . . . thunder?** a popular question in Shakespeare's time

[223] **Theban** Greek philosopher and scholar, perhaps Crates or his master Diogenes, both cynics. The cynics lived in poverty, wore rags, and abjured wealth and power. Equally, it might refer to Tiresias, the Theban prophet and wise man in Homer, Ovid, and Sophocles, and in Eliot's "The Waste Land", who retains his power of sight even in the land of the dead. As a blind seer who paradoxically sees more than those with physical sight, Tiresias corresponds with Edgar's paradoxical role as the wise fool or sane madman whose "reason in madness" outshines in real wisdom the "rationalism" of the blind who will not see.

[224] **study** subject of research

[225] **prevent** avoid

Now outlawed from my blood;[226] he sought my life
But lately, very late.[227] I loved him, friend,
No father his son dearer. True to tell thee,
The grief hath crazed my wits. What a night's this!
I do beseech your Grace———

Lear. O, cry you mercy,[228] sir.
Noble philosopher, your company.

Edgar. Tom's a-cold.

Gloucester. In, fellow, there, into th' hovel; keep thee warm.

Lear. Come, let's in all.

Kent. This way, my lord.

Lear. With him!
I will keep still with my philosopher.

Kent. Good my lord, soothe[229] him; let him take the fellow.

Gloucester. Take him you on.[230]

Kent. Sirrah, come on; go along with us.

Lear. Come, good Athenian.[231]

Gloucester. No words, no words! Hush.

[226] **outlawed from my blood** outlawed, disinherited

[227] **late** (See note at 2.2.118.)

[228] **cry you mercy** I beg your pardon

[229] **soothe** humor

[230] **you on** with you (possibly "take on" in the sense of "engage", i.e., as your court philosopher: see line 183. This may refer either to Edgar or the Fool.)

[231] **Athenian** (perhaps likening him to the Theban. See note at 3.4.160.)

Edgar. Child[232] Rowland[233] to the dark tower[234] came;[235]
His word was still,[236] "Fie, foh, and fum,
I smell the blood of a British[237] man."[238] *Exeunt.*

Scene 5. [*Gloucester's castle.*]

Enter Cornwall and Edmund.

Cornwall. I will have my revenge ere I depart his house.

Edmund. How, my lord, I may be censured,[239] that Nature[240] thus gives way to loyalty,[241] something fears[242] me to think of.

Cornwall. I now perceive it was not altogether your brother's evil disposition made him seek his death; but a provoking merit,[243] set a-work by a reprovable[244] badness in himself.[245]

[232] **Child** title of candidate for knighthood

[233] **Rowland** nephew of Charlemagne and hero of the epic *Song of Roland*

[234] **dark tower** (perhaps a reference to Gloucester's castle)

[235] **Child ... came** (probably a line from a lost ballad)

[236] **His ... still** his motto was always

[237] **British** (The fairy tale has "English man", but Lear was king of Britain; James I liked to style himself "King of Great Brittaine".)

[238] **Fie ... man** purposely incongruous placing of the words of the Giant in "Jack the Giant Killer" into the mouth of the hero Roland

[239] **censured** judged, regarded by others

[240] **Nature** (his love for his father)

[241] **loyalty** (to Cornwall, the ruler)

[242] **something fears** somewhat frightens

[243] **a provoking merit** unclear. Cornwall says that Edgar has been provoked or incited to seek Gloucester's death, but the critics are divided as to the meaning of "merit": "a worthy quality"; "the merit of forestalling Gloucester's treason"; "a sense of his own worth" have all been suggested.

[244] **reprovable** disgraceful; blameworthy

[245] **himself** unclear. It may be either Gloucester or Edgar depending upon the interpretation of the passage.

Edmund. How malicious is my fortune that I must repent to be just! This is the letter which he spoke of, which approves[246] him an intelligent party[247] to the advantages of France. O heavens, that his treason were not! or not I the detector!

Cornwall. Go with me to the Duchess.

Edmund. If the matter of this paper be certain, you have mighty business in hand.

Cornwall. True or false, it hath made thee Earl of Gloucester. Seek out where thy father is, that he may be ready for our apprehension.

Edmund. [*Aside*] If I find him comforting[248] the King, it will stuff his suspicion more fully.—I will persever[249] in my course of loyalty, though the conflict be sore between that and my blood.[250]

Cornwall. I will lay trust upon thee, and thou shalt find a dearer father in my love. *Exeunt.*

Scene 6. [*A chamber in a farmhouse adjoining the castle.*]

Enter Kent and Gloucester.

Gloucester. Here is better than the open air; take it thankfully. I will piece out the comfort with what addition I can. I will not be long from you.

Kent. All the power of his wits have given way to his impatience.[251] The gods reward your kindness.

[246] **approves** proves
[247] **intelligent party** someone bearing intelligence (information): a spy
[248] **comforting** assisting (in legal terms, making one an accessory to a criminal)
[249] **persever** persevere
[250] **blood** natural feeling and duties as son
[251] **impatience** passion or loss of self-control (another allusion to what he lacks most: patience)

Exit [*Gloucester*].

Enter Lear, Edgar, and Fool.

Edgar. Frateretto[252] calls me, and tells me Nero[253] is an angler in the lake of darkness. Pray, innocent,[254] and beware the foul fiend.

Fool. Prithee, Nuncle, tell me whether a madman be a gentleman or a yeoman.[255]

Lear. A king, a king.

Fool. No, he's a yeoman that has a gentleman to his son; for he's a mad yeoman that *sees* his son a gentleman before him.

Lear. To have a thousand with red burning spits
Come hizzing[256] in upon 'em[257]———

Edgar. The foul fiend bites my back.

Fool. He's mad that trusts in the tameness of a wolf, a horse's health,[258] a boy's love, or a whore's oath.

Lear. It shall be done; I will arraign them[259] straight.[260]
[*To Edgar*] Come, sit thou here, most learned justice.[261]

[252] **Frateretto** another fiend listed in Harsnett's *Declaration*

[253] **Nero** (linked with Frateretto in Harsnett's work and depicted by Chaucer as an angler in "The Monk's Tale")

[254] **innocent** simpleton (possibly addressed to the Fool, who speaks for the first time in a while; equally, it could be addressed to Lear)

[255] **yeoman** freeholder of land of lower rank. (Some have suggested that at this point the Fool realizes that Edgar is not truly mad.)

[256] **hizzing** hissing (with an onomatopoetic effect)

[257] **To . . . 'em** (Lear is imagining Goneril and Regan in Hell.)

[258] **a horse's health** (perhaps as reported by the horse-seller)

[259] **arraign them** put them on trial

[260] **straight** (See note at 1.3.26.)

[261] **justice** judge; Justice

[*To the Fool*] Thou, sapient[262] sir, sit here. Now,
you she-foxes——

Edgar. Look, where he[263] stands and glares. Want'st
thou eyes[264] at trial, madam?[265]
Come o'er the bourn,[266] Bessy, to me.[267]

Fool. Her boat hath a leak,
And she must not speak
Why she dares not come over to thee.[268]

Edgar. The foul fiend haunts Poor Tom in the voice of a nightingale.[269] Hoppedance[270] cries in Tom's belly for two white[271] herring. Croak[272] not, black angel; I have no food for thee.

Kent. How do you, sir? Stand you not so amazed.[273]
Will you lie down and rest upon the cushions?

Lear. I'll see their trial first. Bring in their evidence.[274]
[*To Edgar*] Thou, robèd[275] man of justice, take
thy place.
[*To the Fool*] And thou, his yokefellow[276] of equity,[277]

[262] **sapient** wise and discerning
[263] **he** (a demon, or possibly Lear)
[264] **eyes** spectators
[265] **madam** (to Goneril or Regan)
[266] **bourn** brook
[267] **Come . . . me** (a line from a ballad)
[268] **Her . . . thee** (the Fool picks up the song here and improvises)
[269] **voice . . . nightingale** (probably referring to the Fool)
[270] **Hoppedance** (in Harsnett, a fiend associated with music; called Hoberdidance in Harsnett's *Declaration*)
[271] **white** unsmoked: either fresh or pickled
[272] **Croak** rumble (meaning his belly, with hunger)
[273] **amazed** bewildered; dumbfounded
[274] **their evidence** the evidence against them, or those testifying against them
[275] **robèd** (a reference to Edgar's paltry blanket)
[276] **yokefellow** partner
[277] **equity** justice; impartiality

Bench by his side.[278] [*To Kent*] You are o' th' commission;[279]
Sit you too.

Edgar. Let us deal justly.
Sleepest or wakest thou, jolly shepherd?
Thy sheep be in the corn;[280]
And for one blast of thy minikin[281] mouth
Thy sheep shall take no harm.[282]
Purr, the cat is gray.[283]

Lear. Arraign her first. 'Tis Goneril, I here take my oath before this honorable assembly, she kicked the poor King her father.

Fool. Come hither, mistress. Is your name Goneril?

Lear. She cannot deny it.

Fool. Cry you mercy, I took you for a joint stool.[284]

Lear. And here's another,[285] whose warped looks proclaim
What store[286] her heart is made on.[287] Stop her there!
Arms, arms, sword, fire! Corruption in the place!
False justicer, why hast thou let her 'scape?

[278] **Bench . . . side** sit beside him on the bench

[279] **o' th' commission** one of the commissioned justices

[280] **corn** wheat

[281] **minikin** shrill

[282] **Sleepest . . . harm** (probably from a lot song)

[283] **Purr . . . gray** a demon in the form of a gray cat—possibly from Harsnett's devil named Purre. Edgar may also be referring to the sound it is making.

[284] **Cry . . . joint stool** (recalling the phrase about overlooking someone. A "joint stool" was made by a "joiner", distinguishing it from the rougher work of a carpenter. Some have suggested the Fool meant he thought Goneril was one of the bench, i.e., a judge.)

[285] **another** (i.e., Regan)

[286] **store** material; or, ironically, bounty. It may also be an allusion to "For where your treasure is, there will your heart be also" (Mt 6:21).

[287] **on** of

Edgar. Bless thy five wits![288]

Kent. O pity! Sir, where is the patience now
That you so oft have boasted to retain?

Edgar. [*Aside*] My tears begin to take his part so much
They mar my counterfeiting.[289]

Lear. The little dogs and all,
Tray, Blanch, and Sweetheart—see, they bark at me.

Edgar. Tom will throw his head at them. Avaunt, you curs.
Be thy mouth or black or[290] white,
Tooth that poisons if it bite;
Mastiff, greyhound, mongrel grim,
Hound or spaniel, brach[291] or lym,[292]
Or bobtail tike,[293] or trundle-tail[294]—
Tom will make him weep and wail;
For, with throwing thus my head,[295]
Dogs leaped the hatch,[296] and all are fled.
Do, de, de, de.[297] Sessa![298] Come, march to wakes[299] and fairs and market towns.[300] Poor Tom, thy horn[301] is dry.

[288] **Bless ... wits** (See note at 3.4.57.)

[289] **counterfeiting** playing the madman

[290] **or ... or** either ... or

[291] **brach** (See note at 1.4.115.)

[292] **lym** lymmer: a kind of bloodhound

[293] **bobtail tike** mongrel with a bobbed tail

[294] **trundle-tail** long-tailed or curly-tailed dog

[295] **head** (uncertain as to how he does this: perhaps by pantomime or throwing his hat or beggar's horn)

[296] **leaped the hatch** left hurriedly (the hatch was the lower part of a half-door)

[297] **Do ... de** Edgar is perhaps shivering with cold again.

[298] **Sessa** stop

[299] **wakes** annual celebration of a church's dedication

[300] **Come . . . towns** accompany him on his beggar's rounds (possibly from a song)

[301] **horn** Bedlam beggars carried a horn to blow in asking for alms and to fill with a donated drink. (It could also mean that Edgar has "gone dry" and has no more to say—and, indeed, this is his last word in this scene.)

Lear. Then let them anatomize[302] Regan. See what breeds
about her heart.[303] Is there any cause in nature that
make these hard hearts? [*To Edgar*] You, sir,
I entertain[304] for one of my hundred;[305] only I do not
like the fashion of your garments. You will say
they are Persian;[306] but let them be changed.

Kent. Now, good my lord, lie here and rest awhile.

Lear. Make no noise, make no noise; draw the
curtains.[307]
So, so. We'll go to supper i' th' morning.

Fool. And I'll go to bed at noon.[308]

Enter Gloucester.

Gloucester. Come hither, friend. Where is the King
my master?

Kent. Here, sir, but trouble him not; his wits are gone.

Gloucester. Good friend, I prithee take him in thy
arms.
I have o'erheard a plot of death upon[309] him.
There is a litter ready; lay him in't

[302] **anatomize** dissect

[303] **Then . . . heart** (i.e., her heart is as hard as horn)

[304] **entertain** take into my service

[305] **hundred** (i.e., his hundred knights)

[306] **Persian** gorgeous, likely silken (James I had received an embassy from Persia early in his reign. See note at 3.6.36, and Dan 6:8: "What is decreed by the Medes and Persians may not be altered.")

[307] **curtains** i.e., around the bed (as though in his own bed)

[308] **And . . . noon** (from the proverb meaning "I'll play the fool too". These are the Fool's last words and "bed" here may mean the grave. Perhaps the Fool's final words are an allusion to the fact that he was a light to the king in the darkest hours of his "madness" but that he is no longer needed now that the light of sanity, heralded by the coded wisdom of Edgar, approaches. Others have suggested that the Fool's words emphasize Lear's withdrawal into the world of hallucination.)

[309] **upon** against

And drive toward Dover, friend, where thou shalt meet
Both welcome and protection. Take up thy master.
If thou shouldst dally half an hour, his life,
With thine and all that offer to defend him,
Stand in assurèd loss. Take up, take up,
And follow me, that[310] will to some provision
Give thee quick conduct.[311]

Kent. Oppressèd nature sleeps.
This rest might yet have balmed[312] thy broken sinews,[313]
Which, if convenience will not allow,
Stand in hard cure.[314] [*To the Fool*] Come, help to bear thy master.
Thou must not stay behind.

Gloucester. Come, come, away!

Exeunt [*all but Edgar*].

Edgar. When we our betters see bearing our woes,
We scarcely think our miseries our foes.[315]
Who alone suffers suffers most i' th' mind,
Leaving free[316] things and happy shows[317] behind;
But then the mind much sufferance[318] doth o'erskip[319]
When grief hath mates, and bearing[320] fellowship.
How light and portable[321] my pain seems now,

[310] **that** who
[311] **conduct** guidance (i.e., to the provisions)
[312] **balmed** soothed, healed
[313] **sinews** nerves
[314] **Stand . . . cure** are not likely to be cured
[315] **We . . . foes** We are scarcely conscious of our own miseries.
[316] **free** carefree
[317] **shows** scenes; performances; but possibly also masks or pretenses
[318] **sufferance** suffering
[319] **o'erskip** not heed
[320] **bearing** suffering; endurance
[321] **portable** bearable

When that which makes me bend makes the
King bow.
He childed as I fathered. Tom, away.
Mark the high noises,[322] and thyself bewray[323]
When false opinion, whose wrong thoughts[324] defile
thee,
In thy just proof[325] repeals[326] and reconciles thee.[327]
What will hap more tonight, safe 'scape the King![328]
Lurk,[329] lurk. [*Exit.*]

Scene 7. [*Gloucester's castle.*]

Enter Cornwall, Regan, Goneril, Edmund, and Servants.

Cornwall. [*To Goneril*] Post[330] speedily to my Lord your husband; show him this letter.[331] The army of France is landed. [*To Servants*] Seek out the traitor Gloucester. [*Exeunt some of the Servants.*]

Regan. Hang him instantly.

Goneril. Pluck out his eyes.[332]

Cornwall. Leave him to my displeasure. Edmund, keep you our sister company. The revenges we are

[322] **Mark the high noises** Note the rumors about the court.
[323] **bewray** reveal
[324] **wrong thoughts** false reports or opinions
[325] **just proof** proof of integrity
[326] **repeals** i.e., the sentence of outlawry
[327] **reconciles thee** i.e., to your father
[328] **What . . . King!** Whatever else may happen tonight, may the King escape safely!
[329] **Lurk** hide
[330] **Post** ride with haste; hurry
[331] **letter** i.e., the one Edgar took from Gloucester's room
[332] **Pluck out his eyes** (a punishment for rape rather than treason. Perhaps Gloucester is being punished for seeing too much or too clearly.)

bound[333] to take upon your traitorous father are not fit for your beholding. Advise the Duke where you are going, to a most festinate[334] preparation.[335] We are bound to the like. Our posts[336] shall be swift and intelligent[337] betwixt us. Farewell, dear sister; farewell, my Lord of Gloucester.[338]

Enter Oswald.

How now? Where's the King?

Oswald. My Lord of Gloucester hath conveyed him hence.
Some five or six and thirty of his knights,
Hot questrists[339] after him, met him at gate;
Who, with some other of the lords[340] dependants,
Are gone with him toward Dover, where they boast
To have well-armèd friends.

Cornwall. Get horses for your mistress.

[*Exit Oswald.*]

Goneril. Farewell, sweet lord, and sister.

Cornwall. Edmund, farewell.

[*Exeunt Goneril and Edmund.*]

Go seek the traitor Gloucester,
Pinion[341] him like a thief, bring him before us.

[333] **bound** obliged; ready; determined
[334] **festinate** hasty; urgent
[335] **preparation** (i.e., for war)
[336] **posts** messengers
[337] **intelligent** bearing information
[338] **Lord of Gloucester** (Edmund)
[339] **questrists** searchers (those in quest of something: Shakespeare's coinage)
[340] **lords** Gloucester's (or, possibly, Lear's)
[341] **Pinion** bind his arms (as one does the wings of a bird to prevent flight. This treatment is inappropriate for a man of Gloucester's station.)

[*Exeunt other Servants.*]

Though well we may not pass upon his life[342]
Without the form of justice, yet our power
Shall do a court'sy to[343] our wrath, which men
May blame, but not control.

Enter Gloucester, brought in by two or three.

Who's there, the traitor?

Regan. Ingrateful fox, 'tis he.

Cornwall. Bind fast his corky[344] arms.

Gloucester. What means your Graces? Good my friends, consider
You are my guests. Do me no foul play, friends.

Cornwall. Bind him, I say.

[*Servants bind him.*]

Regan. Hard, hard![345] O filthy traitor.

Gloucester. Unmerciful lady as you are, I'm none.

Cornwall. To this chair bind him. Villain, thou shalt find——

[*Regan plucks his beard.*]

Gloucester. By the kind gods, 'tis most ignobly done
To pluck me by the beard.[346]

Regan. So white, and such a traitor?

[342] **pass ... life** sentence him to death

[343] **do a court'sy to** curtsy to (i.e., defer or yield to)

[344] **corky** withered

[345] **Hard, hard** (Gloucester's servants are obviously reluctant to bind him, since Cornwall must say it repeatedly, and, when they do, they try to do so loosely.)

[346] **To pluck me by the beard** (a mortal insult and extreme provocation)

Gloucester. Naughty[347] lady,
These hairs which thou dost ravish[348] from my chin
Will quicken[349] and accuse thee. I am your host.
With robber's hands my hospitable[350] favors[351]
You should not ruffle[352] thus. What will you do?

Cornwall. Come, sir, what letters had you late from France?

Regan. Be simple-answered,[353] for we know the truth.

Cornwall. And what confederacy have you with the traitors
Late footed in the kingdom?

Regan. To whose hands you have sent the lunatic King:
Speak.

Gloucester. I have a letter guessingly set down,[354]
Which came from one that's of a neutral heart,
And not from one opposed.

Cornwall. Cunning.

Regan. And false.

Cornwall. Where hast thou sent the King?

Gloucester. To Dover.

Regan. Wherefore to Dover? Wast thou not charged at
Peril[355] ——

[347] **Naughty** (See note at 3.4.112.)
[348] **ravish** pull out (with the additional meaning, "violate", especially as in rape)
[349] **quicken** come to life
[350] **hospitable** host's
[351] **favors** features; face
[352] **ruffle** handle violently
[353] **Be simple-answered** be straightforward; don't dissimulate
[354] **guessingly set down** written as conjecture
[355] **at Peril** at your peril

Cornwall. Wherefore to Dover? Let him answer that.

Gloucester. I am tied to th' stake, and I must stand
the course.[356]

Regan. Wherefore to Dover?

Gloucester. Because I would not see thy cruel nails
Pluck out his poor old eyes; nor thy fierce sister
In his anointed[357] flesh rash[358] boarish fangs.
The sea, with such a storm as his bare head
In hell-black night endured, would have buoyed[359] up
And quenched the stellèd fires.[360]
Yet, poor old heart, he holp[361] the heavens to rain.
If wolves had at thy gate howled that dearn[362] time,
Thou shouldst have said, "Good porter, turn the
key."[363]
All cruels else subscribe.[364] But I shall see
The wingèd[365] vengeance overtake such children.

[356] **tied . . . course** (A popular entertainment of the time was bear-baiting, in which the bear [or sometimes a bull] was tied to a stake and set upon by dogs in "courses", or series of attacks.)

[357] **anointed** consecrated (Monarchs were—and, in England, still are—anointed with oil in the coronation ceremony, signifying divine election and protection, and the spiritual gifts of kingship.)

[358] **rash** slash obliquely with tusks (Other editions read "stick"—perhaps a change made due to the difficulty of saying the thrice-repeated "sh" sound in "flesh rash boarish".)

[359] **buoyed** risen

[360] **stellèd fires** stars (either "starry fires" or "fixed lights")

[361] **holp** helped

[362] **dearn** dreary; dire

[363] **turn the key** The weather was so dreadful that had even wolves been howling for refuge, you would have commanded the porter to open the gate and let them in for pity's sake.

[364] **All cruels else subscribe** (variously interpreted, with the strongest possibilities being: "Never mind your other cruelties—I will leave them out of consideration; but for the monstrous act of shutting your father out on such a night: I shall see the wingèd vengeance etc."; and, "All cruel creatures but you yield to compassion on such a night.")

[365] **wingèd** heavenly; swift; like a bird of prey

Cornwall. See't shalt thou never. Fellows, hold the chair.
Upon these eyes of thine I'll set my foot.

Gloucester. He that will think to live till he be old,
Give me some help.—O cruel! O you gods!

Regan. One side will mock[366] another. Th' other too.

Cornwall. If you see vengeance[367]———

First Servant. Hold your hand, my lord!
I have served you ever since I was a child;
But better service have I never done you
Than now to bid you hold.

Regan. How now, you dog?

First Servant. If you did wear a beard upon your chin,
I'd shake it[368] on this quarrel. What do you mean![369]

Cornwall. My villain![370]

Draw and fight.

First Servant. Nay, then, come on, and take the chance of anger.

Regan. Give me thy sword.[371] A peasant stand up thus?

She takes a sword and runs at him behind, kills him.

[366] **mock** make ridiculous
[367] **If . . . vengeance** (addressed to Gloucester)
[368] **shake it** fight you
[369] **What . . . mean** i.e., by such behavior
[370] **villain** villain; serf
[371] **Give . . . sword** (addressing another servant)

First Servant. O, I am slain! my lord, you have one eye left
To see some mischief on him.[372] O!

Cornwall. Lest it see more, prevent it. Out, vile jelly.
Where is thy luster now?

Gloucester. All dark and comfortless. Where's my son Edmund?
Edmund, enkindle all the sparks of nature[373]
To quit[374] this horrid act.

Regan. Out, treacherous villain,
Thou call'st on him that hates thee. It was he
That made the overture[375] of thy treasons to us;
Who is too good to pity thee.

Gloucester. O my follies! Then Edgar was abused.[376]
Kind gods, forgive me that, and prosper him.

Regan. Go thrust him out at gates, and let him smell
His way to Dover. *Exit [one] with Gloucester.*

How is't, my lord? How look you?[377]

Cornwall. I have received a hurt. Follow me, lady.
Turn out that eyeless villain. Throw this slave
Upon the dunghill. Regan, I bleed apace.
Untimely comes this hurt. Give me your arm.

Exeunt.

Second Servant. I'll never care what wickedness I do,
If this man come to good.

[372] **mischief on him** harm done to him
[373] **nature** (See note at 3.5.4.)
[374] **quit** avenge
[375] **overture** disclosure
[376] **abused** maligned; wronged
[377] **How look you?** How are you?

Third Servant. If she live long,
And in the end meet the old course of death,[378]
Women will all turn monsters.

Second Servant. Let's follow the old Earl, and get the Bedlam
To lead him where he would. His roguish madness
Allows itself to anything.[379]

Third Servant. Go thou. I'll fetch some flax and whites of eggs
To apply to his bleeding face. Now heaven help
him. [*Exeunt severally.*]

[378] **meet . . . death** die of old age
[379] **His . . . anything** No one will censure him for anything because he is mad.

ACT 4

Scene 1. [*The heath.*]

Enter Edgar.

Edgar. Yet better thus, and known to be contemned,[1]
Than still contemned and flattered.[2] To be worst,
The lowest and most dejected[3] thing of fortune,
Stands still in esperance,[4] lives not in fear:
The lamentable change is from the best,
The worst returns to laughter.[5] Welcome then,
Thou unsubstantial air that I embrace!
The wretch that thou hast blown unto the worst
Owes nothing to thy blasts.[6]

Enter Gloucester, led by an Old Man.[7]

But who comes here?
My father, poorly led?[8] World, world, O world!

[1] **contemned** despised

[2] **Yet . . . flattered** The meaning of this passage is disputed. The most probable reading is: It is better to be despised openly, as I am now, than to be flattered and secretly despised, as I was at court.

[3] **dejected** humbled; cast down

[4] **Stands . . . esperance** remains in hope; always has hope

[5] **The . . . laughter** When things are at their best, any change is lamentable; when things are at their worst, they must improve.

[6] **The . . . blasts** (Edgar refers to the winds of Fortune as his creditors: as he has paid his debts to them, he no longer has anything to fear.)

[7] **Old Man** (There seems to be a peculiar significance to this character: he is the oldest character in the play—older even than Lear. He has seen and lived through more than anyone else and has retained both a sense of time past and the traditional virtues of loyalty and charity strikingly absent from the Britain of Goneril and Regan, and even of Lear as we see him in Act 1.)

[8] **poorly led** "led like a beggar", or "being led by one far below his rank". (Some editions read "parti-eyed" [i.e., with eyes of different colors], though Edgar doesn't appear to notice his father's blindness until 25–26.)

But that thy strange mutations make us hate thee,
Life would not yield to age.[9]

Old Man. O, my good lord, I have been your tenant, and your father's tenant, these fourscore years.

Gloucester. Away, get thee away; good friend, be gone:
Thy comforts[10] can do me no good at all;
Thee they may hurt.[11]

Old Man. You cannot see your way.

Gloucester. I have no way and therefore want[12] no eyes;
I stumbled when I saw. Full oft 'tis seen,
Our means secure us, and our mere defects
Prove our commodities.[13] Oh, dear son Edgar,
The food[14] of thy abusèd[15] father's wrath!
Might I but live to see thee in my touch,[16]
I'd say I had eyes again!

Old Man. How now! Who's there?

Edgar. [*Aside*] O Gods! Who is 't can say "I am at the worst"?
I am worse than e'er I was.

[9] **But . . . age** Only the hateful alterations of life reconcile us to old age and death. (His father's appearance at this moment reveals that things were not yet at their worst for Edgar after all.)

[10] **comforts** assistance; care

[11] **hurt** get you into trouble (since Gloucester is considered a traitor)

[12] **want** need

[13] **Our . . . commodities** Our prosperity gives us false security, and our deficiencies prove to be advantages.

[14] **food** the object (i.e., on which his anger has fed)

[15] **abusèd** misled; deceived

[16] **in my touch** by touching you ("to see you with my fingers")

Old Man. 'Tis poor mad Tom.

Edgar. [*Aside*] And worse I may be yet: the worst is not
So long as we can say "This is the worst."[17]

Old Man. Fellow, where goest?

Gloucester. Is it a beggar-man?

Old Man. Madman and beggar too.

Gloucester. He has some reason,[18] else he could not beg.
I' th' last night's storm I such a fellow saw,
Which made me think a man a worm.[19] My son
Came then into my mind, and yet my mind
Was then scarce friends with him. I have heard more since.
As flies to wanton[20] boys, are we to th' gods,
They kill us for their sport.

Edgar. [*Aside*] How should[21] this be?
Bad is the trade that must play fool to sorrow,
Ang'ring[22] itself and others. Bless thee, master!

Gloucester. Is that the naked fellow?

Old Man. Ay, my lord.

[17] **the ... worst** (i.e., so long as we have hope: the state of despair is the worst condition we can suffer)

[18] **reason** ability to reason

[19] **a man a worm** (Cf. Job 25:6, "[H]ow much less [is man] who is a maggot, and the son of man, who is a worm"—Gloucester's misfortunes also recall those of Job—and Psalms 22:6, "But I am a worm, and no man" from the prophetic psalm of the Suffering Servant, which Christ quoted from the Cross.)

[20] **wanton** capricious; wild

[21] **should** can

[22] **Ang'ring** annoying; upsetting

Gloucester. Then, prithee, get thee gone: if for my sake
Thou wilt o'ertake us hence a mile or twain
I' th' way toward Dover, do it for ancient[23] love,
And bring some covering for this naked soul,
Which I'll entreat to lead me.

Old Man. Alack, sir, he is mad.

Gloucester. 'Tis the times' plague,[24] when madmen lead the blind.
Do as I bid thee, or rather do thy pleasure;[25]
Above the rest,[26] be gone.

Old Man. I'll bring him the best 'parel[27] that I have,
Come on't what will. *Exit.*

Gloucester. Sirrah, naked fellow———

Edgar. Poor Tom's a-cold. [*Aside*] I cannot daub it[28] further.

Gloucester. Come hither, fellow.

Edgar. [*Aside*] And yet I must. —Bless thy sweet eyes, they bleed.

Gloucester. Know'st thou the way to Dover?

Edgar. Both stile and gate, horse-way and footpath.[29]
Poor Tom hath been scared out of his good wits.
Bless thee, good man's son, from the foul fiend!
Five fiends have been in Poor Tom at once; of lust,

[23] **ancient** long-standing; in days gone by
[24] **times' plague** curse of these times
[25] **thy pleasure** whatever you want
[26] **Above the rest** above all
[27] **'parel** apparel; clothes
[28] **daub it** keep up this disguise (literally, "coat it with plaster")
[29] **stile . . . footpath** (He knows every path and every barrier—the gates to the horse-ways and the stiles to the footpaths—on each path.)

as Obidicut;[30] Hobbididence,[31] prince of dumbness;[32] Mahu, of stealing; Modo, of murder; Flibbertigibbet, of mopping[33] and mowing;[34] who since possesses chambermaids and waiting-women.[35] So, bless thee, master!

Gloucester. Here, take this purse, thou whom the heavens' plagues
Have humbled to all strokes:[36] that I am wretched
Makes thee the happier.[37] Heavens, deal so still!
Let the superfluous[38] and lust-dieted[39] man,
That slaves your ordinance,[40] that will not see
Because he does not feel, feel your pow'r quickly;[41]
So distribution should undo excess,[42]
And each man have enough. Dost thou know Dover?

Edgar. Ay, master.

Gloucester. There is a cliff whose high and bending[43] head

[30] **Obidicut** (a devil from Harsnett's *Declaration*, where he appears as Hoberdicut)

[31] **Hobbididence** (See note at 3.6.30. It is not clear whether this is the same devil or another one suggested by Harsnett's original Hoberdidance.)

[32] **dumbness** muteness

[33] **mopping** grimacing

[34] **mowing** making faces

[35] **possesses chambermaids and waiting-women** (This is an allusion to Harsnett's description of the supposed possession of three chambermaids, Sara and Friswood Williams and Anne Smith.)

[36] **to all strokes** i.e., of Fortune

[37] **Makes thee the happier** will be of benefit to you

[38] **superfluous** having more than he needs

[39] **lust-dieted** who has fed to the full on his lusts

[40] **slaves your ordinance** makes your law subservient to his interests

[41] **quickly** soon; keenly; while he lives

[42] **Let . . . excess** (This description fits Gloucester himself; likewise, he wishes to go to Dover to commit suicide, that his death might in some way compensate for his excesses and failure to "see" [i.e., the truth about Edgar].)

[43] **bending** projecting

Looks fearfully[44] in the confinèd deep:[45]
Bring me but to the very brim of it,
And I'll repair the misery thou dost bear
With something rich about me: from that place
I shall no leading need.

Edgar. Give me thy arm:
Poor Tom shall lead thee. *Exeunt.*

Scene 2. [*Before the Duke of Albany's palace.*]

Enter Goneril and Edmund.

Goneril. Welcome,[46] my lord: I marvel our mild husband
Not met[47] us on the way.

Enter Oswald.

Now, where's your master?

Oswald. Madam, within; but never man so changed.
I told him of the army that was landed:
He smiled at it. I told him you were coming;
His answer was, "The worse." Of Gloucester's treachery,
And of the loyal service of his son
When I informed him, then he called me sot,[48]
And told me I had turned the wrong side out:[49]
What most he should dislike seems pleasant to him;
What like,[50] offensive.

[44] **fearfully** terrifyingly; in fear (the cliff is personified)

[45] **confinèd deep** (the English Channel, confined between England and France)

[46] **Welcome** (She welcomes him to her home as they arrive together.)

[47] **Not met** did not meet

[48] **sot** fool

[49] **turned . . . out** (This phrase not only means that Oswald sees things backward morally, but also suggests the word "turn-coat", i.e., that he is a traitor.)

[50] **like** he should like

Goneril. [*To Edmund*] Then shall you go no further.
It is the cowish[51] terror of his spirit,
That dares not undertake:[52] he'll not feel wrongs,
Which tie him to an answer.[53] Our wishes[54] on the way
May prove effects.[55] Back, Edmund, to my brother;
Hasten his musters[56] and conduct his pow'rs.[57]
I must change names[58] at home and give the distaff[59]
Into my husband's hands. This trusty servant
Shall pass between us: ere long you are like to hear,
If you dare venture in your own behalf,
A mistress's[60] command.[61] Wear this; spare speech;

[*Giving a favor*]

Decline your head.[62] This kiss, if it durst speak,
Would stretch thy spirits up into the air:
Conceive,[63] and fare thee well.

Edmund. Yours in the ranks of death.[64]

[51] **cowish** cowardly
[52] **undertake** take charge; assume responsibility
[53] **tie him to an answer** demand response or retaliation
[54] **wishes** desire for one another; plans to get rid of my husband
[55] **effects** come to be fulfilled
[56] **musters** assembling of soldiers
[57] **conduct his pow'rs** lead his army
[58] **change names** exchange roles (i.e., with her husband. Some editions have "change arms"—as in weapons—instead, which works well with what follows.)
[59] **distaff** cleft stick used in spinning (a symbol of a wife's work)
[60] **mistress** lover; wife; ruler
[61] **If . . . command** (suggesting she will reward him if he is daring enough to kill her husband)
[62] **Decline your head** (so that she can give him the "favor" referred to in the stage direction: a chain, a kiss, a ribbon for his hat, etc.)
[63] **Conceive** imagine; comprehend my meaning (with a punning sexual innuendo)
[64] **stretch . . . death** "stretch thy spirits", "conceive", and "death" are sexual innuendoes

Goneril. My most dear Gloucester!

Exit [Edmund].

O, the difference of man and man!
To thee a woman's services are due:
My fool[65] usurps my body.[66]

Oswald. Madam, here comes my lord.

Exit.

Enter Albany.

Goneril. I have been worth the whistle.[67]

Albany. O Goneril!
You are not worth the dust which the rude wind
Blows in your face. I fear your disposition:
That nature which contemns[68] its origin
Cannot be bordered certain in itself;[69]
She that herself will sliver[70, 71] and disbranch
From her material[72] sap[73] perforce must wither
And come to deadly use.[74]

Goneril. No more; the text[75] is foolish.

[65] **My fool** my husband, but also, possibly, Edmund (if he is being used cynically by Goneril) and, unwittingly, Goneril's own lustful desires

[66] **body** (other editions have "bed" instead of "body", with the same meaning)

[67] **worth the whistle** worth seeking (i.e., coming to meet on my return journey. From the proverb "It is a poor dog that is not worth the whistling.")

[68] **contemns** scornfully rejects; despises

[69] **bordered ... itself** trusted to keep within fixed bounds

[70] **sliver** piece of wood torn from a tree; to tear a sliver from a tree

[71] **herself ... sliver** (like a branch cutting itself off a tree)

[72] **material** essential; source of her substance

[73] **disbranch ... sap** cut herself off from the source of her lifeblood

[74] **come to deadly use** used as dead wood for burning; become a deadly thing

[75] **text** i.e., basis of your sermon. (That is, the Fourth Commandment: Honor your father and your mother. See Exodus 20:12 and Ephesians 6:2–3.)

Albany. Wisdom and goodness to the vile seem vile:
Filths savor but themselves.[76] What have you done?
Tigers, not daughters, what have you performed?
A father, and a gracious agèd man,
Whose reverence even the head-lugged[77] bear would lick,
Most barbarous, most degenerate, have you madded.[78]
Could my good brother[79] suffer you to do it?
A man, a prince, by him so benefited!
If that the heavens do not their visible spirits[80]
Send quickly down to tame these vile offenses,
It will come,
Humanity must perforce prey on itself,
Like monsters of the deep.

Goneril. Milk-livered[81] man!
That bear'st a cheek for blows,[82] a head for wrongs;
Who hast not in thy brows an eye discerning
Thine honor from thy suffering;[83] that not know'st
Fools do those villains pity who are punished
Ere they have done their mischief.[84] Where's thy drum?

[76] **Filths ... themselves** those who are filthy enjoy only what is filthy. (See Titus 1:15.)

[77] **head-lugged** pulled about by the head (as in bear-baiting)

[78] **madded** driven insane

[79] **brother** brother-in-law (Cornwall)

[80] **visible spirits** spirits in visible form

[81] **Milk-livered** cowardly. (See note at 2.2.17. It is also suggestive of effeminacy, as "milk" is associated with such feminine traits as nurture and compassion.)

[82] **bear'st ... blows** (recalling Christ's injunction: "If any one strikes you on the right cheek, turn to him the other also" [Mt 5:39])

[83] **discerning ... suffering** You cannot distinguish between insults that must be avenged and inconveniences that can be honorably tolerated.

[84] **Fools ... mischief** Only fools pity villains (such as Lear and Gloucester) for being punished before they have carried out their crimes.

France spreads his banners in our noiseless[85]
land,
With plumèd helm[86] thy state begins to threat,[87]
Whilst thou, a moral fool,[88] sits still and cries
"Alack, why does he so?"

Albany. See thyself, devil![89]
Proper deformity seems not in the fiend
So horrid as in woman.[90]

Goneril. O vain[91] fool!

Albany. Thou changèd and self-covered[92] thing,
for shame,
Be-monster[93] not thy feature.[94] Were 't my fitness[95]
To let these hands obey my blood,[96]
They are apt enough to dislocate and tear
Thy flesh and bones: howe'er[97] thou art a fiend,
A woman's shape doth shield thee.

[85] **noiseless** without the sound of a drum (i.e., with no sign that it is preparing for war)

[86] **helm** helmet

[87] **thy . . . threat** Albany's rule is threatened by the landing of the French forces.

[88] **moral fool** moralizing fool; a fool for being moral

[89] **See thyself devil!** (possibly holding up her hand-mirror to her face, and meaning either that a devil was visible in her face distorted by evil passions; that she herself was a devil; or that a devil was behind her. A devil was sometimes portrayed as standing behind Lady Vanity with his face rather than hers in the reflection.)

[90] **Proper . . . woman** Moral and physical deformity is more horrid in a woman than in a fiend since it is proper or fitting to the fiend.

[91] **vain** worthless

[92] **changèd and self-covered** unclear; possibly, "distorted by your own selfishness and evil actions"; alternatively, "you have become a fiend and covered your womanly features"

[93] **Be-monster** make monstrous, fiendish, repulsive

[94] **feature** appearance

[95] **my fitness** fitting for me

[96] **blood** anger; instinct

[97] **howe'er** even though; but although

Goneril. Marry,[98] your manhood mew[99]——

Enter a Messenger.

Albany. What news?

Messenger. O, my good lord, the Duke of Cornwall's dead,
Slain by his servant, going to[100] put out
The other eye of Gloucester.

Albany. Gloucester's eyes!

Messenger. A servant that he bred,[101] thrilled with remorse,[102]
Opposed against the act, bending his sword
To his great master, who thereat enraged
Flew on him, and amongst them felled him[103] dead,
But not without that harmful stroke[104] which since
Hath plucked him after.[105]

Albany. This shows you are above,
You justicers,[106] that these our nether[107] crimes
So speedily can venge.[108] But, O poor Gloucester!
Lost he his other eye?

Messenger. Both, both, my lord.
This letter, madam, craves a speedy answer;
'Tis from your sister.

[98] **Marry** (See note at 3.2.40.)
[99] **mew** confine; shed; miaow! (ridiculing his manhood)
[100] **going to** as he was going to
[101] **bred** brought up
[102] **thrilled with remorse** pierced or suddenly moved with compassion
[103] **amongst them felled him** between them, they struck him down
[104] **harmful stroke** mortal wound
[105] **plucked him after** drawn Cornwall after (into death)
[106] **justicers** judges
[107] **nether** here below (i.e., on earth)
[108] **venge** avenge

Goneril. [*Aside*] One way I like this well;
But being widow,[109] and my Gloucester with her,
May all the building in my fancy pluck[110]
Upon my hateful life.[111] Another way,[112]
The news is not so tart.[113]—I'll read, and answer.

Exit.

Albany. Where was his son when they did take his eyes?

Messenger. Come with my lady hither.

Albany. He is not here.

Messenger. No, my good lord; I met him back[114] again.

Albany. Knows he the wickedness?

Messenger. Ay, my good lord; 'twas he informed against him,
And quit the house on purpose, that their punishment
Might have the freer course.

Albany. Gloucester, I live
To thank thee for the love thou showed'st the King,
And to revenge thine eyes. Come hither, friend:
Tell me what more thou know'st. *Exeunt.*

[109] **being widow** Regan being a widow

[110] **May . . . pluck** may pull all my cherished designs (castles in the air) crashing down

[111] **hateful life** (hateful without the realization of her designs)

[112] **Another way** in another way

[113] **tart** sharp-tasting; grievous (in that Cornwall's death brings her one step closer to ruling the whole of Britain)

[114] **back** on his way back

[Scene 3. *The French camp near Dover.*]

Enter Kent and a Gentleman.

Kent. Why the King of France is so suddenly gone back, know you no reason?

Gentleman. Something he left imperfect[115] in the state,[116] which since his coming forth is thought of, which imports[117] to the kingdom so much fear and danger that his personal return was most required and necessary.[118]

Kent. Who hath he left behind him general?

Gentleman. The Marshal of France, Monsieur La Far.

Kent. Did your letters pierce the queen to any demonstration of grief?

Gentleman. Ay, sir; she took them, read them in my presence,
And now and then an ample tear trilled[119] down
Her delicate cheek: it seemed she was a queen
Over her passion, who most rebel-like
Sought to be king o'er her.

Kent. O, then it moved her.

Gentleman. Not to a rage: patience and sorrow strove

[115] **imperfect** unfinished

[116] **state** i.e., France

[117] **imports** carries with it; portends

[118] **Something . . . necessary** (More likely, Cordelia persuaded him to return, so the endeavor would be limited to redressing her father's wrongs. It has been pointed out that Shakespeare and his contemporaries would have had to be very cautious in writing of a foreign invasion: this "foreign" invasion is led by a native of proven virtue.)

[119] **trilled** trickled

Who should express her goodliest.[120] You have seen
Sunshine and rain at once: her smiles and tears
Were like a better way:[121] those happy smilets[122]
That played on her ripe lip seemed not to know
What guests were in her eyes, which parted thence
As pearls from diamonds dropped. In brief,
Sorrow would be a rarity most belovèd,
If all could so become it.[123]

Kent. Made she no verbal question?[124]

Gentleman. Faith, once or twice she heaved the name of "father"
Pantingly forth, as if it pressed her heart;
Cried "Sisters! Sisters! Shame of ladies! Sisters!
Kent! Father! Sisters! What, i' th' storm? i' th' night?
Let pity not be believed!"[125] There she shook
The holy water from her heavenly eyes,
And clamor moistened:[126] then away she started
To deal with grief alone.

Kent. It is the stars,
The stars above us, govern our conditions;[127]
Else one self[128] mate and make[129] could not beget

[120] **Who . . . goodliest** which should portray her most best

[121] **like a better way** like rain breaking through sunshine, but in a better way

[122] **smilets** little smiles

[123] **If . . . it** if it were so becoming to everyone

[124] **Made . . . question?** Did she put anything into words?

[125] **Let pity not be believed** (Perhaps this means that although pity for her sisters urges her to find some way of exculpating them, such pity should not be heeded.)

[126] **clamor moistened** (There is no consensus on the meaning here, except that she broke into tears; some suggest that "moistened" should read "mastered her".)

[127] **conditions** natures; characters

[128] **one self** one and the same

[129] **mate and make** (Both words mean "mate" or "spouse", thus meaning here "the very same husband and wife".)

Such different issues.[130] You spoke not with her
since?

Gentleman. No.

Kent. Was this before the King returned?

Gentleman. No, since.

Kent. Well, sir, the poor distressèd Lear's i' th'
town;
Who sometime[131] in his better tune[132] remembers
What we are come about, and by no means
Will yield to see his daughter.

Gentleman. Why, good sir?

Kent. A sovereign[133] shame so elbows[134] him: his own
unkindness
That stripped her from his benediction, turned her
To foreign casualties,[135] gave her dear rights
To his dog-hearted[136] daughters: these things sting
His mind so venomously that burning shame
Detains him from Cordelia.

Gentleman. Alack, poor gentleman!

Kent. Of Albany's and Cornwall's powers[137] you heard
not?

Gentleman. 'Tis so;[138] they are afoot.

[130] **issues** children
[131] **sometime** sometimes
[132] **tune** intervals
[133] **sovereign** overwhelming
[134] **elbows** keeps thrusting him back (with his elbow); continually reminding him
[135] **casualties** uncertainties
[136] **dog-hearted** pitiless
[137] **powers** armies
[138] **'Tis so** I have heard

Kent. Well, sir, I'll bring you to our master Lear,
And leave you to attend him: some dear cause[139]
Will in concealment wrap me up awhile;
When I am known aright, you shall not grieve
Lending me this acquaintance. I pray you, go
Along with me. [*Exeunt.*]

[Scene 4. *The same. A tent.*]

Enter, with drum and colors,[140] *Cordelia, Doctor, and Soldiers.*

Cordelia. Alack, 'tis he: why, he was met even now
As mad as the vexed sea; singing aloud;
Crowned with rank femiter[141] and furrow-weeds,[142]
With hardocks,[143] hemlock,[144] nettles,[145]
cuckoo-flow'rs,[146]
Darnel,[147] and all the idle[148] weeds that grow
In our sustaining corn.[149] A century[150] send forth;
Search every acre in the high-grown field,
And bring him to our eye [*Exit an Officer.*] What
can man's wisdom[151]

[139] **dear cause** important purpose (we are not told what)

[140] **drum and colors** drummer and standard-bearers. ("Colors" are banners or flags, bearing the colors of nation, party, family, etc.)

[141] **femiter** fumitory, a bitter herb. (It is also associated with hemlock and darnel in *Henry V* [5.2.45].)

[142] **furrow-weeds** weeds growing in a furrow

[143] **hardocks** burdocks, a common weed, with burrs

[144] **hemlock** both a poison and a narcotic

[145] **nettles** a stinging plant, which grows about graves

[146] **cuckoo-flow'rs** perhaps the Bedlam Cowslip or *Cardamine pratensis*, which were remedies for brain diseases

[147] **Darnel** weeds that injure wheat crops; also a narcotic

[148] **idle** worthless (in contrast to the "sustaining" corn)

[149] **sustaining corn** wheat, the staple of life

[150] **century** one hundred soldiers (recalling—or perhaps restoring—Lear's reservation of knights)

[151] **What can man's wisdom** What can natural science do

In the restoring his bereavèd[152] sense?
He that helps him take all my outward worth.[153]

Doctor. There is means, madam:
Our foster-nurse of nature is repose,[154]
The which he lacks: that to provoke[155] in him,
Are many simples operative,[156] whose power
Will close the eye of anguish.[157]

Cordelia. All blest secrets,
All you unpublished virtues of the earth,
Spring with my tears![158] be aidant[159] and remediate[160]
In the good man's distress! Seek, seek for him,
Lest his ungoverned rage dissolve the life
That wants[161] the means[162] to lead it.[163]

Enter Messenger.

Messenger. News, madam;
The Brittish pow'rs are marching hitherward.

Cordelia. 'Tis known before. Our preparation[164] stands
In expectation of them, O dear father,
It is thy business that I go about;[165]

[152] **bereavèd** impaired, robbed of its powers

[153] **outward worth** material possessions; wealth

[154] **Our ... repose** the best nurse Nature has is rest

[155] **provoke** induce

[156] **simples operative** herbs with effective medicinal properties

[157] **anguish** pain

[158] **virtues ... tears!** powerful medicinal herbs, spring up, grow quickly, watered by my tears!

[159] **aidant** helpful

[160] **remediate** remedial (possibly a word coined by Shakespeare, perhaps to avoid the repetition of sounds that would occur if he had used the more common term "remediant")

[161] **wants** lacks

[162] **the means** reason

[163] **lead it** be in command of his rage

[164] **preparation** readied troops

[165] **O ... about** (recalling Christ's words in Lk 2:49: "I must be about my Father's business.")

Therefore great France
My mourning and importuned[166] tears hath pitied.
No blown[167] ambition doth our arms incite,
But love, dear love, and our aged father's right:
Soon may I hear and see him! *Exeunt.*

[Scene 5. *Gloucester's castle.*]

Enter Regan and Oswald.

Regan. But are my brother's pow'rs set forth?

Oswald. Ay, madam.

Regan. Himself in person there?

Oswald. Madam, with much ado:[168]
Your sister is the better soldier.

Regan. Lord Edmund spake not with your lord at home?

Oswald. No, madam.

Regan. What might import[169] my sister's letter to him?

Oswald. I know not, lady.

Regan. Faith, he is posted[170] hence on serious matter.
It was great ignorance,[171] Gloucester's eyes being out,
To let him live. Where he arrives he moves
All hearts against us: Edmund, I think, is gone,
In pity of his misery, to dispatch[172]

[166] **importuned** pressingly solicitous
[167] **blown** swollen, inflated (with pride)
[168] **ado** after much fuss or trouble. (Albany required a good deal of persuasion, not being sure what was the dutiful thing to do.)
[169] **import** signify; express
[170] **is posted** has departed in haste
[171] **ignorance** foolishness; ignorance of the consequences
[172] **dispatch** do away with; kill

His nighted[173] life; moreover, to descry
The strength o' th' enemy.

Oswald. I must needs after him, madam, with my
letter.

Regan. Our troops set forth tomorrow: stay with us;[174]
The ways are dangerous.

Oswald. I may not, madam:
My lady charged my duty[175] in this business.

Regan. Why should she write to Edmund? Might not
you
Transport her purposes by word? Belike,[176]
Some things I know not what. I'll love thee much,
Let me unseal the letter.

Oswald. Madam, I had rather——

Regan. I know your lady does not love her husband;
I am sure of that: and at her late being here[177]
She gave strange eliads[178] and most speaking looks
To noble Edmund. I know you are of her bosom.[179]

Oswald. I, madam?

Regan. I speak in understanding: y'are; I know 't:
Therefore I do advise you, take this note:[180]
My lord is dead; Edmund and I have talked;
And more convenient[181] is he for my hand
Than for your lady's: you may gather more.[182]

[173] **nighted** darkened (i.e., blinded, but also darkened with misfortune)

[174] **stay with us** (Regan wants to delay the delivery of Goneril's letter to Edmund.)

[175] **charged my duty** bound me to follow her orders strictly

[176] **Belike** probably

[177] **at . . . here** when she was last here

[178] **eliads** (oeillads) amorous glances

[179] **of her bosom** in her confidence

[180] **take this note** take note of what I am about to say

[181] **convenient** appropriate; suitable

[182] **gather more** deduce more about this yourself

If you do find him, pray you, give him this;[183]
And when your mistress hears thus much[184] from you,
I pray, desire her call her wisdom to her.
So, fare you well.
If you do chance to hear of that blind traitor,
Perferment[185] falls on him that cuts him off.

Oswald. Would I could meet him, madam! I should show
What party I do follow.

Regan. Fare thee well.

Exeunt.

[Scene 6. *Fields near Dover.*]

Enter Gloucester and Edgar

Gloucester. When shall I come to th' top of that same hill?

Edgar. You do climb up it now. Look, how we labor.

Gloucester. Methinks the ground is even.

Edgar. Horrible steep.
Hark, do you hear the sea?

Gloucester. No, truly.

Edgar. Why then your other senses grow imperfect
By your eyes' anguish.[186]

[183] **this** (Exactly what she gives him is not clear, perhaps a token but probably a letter, since in 4.6.252 Oswald speaks of having letters [plural] to deliver to Edmund.)

[184] **thus much** (i.e., what I have said)

[185] **Perferment** advancement; promotion

[186] **anguish** physical pain

Gloucester. So may it be indeed.
Methinks thy voice is altered, and thou speak'st
In better phrase and matter than thou didst.[187]

Edgar. Y'are much deceived: in nothing am I changed
But in my garments.

Gloucester. Methinks y'are better spoken.

Edgar. Come on, sir; here's the place: stand still. How fearful
And dizzy 'tis to cast one's eyes so low!
The crows and choughs[188] that wing the midway air[189]
Show scarce so gross[190] as beetles. Half way down
Hangs one that gathers sampire,[191] dreadful trade!
Methinks he seems no bigger than his head.
The fishermen that walk upon the beach
Appear like mice; and yond tall anchoring bark[192]
Diminished to her cock;[193] her cock, a buoy
Almost too small for sight. The murmuring surge
That on th' unnumb'red[194] idle[195] pebble[196] chafes
Cannot be heard so high. I'll look no more,
Lest my brain turn and the deficient sight[197]
Topple down headlong.

Gloucester. Set me where you stand.

[187] **In . . . didst** (This is, of course, true, as Edgar is not only speaking sanely, but has moved from prose to verse.)

[188] **choughs** jackdaws

[189] **midway air** the air midway down to the bottom

[190] **Show . . . gross** look scarcely as big

[191] **sampire** samphire (herbe de Saint Pierre, or St. Peter's herb: a plant with aromatic leaves used in pickling and gathered from cliffs by men on ropes)

[192] **bark** a small sailing vessel

[193] **cock** cock-boat (a small ship's rowboat)

[194] **unnumb'red** innumerable

[195] **idle** barren; moving uselessly

[196] **pebble** (not infrequently used as a plural)

[197] **my . . . sight** I become dizzy and (not seeing properly)

Edgar. Give me your hand: you are now within a foot
Of th' extreme verge: for all beneath the moon
Would I not leap upright.[198]

Gloucester. Let go my hand.
Here, friend, 's another purse; in it a jewel
Well worth a poor man's taking. Fairies[199] and gods
Prosper it with thee! Go thou further off;
Bid me farewell, and let me hear thee going.

Edgar. Now fare ye well, good sir.

Gloucester. With all my heart.

Edgar. [*Aside*] Why I do trifle thus with his despair
Is done[200] to cure it.

Gloucester. O you mighty gods!

He kneels.

This world I do renounce, and in your sights
Shake patiently my great affliction off:
If I could bear it longer and not fall
To quarrel with[201] your great opposeless wills,[202]
My snuff[203] and loathèd part of nature should
Burn itself out. If Edgar live, O bless him!
Now, fellow, fare thee well.

He falls.

[198] **upright** even straight up into the air (lest I lose my footing and fall)

[199] **Fairies** (Referring to the legend that fairies magically multiply hidden treasure for the one who finds it. Gloucester might also be binding Edgar to secrecy, since it was also a popular belief that those who were indiscreet about finding fairy treasure brought ruin upon themselves.)

[200] **Is done** is done in order to (the redundancy of "I do" and "is done" was common in colloquial speech)

[201] **To quarrel with** into rebelling against

[202] **opposeless wills** (Opposition to the will of the gods is both futile and impious—although, in fact, committing suicide might well be seen as an attempt to thwart the will of the gods.)

[203] **snuff** smoldering wick

Edgar. Gone, sir, farewell.
And yet I know not how[204] conceit[205] may rob
The treasury of life, when life itself
Yields to[206] the theft.[207] Had he been where he thought,
By this had thought been past. Alive or dead?
Ho, you sir! friend! Hear you, sir! speak!
Thus might he pass[208] indeed: yet he revives.
What are you, sir?

Gloucester. Away, and let me die.

Edgar. Hadst thou been aught but gossamer, feathers, air,
So many fathom down precipitating,[209]
Thou'dst shivered[210] like an egg: but thou dost breathe;
Hast heavy substance; bleed'st not; speak'st; art sound.
Ten masts at each[211] make not the altitude
Which thou hast perpendicularly fell:
Thy life's a miracle. Speak yet again.

Gloucester. But have I fall'n, or no?

Edgar. From the dread summit of this chalky bourn.[212]
Look up a-height;[213] the shrill-gorged[214] lark so far
Cannot be seen or heard: do but look up.

[204] **how** if (or, possibly, "at what price")
[205] **conceit** imagination, deluded belief
[206] **Yields to** consents
[207] **I know . . . theft** (Edgar fears his father's belief that he has jumped off the cliff, coupled with his desire to die, may actually kill him.)
[208] **pass** die
[209] **precipitating** hurtling
[210] **shivered** been shattered
[211] **at each** end to end
[212] **chalky bourn** (the cliffs of Dover)
[213] **a-height** on high
[214] **shrill-gorged** shrill-voiced

Gloucester. Alack, I have no eyes.
Is wretchedness deprived that benefit,
To end itself by death? 'Twas yet some comfort,
When misery could beguile[215] the tyrant's rage[216]
And frustrate his proud will.

Edgar. Give me your arm.
Up, so. How is 't? Feel you[217] your legs? You stand.

Gloucester. Too well, too well.

Edgar. This is above all strangeness.
Upon the crown o' th' cliff, what thing was that
Which parted from you?

Gloucester. A poor unfortunate beggar.

Edgar. As I stood here below, methought his eyes
Were two full moons; he had a thousand noses,
Horns whelked[218] and waved like the enridgèd[219] sea:
It was some fiend; therefore, thou happy[220] father,[221]
Think that the clearest[222] gods, who make them honors
Of men's impossibilities,[223] have preserved thee,

Gloucester. I do remember now: henceforth I'll bear
Affliction till it do cry out itself

[215] **beguile** cheat
[216] **the tyrant's rage** (alluding to the Stoics' defense of suicide)
[217] **Feel you** do you have any feeling in; can you use
[218] **whelked** twisted, coiled (like the shell of a whelk)
[219] **enridgèd** with waves like ridges; furrowed (Some editions read "enraged".)
[220] **happy** (See note at 2.3.2.)
[221] **father** old man (a respectful term of address, which did not necessarily imply a close or blood relationship)
[222] **clearest** purest; most glorious; clear-sighted
[223] **who . . . impossibilities** who win men's reverence and admiration by doing what is impossible to man (Cf. Lk 18:27: "What is impossible with men is possible with God.")

"Enough, enough," and die. That thing you speak of,
I took it for a man; often 'twould say
"The fiend, the fiend"—he led me to that place.

Edgar. Bear free[224] and patient thoughts.

Enter Lear [fantastically dressed with wild flowers].

But who comes here?
The safer[225] sense will ne'er accommodate[226]
His master thus.[227]

Lear. No, they cannot touch[228] me for coining;[229] I am the King himself.

Edgar. O thou side-piercing[230] sight!

Lear. Nature's above art in that respect.[231] There's your press-money.[232] That fellow handles his bow like a crow-keeper;[233] draw me a clothier's yard.[234] Look, look, a mouse! Peace, peace; this piece of

[224] **free** (i.e., from sorrow, despair)

[225] **safer** more mentally sound

[226] **accommodate** dress; equip

[227] **The safer . . . thus** No one in his right mind would dress himself like this.

[228] **touch** lay hands on. (There is a pun here for another meaning of "touch" was "to test gold by rubbing it in a touchstone".)

[229] **coining** minting coins (which was a Royal prerogative)

[230] **side-piercing** heart-piercing (perhaps recalling Longinus's piercing Christ's heart on the Cross [Jn 19:34])

[231] **Nature's . . . respect** (A common theme for debate in Renaissance times was the relation between nature and art, here perhaps referring to his natural rights as one born king.)

[232] **press-money** money paid to recruits when they were "impressed", or enlisted in the army

[233] **crow-keeper** unclear; possibly a farmboy assigned with the task of scaring away crows (and thus probably an inept archer); perhaps a scarecrow (see *Romeo and Juliet* [1.4.6])

[234] **clothier's yard** (the length of a standard English arrow)

toasted cheese will do 't. There's my gauntlet;[235] I'll prove it on[236] a giant. Bring up the brown bills.[237] O, well flown,[238] bird! i' th' clout,[239] i' th' clout: hewgh![240] Give the word.[241]

Edgar. Sweet marjoram.[242]

Lear. Pass.

Gloucester. I know that voice.

Lear. Ha! Goneril, with a white beard![243] They flattered me like a dog,[244] and told me I had white hairs in my beard[245] ere the black ones were there.[246] To say "ay" and "no" to everything that I said! "Ay" and "no" too was no good divinity.[247] When the rain came to wet me once and the wind to make me chatter; when the thunder would not peace at my bidding; there I found 'em, there I smelt 'em out. Go to, they are not men o' their words: they

[235] **gauntlet** armored glove (to throw down a gauntlet was to issue a challenge to a duel)

[236] **prove it on** make good my challenge

[237] **brown bills** soldiers who carry halberds, a combined spear and battle-axe. (They were called "brown" because they were painted to prevent rust.)

[238] **well flown** (call of a falconer to a successful hawk, though perhaps here referring to an imaginary arrow)

[239] **clout** target (perhaps a conflation of the hawk and the arrow)

[240] **hewgh** (an imitation of the sound of a whizzing arrow, or perhaps a sound of astonishment)

[241] **word** watchword; password

[242] **Sweet marjoram** medicinal herb used to cure illnesses of the brain

[243] **Goneril . . . beard** (either mistaking Gloucester for Goneril, or reproaching Goneril for treating an old man so cruelly)

[244] **like a dog** like a dog fawning on its master (perhaps prompted by Gloucester's falling to his knees)

[245] **white . . . beard** (signs of wisdom)

[246] **ere . . . there** before I even had a beard

[247] **divinity** theology. (See Matthew 5:37, "Say 'Yes' when you mean 'Yes' and 'No' when you mean 'No.' Anything beyond that is from the evil one." Cf. also James 5:12 and 2 Corinthians 1:18. Interestingly, the previous verse in Matthew reads "Do not swear by your head [you cannot make a single hair white or black].")

told me I was everything; 'tis a lie, I am not ague-proof.[248, 249]

Gloucester. The trick[250] of that voice I do well remember: Is't not the king?

Lear. Ay, every inch a king.
When I do stare, see how the subject quakes.
I pardon that man's life. What was thy cause?[251]
Adultery?
Thou shalt not die: die for adultery! No:
The wren goes to 't, and the small gilded fly
Does lecher[252] in my sight.
Let copulation thrive; for Gloucester's bastard son
Was kinder to his father than my daughters
Got[253] 'tween the lawful sheets.
To 't, luxury,[254] pell-mell![255] for I lack soldiers.
Behold yond simp'ring dame,
Whose face between her forks[256] presages snow,[257]
That minces[258] virtue and does shake the head
To hear of pleasure's name.
The fitchew,[259] nor the soilèd[260] horse, goes to 't[261]
With a more riotous appetite.

[248] **ague-proof** immune to fever

[249] **When the . . . ague-proof** (These words allude to the sycophantic ascribing of godlike powers to Lear at the start of the play and describe his abandonment to the storm on the part of his daughters and Cornwall, which revealed their disloyalty and his own mortality.)

[250] **trick** characteristic manner

[251] **thy cause** the charge brought against you

[252] **lecher** copulate

[253] **Got** begotten

[254] **luxury** lust

[255] **pell-mell** in abandoned promiscuity

[256] **forks** legs

[257] **Whose . . . snow** who appears to be cold and thus chaste

[258] **minces** affects virtue by the coy delicacy of her walk

[259] **fitchew** polecat (slang for "prostitute")

[260] **soilèd** lustful with rich feeding

[261] **goes to 't** takes to sexual intercourse

Down from the waist they are Centaurs,[262]
Though women all above:
But to[263] the girdle do the gods inherit,[264]
Beneath is all the fiend's.
There's hell, there's darkness, there is the sulphurous pit,
Burning, scalding, stench, consumption; fie, fie, fie!
pah, pah! Give me an ounce of civet;[265] good apothecary, sweeten my imagination: there's money for thee.

Gloucester. O, let me kiss that hand!

Lear. Let me wipe it first; it smells of mortality.[266]

Gloucester. O ruined piece of nature! This great world
Shall so wear out to nought.[267] Dost thou know me?

Lear. I remember thine eyes well enough. Dost thou Squiny[268] at me? No, do thy worst, blind Cupid;[269] I'll not love. Read thou this challenge;[270] mark but the penning[271] of it.

Gloucester. Were all thy letters suns, I could not see.

[262] **Centaurs** (mythical creatures, half-horse—and thus half-animal—and half-man, that were associated with lust)

[263] **But to** only as far as

[264] **But . . . inherit** the gods only rule what's above the waist

[265] **civet** (See note at 3.4.107.)

[266] **mortality** death; the human condition

[267] **This . . . nought** The world—or, indeed, the whole of creation—will wear out to nothing in the same way that man does.

[268] **Squiny** squint

[269] **blind Cupid** (Blindfolded Cupid was thought to shoot randomly his arrows that caused his victims to fall in love; the image of a blindfolded Cupid appeared on brothel signs.)

[270] **challenge** (this time a written challenge, either completely imaginary or some other paper. There is irony in the blind Gloucester being asked to read this letter, as he had been disastrously "blind" when he read the letter Edmund ascribed to Edgar [1.2.45ff.])

[271] **penning** style of writing (again recalling Gloucester's examination of the false letter from Edgar)

Edgar. I would not take[272] this from report: it is,
And my heart breaks at it.

Lear. Read.

Gloucester. What, with the case of eyes?[273]

Lear. O, ho, are you there with me?[274] No eyes in your head, nor no money in your purse? Your eyes are in a heavy case,[275] your purse in a light,[276] yet you see how this world goes.

Gloucester. I see it feelingly.[277]

Lear. What, art mad? A man may see how this world goes with no eyes. Look with thine ears: see how yond justice rails upon yond simple[278] thief. Hark, in thine ear: change places, and, handy-dandy,[279] which is the justice, which is the thief? Thou hast seen a farmer's dog bark at a beggar?

Gloucester. Ay, sir.

Lear. And the creature[280] run from the cur? There thou mightst behold the great image of authority: a dog's obeyed in office.[281]
Thou rascal beadle,[282] hold[283] thy bloody hand!

[272] **take** believe
[273] **case of eyes** eye-sockets
[274] **are . . . me?** Is that what you mean? Is that your excuse?
[275] **heavy case** grievous condition (punning on Gloucester's word)
[276] **light** empty; light-hearted
[277] **feelingly** by sense of touch; keenly
[278] **simple** common; humble; mere
[279] **handy-dandy** take your pick (a phrase from a children's game in which one must pick the correct hand, here indicating that the justice and thief are indistinguishable)
[280] **creature** (i.e., the beggar)
[281] **office** his official position
[282] **beadle** parish constable who whipped wrongdoers
[283] **hold** restrain

Why dost thou lash that whore? Strip thy own back;
Thou hotly lusts to use her in that kind[284]
For which thou whip'st her. The usurer[285] hangs the cozener.[286]
Through tattered clothes small vices do appear;
Robes and furred gowns[287] hide all. Plate[288] sin with gold,
And the strong lance of justice hurtless[289] breaks;
Arm it in rags, a pygmy's straw does pierce it.
None does offend, none, I say, none; I'll able[290] 'em:
Take that of[291] me, my friend, who have the power
To seal th' accuser's lips. Get thee glass eyes,[292]
And, like a scurvy[293] politician,[294] seem
To see the things thou dost not. Now, now, now, now.
Pull off my boots: harder, harder: so.

Edgar. O, matter and impertinency[295] mixed!
Reason in madness!

Lear. If thou wilt weep my fortunes, take my eyes.
I know thee well enough; thy name is Gloucester:

[284] **kind** the same way

[285] **usurer** a moneylender (at exorbitant interest) who in this case is also a magistrate

[286] **cozener** petty swindler (usury is a more serious crime than petty swindling)

[287] **Robes and furred gowns** (the clothing of the rich and powerful, and also of judges)

[288] **Plate** plate mail

[289] **hurtless** without effect

[290] **able** vouch for; authorize

[291] **Take that of** (various possibilities, including "Learn that from me"; "that" has also been taken to mean an imaginary document, or money, or the pardon mentioned earlier)

[292] **glass eyes** spectacles

[293] **scurvy** contemptible; dishonorable; vile

[294] **politician** manipulator

[295] **matter and impertinency** sense and nonsense

Thou must be patient; we came crying hither:
Thou know'st, the first time that we smell the air[296]
We wawl[297] and cry. I will preach to thee: mark.

Gloucester. Alack, alack the day!

Lear. When we are born, we cry that we are come
To this great stage of fools. This'[298] a good block.[299]
It were a delicate[300] stratagem, to shoe
A troop of horse with felt: I'll put 't in proof;[301]
And when I have stol'n upon these son-in-laws,
Then, kill, kill, kill, kill, kill, kill!

Enter a Gentleman [with Attendants].

Gentleman. O, here he is: lay hand upon him. Sir,
Your most dear daughter—

Lear. No rescue? What, a prisoner? I am even
The natural[302] fool of fortune. Use me well;
You shall have ransom. Let me have surgeons;
I am cut to th' brains.[303]

Gentleman. You shall have anything.

Lear. No seconds?[304] all myself?
Why, this would make a man a man of salt,[305]

[296] **the . . . air** (at birth)

[297] **wawl** bawl

[298] **This'** this is

[299] **block** (several possible meanings, most notably, the mold used in making a hat [Lear taking off his—possibly imaginary—hat, or crown of flowers, to preach]; a mounting-block or tree-stump or a target for jousting practice)

[300] **delicate** ingenious

[301] **put 't in proof** put it to the test

[302] **natural** born

[303] **cut . . . brains** (meaning both "driven to madness" and an imaginary head wound. It also suggests a crown of thorns.)

[304] **seconds** (In a duel, each duelist is supported by a "second" who serves as a witness, ensures fair play, and provides whatever aid necessary afterward [Lear threw down his gauntlet at 4.6.90].)

[305] **man of salt** tears

To use his eyes for garden water-pots,
Ay, and laying autumn's dust.

Gentleman. Good sir—

Lear. I will die bravely,[306] like a smug[307] bridegroom.[308]
What!
I will be jovial: come, come; I am a king;
Masters, know you that?

Gentleman. You are a royal one, and we obey you.

Lear. Then there's life in 't.[309] Come, and you get it,
you shall get it by running. Sa, sa, sa, sa.[310,311]

Exit [*running; Attendants follow*].

Gentleman. A sight most pitiful in the meanest wretch,
Past speaking of in a king! Thou hast one daughter
Who redeems nature from the general curse
Which twain[312] have brought her to.

Edgar. Hail, gentle[313] sir.

Gentleman. Sir, speed you:[314] what's your will?

Edgar. Do you hear aught, sir, of a battle toward?[315]

[306] **bravely** courageously; finely arrayed

[307] **smug** spruce

[308] **bridegroom** (punning on "die", a word with sexual innuendo, but, also, paradoxically, an allusion to Christ in the context of the scriptural applicability of the previous lines)

[309] **life in 't** still some hope

[310] **Sa . . . sa** (from French "ça, ça!" meaning "there, there!"—a hunting cry to urge dogs in the chase; also a cry of defiance)

[311] **No rescue . . . Sa, sa, sa, sa** These lines are awash with oblique references to the Passion of Christ, from the Agony in the Garden to the Resurrection, hinting at the redemptive aspects of Lear's suffering.

[312] **twain** Goneril and Regan (with Adam and Eve as a possible secondary meaning, which would make "one daughter who redeems nature from the general curse" a reference to the Virgin Mary)

[313] **gentle** well-born; noble

[314] **speed you** God speed (prosper) you

[315] **toward** impending

Gentleman. Most sure and vulgar:[316] every one hears that,
Which can distinguish sound.

Edgar. But, by your favor,
How near's the other army?

Gentleman. Near and on speedy foot; the main descry
Stands on the hourly thought.[317]

Edgar. I thank you, sir: that's all.

Gentleman. Though that the Queen on special cause is here,
Her army is moved on.

Edgar. I thank you, sir.

Exit [*Gentleman*].

Gloucester. You ever-gentle gods, take my breath from me;
Let not my worser spirit[318] tempt me again
To die before you please.

Edgar. Well pray you, father.

Gloucester. Now, good sir, what are you?

Edgar. A most poor man, made tame[319] to fortune's blows;
Who, by the art of known and feeling sorrows,[320]
Am pregnant[321] to good pity. Give me your hand,
I'll lead you to some biding.[322]

[316] **vulgar** commonly known

[317] **the . . . thought** We expect to catch sight of the main body of troops any hour now.

[318] **worser spirit** evil angel; evil side

[319] **tame** grown used; submissive

[320] **art . . . sorrows** taught by experiencing heartfelt sorrows

[321] **pregnant** inclined; big with

[322] **biding** abode

Gloucester. Hearty thanks;
The bounty and the benison[323] of heaven
To boot, and boot.[324]

Enter Oswald.

Oswald. A proclaimed prize![325] Most happy![326]
That eyeless head of thine was first framed[327] flesh
To raise my fortunes. Thou old unhappy traitor,
Briefly thyself remember:[328] the sword is out
That must destroy thee.

Gloucester. Now let thy friendly[329] hand
Put strength enough to 't.

[*Edgar interposes.*]

Oswald. Wherefore, bold peasant,
Dar'st thou support a published[330] traitor? Hence!
Lest that th' infection of his fortune take
Like hold on thee. Let go his arm.

Edgar. Chill[331] not let go, zir, without vurther 'casion.[332]

Oswald. Let go, slave, or thou diest![333]

Edgar. Good gentleman, go your gait,[334] and let poor Volk[335] pass. And chud ha' bin zwaggered out of my life, 'twould not ha' bin zo long as 'tis by a

[323] **benison** blessing
[324] **To boot, and boot** To reward you in addition (to his thanks)
[325] **proclaimed prize** (i.e., a man with a price on his head)
[326] **happy** fortunate (for Oswald)
[327] **framed** fashioned (i.e., born)
[328] **thyself remember** repent your sins and prepare to die
[329] **friendly** (since Gloucester does not wish to live)
[330] **published** proclaimed
[331] **Chill** I will (Edgar acts the yokel here, speaking in a typical rustic stage dialect, based on that of Somerset.)
[332] **vurther 'casion** further occasion (i.e., reason)
[333] **thou diest** (Note Oswald's willingness to fight if the odds are in his favor: a blind old man, or one he takes for a peasant armed only with a cudgel.)
[334] **gait** way
[335] **Volk** folk

vortnight.[336] Nay, come not near th' old man; keep out, che vor' ye,[337] or I'se[338] try whether your costard[339] or my ballow[340] be the harder: chill be plain with you.

Oswald. Out,[341] dunghill![342]

They fight.

Edgar. Chill pick your teeth,[343] zir: come; no matter vor your foins.[344]

[*Oswald falls.*]

Oswald. Slave, thou hast slain me. Villain,[345] take my purse:
If ever thou wilt thrive, bury my body,
And give the letters which thou find'st about[346] me
To Edmund Earl of Gloucester; seek him out
Upon the English[347] party.[348] O, untimely death!
Death!

He dies.

Edgar. I know thee well. A serviceable[349] villain,
As duteous to the vices of thy mistress
As badness would desire.

[336] **And . . . vortnight** If I could have been swaggered out of my life, it would not have been so long as it is by a fortnight (i.e., If I could have been bullied out of my life, I would not have lasted two weeks).

[337] **che vor' ye** "I warn you" or "I warrant you"

[338] **I'se** I shall

[339] **costard** large apple (at times used humorously to mean the "head")

[340] **ballow** cudgel

[341] **Out** (interjection conveying indignation and reproach)

[342] **dunghill** born on a dunghill; lowborn

[343] **Chill pick your teeth** (perhaps with Oswald's dagger. The phrase is thought to be proverbial, meaning "You'll find me more than a match for you.")

[344] **foins** sword thrusts

[345] **Villain** serf; peasant

[346] **about** upon

[347] **English** (Some editions read "British".)

[348] **party** side

[349] **serviceable** diligent in service

Gloucester. What, is he dead?

Edgar. Sit you down, father; rest you.
Let's see these pockets: the letters that he speaks of
May be my friends. He's dead; I am only sorry
He had no other deathsman.[350] Let us see:
Leave,[351] gentle wax;[352] and, manners, blame us not:
To know our enemies' minds, we rip their hearts;
Their papers[353] is more lawful.

Reads the letter.

"Let our reciprocal vows be remembered. You have many opportunities to cut him[354] off:[355] if your will[356] want not,[357] time and place will be fruitfully[358] offered. There is nothing done, if he return the conqueror: then am I the prisoner, and his bed my jail; from the loathed warmth whereof deliver me, and supply the place for your labor.

"Your—wife, so I would say—affectionate servant,[359] and for you her own for venture,[360] 'Goneril.' "

O indistinguished space[361] of woman's will![362]
A plot upon her virtuous husband's life;

[350] **deathsman** executioner
[351] **Leave** by your leave
[352] **wax** (breaking the seal on the letter)
[353] **Their papers** Ripping open their papers
[354] **him** (Albany)
[355] **to . . . off** to kill him
[356] **will** intention; carnal appetite; lust
[357] **want not** is not lacking; is sufficient
[358] **fruitfully** copiously (suggesting also sexual reward)
[359] **servant** lover
[360] **and . . . venture** (This phrase does not appear in many editions, perhaps because it is awkward and/or thought to be an actor's interpolation. It may mean "yours for the venturing".)
[361] **indistinguished space** limitless expanse
[362] **will** lust; carnal appetite

And the exchange[363] my brother! Here in the sands
Thee I'll rake up,[364] the post unsanctified[365]
Of murderous lechers; and in the mature time,[366]
With this ungracious[367] paper[368] strike[369] the sight
Of the death-practiced[370] Duke: for him 'tis well
That of thy death and business I can tell.[371]

Gloucester. The King is mad: how stiff[372] is my vile sense,[373]
That I stand up, and have ingenious[374] feeling
Of my huge sorrows! Better I were distract:[375]
So should my thoughts be severed from my griefs,
And woes by wrong imaginations[376] lose
The knowledge of themselves.

Drum afar off.

Edgar. Give me your hand:
Far off, methinks, I hear the beaten drum.
Come, father, I'll bestow[377] you with a friend.[378]

Exeunt.

[363] **exchange** substitute
[364] **rake up** bury; cover up
[365] **post unsanctified** unholy messenger
[366] **in the mature time** when the time is ripe
[367] **ungracious** without grace (thus wicked); profane
[368] **paper** letter
[369] **strike** blast
[370] **death-practiced** with a plot against his life
[371] **tell** (Some editions add the stage direction "*Exit: dragging out the body*", with Edgar reentering as Gloucester ends his line, which makes good on Edgar's intention and explains his not responding to his father's words.)
[372] **stiff** obstinately unyielding
[373] **sense** capacity for feeling
[374] **ingenious** conscious
[375] **distract** insane
[376] **wrong imaginations** illusions
[377] **bestow** lodge
[378] **friend** (Evidently they never reach this person.)

Scene 7. [*A tent in the French camp.*]

Enter Cordelia, Kent, Doctor, and Gentleman.

Cordelia. O thou good Kent, how shall I live and work,
To match thy goodness? My life will be too short,
And every measure fail me.

Kent. To be acknowledged, madam, is o'erpaid.
All my reports go[379] with the modest[380] truth,
Nor more nor clipped,[381] but so.

Cordelia. Be better suited:[382]
These weeds[383] are memories[384] of those worser hours:
I prithee, put them off.

Kent. Pardon, dear madam;
Yet to be known shortens my made intent:[385]
My boon I make it,[386] that you know me not
Till time and I think meet.[387]

Cordelia. Then be 't so, my good lord. [*To the Doctor.*] How does the King?

Doctor. Madam, sleeps still.

Cordelia. O you kind gods![388]
Cure this great breach in his abusèd[389] nature.

[379] **go** agree
[380] **modest** unexaggerated
[381] **Nor . . . clipped** neither more nor less than the truth ("clipped", meaning "abbreviated")
[382] **suited** dressed
[383] **weeds** clothes
[384] **memories** reminders
[385] **shortens . . . intent** interferes with my plans
[386] **My boon I make it** I ask this favor
[387] **meet** appropriate
[388] **O you kind gods!** (Note the difference between Cordelia's attitude to the gods and that of all others in the play.)
[389] **abusèd** maltreated

Th' untuned and jarring senses, O, wind[390] up
Of this child-changèd[391] father.

Doctor. So please your Majesty
That we may wake the King: he hath slept long.

Cordelia. Be governed by your knowledge, and proceed
I' th' sway[392] of your own will. Is he arrayed?

Enter Lear in a chair carried by Servants.

Gentleman. Ay, madam; in the heaviness of sleep
We put fresh garments on him.

Doctor. Be by, good madam, when we do awake him;
I doubt not of his temperance.[393]

Cordelia. Very well.

Doctor. Please you, draw near. Louder the music there!

Cordelia. O my dear father, restoration[394] hang
Thy medicine on my lips, and let this kiss
Repair those violent harms that my two sisters
Have in thy reverence[395] made.

Kent. Kind and dear Princess.

Cordelia. Had you not been their father, these white Flakes[396]
Did challenge[397] pity of them. Was this a face
To be opposed against the warring winds?

[390] **wind** tune (i.e., by winding the strings)

[391] **child-changèd** changed by the maltreatment of his children; also, his change from the *childish* arrogance of the beginning of the play to the *childlike* innocence and wisdom of his conversion from pride to humility at the play's end

[392] **I' th' sway** according to the direction

[393] **temperance** sanity; self-control

[394] **restoration** of his health (and, perhaps, of his kingdom)

[395] **reverence** venerable person

[396] **Flakes** locks

[397] **challenge** claim

To stand against the deep dread-bolted[398] thunder?
In the most terrible and nimble stroke
Of quick, cross[399] lightning to watch—poor
perdu![400]—
With this thin helm?[401] Mine enemy's dog,
Though he had bit me, should have stood that night
Against my fire; and wast thou fain,[402] poor father,
To hovel thee[403] with swine and rogues forlorn,[404]
In short[405] and musty straw?[406] Alack, alack!
'Tis wonder that thy life and wits at once
Had not concluded all.[407] He wakes; speak to him.

Doctor. Madam, do you; 'tis fittest.

Cordelia. How does my royal lord? How fares your
Majesty?

Lear. You do me wrong to take me out o' th' grave:
Thou art a soul in bliss; but I am bound
Upon a wheel of fire,[408] that[409] mine own tears
Do scald like molten lead.

Cordelia. Sir, do you know me?

Lear. You are a spirit, I know. Where did you die?

[398] **dread-bolted** equipped with dreaded, or awe-inspiring, thunderbolts

[399] **cross** forked

[400] **perdu** sentinel in such an exposed position that he can hardly escape death; lost one (Frenh)

[401] **helm** (The little hair he had left was his only helmet.)

[402] **fain** (See note at 1.2.70.)

[403] **To hovel thee** to lodge yourself in a hovel

[404] **rogues forlorn** vagrants; outcasts

[405] **short** insufficient; broken up with long use, thus old

[406] **To ... straw** (The images here—hovel, swine, rogues, straw—allude to the story of the Prodigal Son [see Lk 15:11–32]; Lear is the Prodigal Father, Cordelia the forgiving daughter.)

[407] **all** altogether; together

[408] **wheel of fire** (One of the torments in Purgatory, where Lear, shedding penitential tears, believes himself to be. Equally, there are suggestions of the revolutions of the wheel of Fortune, and the punishment of Ixion in Greek mythology.)

[409] **that** so that

Cordelia. Still, still, far wide.[410]

Doctor. He's scarce awake: let him alone awhile.

Lear. Where have I been? Where am I? Fair daylight?
I am mightily abused.[411] I should ev'n die with pity,
To see another thus.[412] I know not what to say.
I will not swear these are my hands: let's see;
I feel this pin prick.[413] Would I were assured
Of my condition.

Cordelia. O, look upon me, sir,
And hold your hand in benediction o'er me.
You must not kneel.[414]

Lear. Pray, do not mock me:
I am a very foolish fond[415] old man,
Fourscore and upward, not an hour more nor less;
And, to deal plainly,
I fear I am not in my perfect mind.
Methinks I should know you and know this man,[416]
Yet I am doubtful; for I am mainly[417] ignorant
What place this is, and all the skill I have
Remembers not these garments, nor I know not
Where I did lodge last night. Do not laugh at me,
For, as I am a man, I think this lady
To be my child Cordelia.

Cordelia. And so I am, I am.

[410] **Still . . . wide** (i.e., wide of the mark: Lear's wits still wander far astray)

[411] **abused** deluded; mistreated

[412] **another thus** someone else in my state

[413] **pin prick** (using a broach or ornament)

[414] **kneel** (Cordelia has knelt to receive his blessing; now Lear tries to kneel before her. At this point in the story, the original *King Leir* included excessive kneeling, which Shakespeare abbreviated to more effective use.)

[415] **fond** silly; senile

[416] **this man** (Kent)

[417] **mainly** entirely

Lear. Be your tears wet? Yes, faith. I pray, weep not.
If you have poison for me, I will drink it.
I know you do not love me; for your sisters
Have, as I do remember, done me wrong.
You have some cause, they have not.

Cordelia. No cause, no cause.

Lear. Am I in France?

Kent. In your own kingdom, sir.

Lear. Do not abuse[418] me.

Doctor. Be comforted, good madam: the great rage,[419]
You see, is killed in him: and yet it is danger
To make him even o'er[420] the time he has lost.
Desire him to go in; trouble him no more
Till further settling.[421]

Cordelia. Will 't please your Highness walk?[422]

Lear. You must bear with me. Pray you now, forget and forgive. I am old and foolish.

Exeunt. Mane[n]t[423] *Kent and Gentleman.*

Gentleman. Holds it true, sir, that the Duke of Cornwall was so slain?

Kent. Most certain, sir.

Gentleman. Who is conductor[424] of his people?

Kent. As 'tis said, the bastard son of Gloucester.

[418] **abuse** deceive
[419] **rage** madness
[420] **even o'er** smooth over: to restore an unbroken sequence of events to his mind
[421] **further settling** his wits are more composed
[422] **walk** (perhaps in the sense of "withdraw")
[423] **Mane[n]t** remain
[424] **conductor** the leader; commander

Gentleman. They say Edgar, his banished son, is with the Earl of Kent in Germany.

Kent. Report[425] is changeable.[426] 'Tis time to look about; the powers[427] of the kingdom approach apace.

Gentleman. The arbitrement[428] is like to be bloody. Fare you well, sir. [*Exit.*]

Kent. My point[429] and period[430] will be throughly[431] wrought,
Or[432] well or ill, as this day's battle's fought.[433]

Exit.

[425] **Report** common talk; rumor
[426] **changeable** always changing; unreliable
[427] **powers** (See note at 4.3.49.)
[428] **arbitrement** settling of the contest (i.e., decisive battle)
[429] **point** object
[430] **period** conclusion; end
[431] **throughly** thoroughly
[432] **Or** either
[433] **as ... fought** in accord with the outcome of this battle

ACT 5

Scene 1. [*The British camp near Dover.*]

Enter, with drum and colors, Edmund, Regan, Gentlemen, and Soldiers.

Edmund. Know of[1] the Duke if his last purpose hold,[2]
Or whether since he is[3] advised[4] by aught[5]
To change the course: he's full of alteration[6]
And self-reproving: bring his constant pleasure.[7]

[*To a Gentleman, who goes out.*]

Regan. Our sister's man is certainly miscarried.[8]

Edmund. 'Tis to be doubted,[9] madam.

Regan. Now, sweet lord,
You know the goodness I intend upon you:[10]
Tell me, but truly, but then speak the truth,
Do you not love my sister?

Edmund. In honored[11] love.

Regan. But have you never found my brother's way
To the forfended[12] place?[13]

Edmund. That thought abuses[14] you.

[1] **Know of** find out from
[2] **his . . . hold** holds to his most recent decision (to fight)
[3] **since he is** he has since been
[4] **advised** induced; persuaded
[5] **aught** anything
[6] **alteration** vacillation
[7] **constant pleasure** definitive choice; final resolution
[8] **miscarried** come to some harm
[9] **doubted** feared; suspected
[10] **goodness . . . you** (i.e., to marry you and give you ruling power)
[11] **honored** honorable
[12] **forfended** forbidden (by her marriage to Albany)
[13] **place** (Goneril's bed or body)
[14] **abuses** dishonors

Regan. I am doubtful[15] that you have been conjunct[16]
And bosomed with her, as far as we call hers.[17]

Edmund. No, by mine honor, madam.

Regan. I shall never endure her: dear my lord,
Be not familiar[18] with her.

Edmund. Fear me not.[19]—
She and the Duke her husband!

Enter, with drum and colors, Albany, Goneril [and] Soldiers.

Goneril. [*Aside*] I had rather lose the battle than that sister
Should loosen[20] him and me.

Albany. Our very loving sister, well be-met.[21]
Sir, this I heard, the King is come to his daughter,
With others whom the rigor of our state[22]
Forced to cry out. Where I could not be honest,[23]
I never yet was valiant: for this business,
It touches[24] us, as[25] France invades our land,
Not bolds the King, with others,[26] whom, I fear,
Most just and heavy causes make oppose.[27]

Edmund. Sir, you speak nobly.

[15] **doubtful** fearful; suspicious

[16] **conjunct** closely joined

[17] **bosomed ... hers** (i.e., not merely in her confidence, but in the fullest respect)

[18] **familiar** intimate

[19] **Fear me not** Harbor no doubts about me.

[20] **loosen** cause a breach between (with a pun on "lose")

[21] **be-met** met

[22] **rigor ... state** harshness of our rule

[23] **honest** honest; honorable

[24] **touches** concerns

[25] **as** only inasmuch as

[26] **Not ... others** not insofar as ("this business" or "France"—the meaning is not altogether clear) emboldens King Lear and his supporters

[27] **make oppose** incite them to oppose us

Regan. Why is this reasoned?[28]

Goneril. Combine together 'gainst the enemy;
For these domestic and particular broils[29]
Are not the question[30] here.

Albany. Let's then determine
With th' ancient of war[31] on our proceeding.[32]

Edmund. I shall attend you presently at your tent.

Regan. Sister, you'll go with us?[33]

Goneril. No.

Regan. 'Tis most convenient;[34] pray you, go with us.

Goneril. [*Aside*] O, ho, I know the riddle.[35]—I will go.

Exeunt both the Armies. Enter Edgar [*disguised*].

Edgar. If e'er your Grace had speech with man so poor,
Hear me one word.

Albany. [*To those going out*] I'll overtake you. [*To Edgar*] Speak:

Exeunt [*all but Albany and Edgar*].

Edgar. Before you fight the battle, ope[36] this letter.
If you have victory, let the trumpet sound

[28] **Why . . . reasoned?** Why do you raise this issue? What is the point of going over this?
[29] **particular broils** personal squabbles
[30] **question** issue
[31] **th' ancient of war** veteran officers
[32] **our proceeding** our course of action
[33] **us** me (attempting to keep her away from Edmund)
[34] **convenient** appropriate; proper
[35] **riddle** meaning of this riddle (why she wants this)
[36] **ope** open

For[37] him that brought it: wretched though I seem,
I can produce a champion[38] that will prove[39]
What is avouchèd[40] there. If you miscarry,[41]
Your business of[42] the world hath so an end,
And machination[43] ceases. Fortune love you.

Albany. Stay till I have read the letter.

Edgar. I was forbid it.[44]
When time shall serve, let but the herald cry,
And I'll appear again.

Albany. Why, fare thee well: I will o'erlook thy
paper.[45] *Exit* [*Edgar*].

Enter Edmund.

Edmund. The enemy's in view: draw up your powers.[46]
Here is the guess[47] of their true strength and
forces
By diligent discovery;[48] but your haste
Is now urged on you.

Albany. We will greet[49] the time. *Exit.*

Edmund. To both these sisters have I sworn my love;
Each jealous[50] of the other, as the stung
Are of the adder. Which of them shall I take?

[37] **let . . . For** let the trumpet call for, summon
[38] **champion** one who fights in single combat for his own or another's cause
[39] **prove** in combat
[40] **avouchèd** avowed; asserted
[41] **miscarry** lose the battle
[42] **of** in
[43] **machination** scheming
[44] **I was forbid it** (evidently by himself)
[45] **o'erlook thy paper** look it over. (The director can choose whether Albany has any time to read part of the letter before Edmund's entrance—which, if so, would heighten the tension and explain Albany's curt response.)
[46] **powers** troops
[47] **guess** estimate
[48] **discovery** reconnaissance
[49] **greet** respond to the needs of
[50] **jealous** suspicious

Both? One? Or neither? Neither can be enjoyed,
If both remain alive: to take the widow
Exasperates, makes mad her sister Goneril;
And hardly shall I[51] carry out my side,[52]
Her husband being alive. Now then, we'll use
His countenance[53] for the battle; which being done,
Let her who would be rid of him devise
His speedy taking off. As for the mercy
Which he intends to Lear and to Cordelia,
The battle done, and they within our power,
Shall[54] never see his pardon; for my state[55]
Stands on[56] me to defend, not to debate.[57,58] *Exit.*

Scene 2. [*A field between the two camps.*]

Alarum[59] *within. Enter, with drum and colors, Lear, Cordelia, and Soldiers, over the stage; and exeunt.*

Enter Edgar and Gloucester.

Edgar. Here, father,[60] take the shadow of this tree
For your good host; pray that the right may thrive.
If ever I return to you again,
I'll bring you comfort.

Gloucester. Grace go with you, sir.

[51] **hardly shall I** it will be hard for me to

[52] **carry ... side** achieve my ambitions (the expression comes from a card game)

[53] **countenance** authority; prestige

[54] **Shall** (i.e., Lear and Cordelia)

[55] **state** position; state of affairs

[56] **Stands on** concerns; depends

[57] **debate** (i.e., with himself about what is right and what is wrong)

[58] **As ... debate** (Having already betrayed his own brother and father, there is no reason to be just toward Lear and Cordelia, who pose a threat to his new ambition: ruling a united kingdom.)

[59] **Alarum** call to arms

[60] **father** (Still the generic address to an old man: Edgar has not yet disclosed himself to his father.)

Exit [Edgar].[61]

Alarum and retreat[62] *within. [Re-]enter Edgar.*

Edgar. Away, old man; give me thy hand; away!
King Lear hath lost, he and his daughter ta'en:[63]
Give me thy hand; come on.

Gloucester. No further, sir; a man may rot even here.

Edgar. What, in ill thoughts again? Men must endure
Their going hence, even as their coming hither:
Ripeness[64] is all.[65] Come on.

Gloucester. And that's true too.

Exeunt.

Scene 3. [*The British camp near Dover.*]

Enter, in conquest, with drum and colors, Edmund; Lear and Cordelia, as prisoners; Soldiers, Captain.

Edmund. Some officers take them away: good guard,[66]
Until their greater pleasures[67] first be known
That are to censure[68] them.

[61] **Exit [Edgar]** (leaving Gloucester alone on stage while the sounds of battle occur offstage, and letting the audience experience it from the point of view of a blind, wretched, and isolated old man)

[62] **Alarum and retreat** (trumpet signals)

[63] **ta'en** taken

[64] **Ripeness** waiting for the proper time

[65] **Men . . . all** (Edgar's words reflect both Greek and Christian thought, that man must depend on Providence as much in his death as in his birth. The "ripeness" he speaks of may not only mean waiting for the divine plan to ripen, but also be advice to make oneself "ripe"—or ready—for death whenever it should occur.)

[66] **good guard** keep a close watch on them, with sufficient guard

[67] **their greater pleasures** the pleasure or intentions of those with greater authority

[68] **censure** pass judgment on

Cordelia. We are not the first
Who with best meaning[69] have incurred the worst.
For thee, oppressèd King, I am cast down;
Myself could else out-frown false fortune's frown.
Shall we not see these daughters and these sisters?

Lear. No, no, no, no! Come, let's away to prison:
We two alone will sing like birds i' th' cage:
When thou dost ask me blessing, I'll kneel down
And ask of thee forgiveness: so we'll live,
And pray, and sing, and tell old tales, and laugh
At gilded butterflies,[70] and hear poor rogues
Talk of court news; and we'll talk with them too,
Who loses and who wins, who's in, who's out;
And take upon's the mystery of things,
As if we were God's spies:[71] and we'll wear out,[72]
In a walled prison, packs and sects[73] of great ones
That ebb and flow by th' moon.

Edmund. Take them away.

Lear. Upon such sacrifices,[74] my Cordelia,
The gods themselves throw incense.[75] Have I caught
thee?

[69] **meaning** intentions

[70] **gilded butterflies** gaily clad courtiers (though it is possible Lear is referring to real butterflies)

[71] **God's spies** privy to divine secrets; commissioned to spy and report on men by God or the gods. (It is singularly curious that in this play, set in pagan times, this is the only reference to "God", and curious also that "God" is capitalized. This fact, coupled with the context in which the word is used, has led several scholars to conclude that this is a coded reference to the Jesuit priests who, as "outlaws for Christ" hiding from the Elizabethan authorities, could be considered "God's spies".)

[72] **wear out** outlive

[73] **packs and sects** cliques and factions

[74] **such sacrifices** (most likely their renouncing of the world, but perhaps Cordelia's sacrifices in helping Lear)

[75] **throw incense** (That is, such sacrifice is worthy of the gods and makes us like the gods, who alone are entitled to receive incense.)

He that parts us shall bring a brand from heaven,[76]
And fire us hence like foxes.[77] Wipe thine eyes;
The good years[78] shall devour them,[79] flesh and fell,[80]
Ere they shall make us weep.[81] We'll see 'em starved first.
Come. [*Exeunt Lear and Cordelia, guarded.*]

Edmund. Come hither, captain; hark.
Take thou this note:[82] go follow them to prison:
One step I have advanced thee; if thou dost
As this instructs thee, thou dost make thy way
To noble fortunes: know thou this, that men
Are as the time is:[83] to be tender-minded
Does not become a sword:[84] thy great employment
Will not bear question;[85] either say thou'lt do 't,
Or thrive by other means.

Captain. I'll do 't, my lord.

Edmund. About it; and write happy[86] when th' hast done.

[76] **He ... heaven** (That is, how Heaven alone has the power to part us.)

[77] **fire ... foxes** (Fire and smoke were used to drive foxes from their dens or from hiding.)

[78] **good years** (Some critics have seen in this a reference to "goodyear": an undefined malignant power.)

[79] **good ... them** (a possible allusion to Pharaoh's dream in the time of Joseph: where seven lean cows devoured seven fat cows [the latter representing years of good harvest, or "good years"]; see Genesis 41:1–7)

[80] **fell** skin

[81] **Ere ... weep** (Indeed Goneril and Regan are dead by the time Lear weeps again.)

[82] **note** (a directive arranging the deaths of Lear and Cordelia)

[83] **men ... is** Men are slaves to the times in which they find themselves and are governed by the exigencies of the moment. (Edmund's cynical pragmatism stands in stark contradistinction to the Christian idealism of Lear's words that precede it; if Lear and Cordelia are cast in the role of Christian martyrs, Edmund takes the role of a Machiavellian villain, a secular humanist in the spirit of the emerging Enlightenment.)

[84] **sword** soldier

[85] **question** consideration; discussion

[86] **write happy** consider yourself lucky, fortunate

Mark; I say, instantly, and carry it so
As I have set it down.[87]

Captain. I cannot draw a cart, nor eat dried oats;
If it be man's work, I'll do 't. *Exit Captain.*

Flourish. Enter Albany, Goneril, Regan [another Captain, and] Soldiers.

Albany. Sir, you have showed today your valiant strain,[88]
And fortune led you well: you have the captives
Who were the opposites of[89] this day's strife:
I do require them of you, so to use[90] them
As we shall find their merits[91] and our safety
May equally determine.

Edmund. Sir, I thought it fit
To send the old and miserable King
To some retention[92] and appointed guard;
Whose[93] age had charms in it, whose title more,
To pluck the common bosom on his side,[94]
And turn our impressed lances[95] in our eyes[96]
Which do command them. With him I sent the Queen:
My reason all the same; and they are ready
Tomorrow, or at further space,[97] t' appear

[87] **carry . . . down** carry it out precisely as I have written (i.e., making it appear that Cordelia has committed suicide)
[88] **strain** lineage; natural disposition
[89] **opposites of** opponents in
[90] **use** treat
[91] **their merits** what they deserve
[92] **retention** confinement
[93] **Whose** he whose
[94] **pluck . . . side** draw the sympathy of the common people to himself
[95] **our impressed lances** our conscripted soldiers
[96] **in our eyes** against us
[97] **space** span of time

Where you shall hold your session.[98] At this time
We sweat and bleed: the friend hath lost his friend;
And the best quarrels,[99] in the heat,[100] are cursed
By those that feel their sharpness.[101]
The question of Cordelia and her father
Requires a fitter place.

Albany. Sir, by your patience,
I hold you but a subject of[102] this war,
Not as a brother.

Regan. That's as we[103] list[104] to grace[105] him.
Methinks our pleasure might have been demanded,[106]
Ere you had spoke so far. He led our powers,
Bore the commission[107] of my place[108] and person;
The which immediacy[109] may well stand up
And call itself your brother.

Goneril. Not so hot:
In his own grace he doth exalt himself
More than in your addition.[110]

Regan. In my rights,
By me invested, he compeers[111] the best.

[98] **session** judicial proceedings
[99] **quarrels** causes
[100] **in the heat** (i.e., while passions are still running high)
[101] **At ... sharpness** (Edmund appears to be trying to obtain a fair trial for Lear and Cordelia, but his real concern is to give the soldier sufficient time to kill them.)
[102] **of** in
[103] **we** (Regan is perhaps using the royal "we" here.)
[104] **list** choose
[105] **to grace** to honor
[106] **demanded** asked
[107] **commission** authority
[108] **place** rank
[109] **immediacy** position of being Regan's direct representative
[110] **your addition** the honors you have given him
[111] **compeers** equals; is the peer of

Goneril. That were the most, if he should husband
you.[112]

Regan. Jesters do oft prove prophets.[113]

Goneril. Holla, holla![114]
That eye that told you so looked but a-squint.[115]

Regan. Lady, I am not well; else I should answer
From a full-flowing stomach.[116] General,
Take thou my soldiers, prisoners, patrimony;[117]
Dispose of them, of me; the walls is thine:[118]
Witness the world, that I create thee here
My lord, and master.

Goneril. Mean you to enjoy him?

Albany. The let-alone[119] lies not in your good will.

Edmund. Nor in thine, lord.

Albany. Half-blooded[120] fellow, yes.

Regan. [*To Edmund*] Let the drum strike, and prove[121]
my title thine.

Albany. Stay yet; hear reason. Edmund, I arrest thee
On capital treason; and in thy attaint[122]

[112] **That . . . you** That would be fully realized only if he became your husband (some editions give this line to Albany).

[113] **Jesters . . . prophets** (proverbial)

[114] **Holla, holla!** Stop, stop!

[115] **That . . . a-squint** recalling the proverb "Love being jealous, makes a good eye look a-squint", i.e., see with distorted vision

[116] **From . . . stomach** exceedingly abundant anger ("stomach" could refer to anger or resentment)

[117] **patrimony** legacy; inheritance

[118] **walls is thine** I myself am yours ("walls" could refer to one's heart. Also, when an army had gained the walls, the fortress was lost, and winning a lady's heart had long been compared to capturing a fortress.)

[119] **let-alone** authority to deny

[120] **Half-blooded** bastard, and with only one parent of noble blood

[121] **prove** (by combat)

[122] **attaint** impeachment

This gilded serpent [*pointing to Goneril*]. For
your claim, fair sister,
I bar it in the interest of my wife.[123]
'Tis she is subcontracted[124] to this lord,
And I, her husband, contradict your banes.[125]

If you will marry, make your loves[126] to me;
My Lady is bespoke.[127]

Goneril. An interlude![128]

Albany. Thou art armed, Gloucester: let the trumpet
sound:
If none appear to prove upon thy person
Thy heinous, manifest, and many treasons,

There is my pledge[129] [*throwing down a glove*]:
I'll make[130] it on thy heart,
Ere I taste bread, thou art in nothing less
Than I have here proclaimed thee.

Regan. Sick, O, sick!

Goneril. [*Aside*] If not, I'll ne'er trust medicine.[131]

Edmund. [*Throwing down a glove*] There's my
exchange:[132] what in the world[133] he is
That names me traitor, villain-like he lies:
Call by the trumpet: he that dares approach,

[123] **I ... wife** (said with extreme irony)

[124] **subcontracted** already engaged (Shakespeare's coinage)

[125] **banes** wedding banns (proclamation of intention to marry, read out in church on three consecutive Sundays to give opportunity of objection)

[126] **loves** overtures

[127] **bespoke** spoken for; engaged

[128] **interlude** a brief drama, often a farce, performed between the acts of a longer play

[129] **pledge** i.e., to fight in proof of his assertions; challenge

[130] **make** make good on; prove

[131] **medicine** poison

[132] **exchange** my glove in return (technical term for answering a challenge)

[133] **what in the world** of whatever rank

On him, on you—who not?—I will maintain
My truth and honor firmly.

Albany. A herald, ho!

Edmund. A herald, ho, a herald!

Albany. Trust to thy single virtue;[134] for thy soldiers,
All levied in my name, have in my name
Took their discharge.

Regan. My sickness grows upon me.

Albany. She is not well; convey her to my tent.

[*Exit Regan, led*.]

Enter a Herald.

Come hither, herald. Let the trumpet sound—
And read out this.

Captain. Sound, trumpet!

A trumpet sounds.

Herald. (*Reads*.) "If any man of quality or degree[135] within the lists of[136] the army will maintain upon Edmund, supposed Earl of Gloucester, that he is a manifold traitor, let him appear by the third sound of the trumpet: he is bold in his defense."

Edmund. Sound!

First trumpet.

Herald. Again!

Second trumpet.

Herald. Again!

[134] **single virtue** unaided valor, strength
[135] **quality or degree** birth or rank
[136] **lists of** i.e., of those enlisted in

Third trumpet.

Trumpet answers within. Enter Edgar, at the third sound, armed,[137] *a trumpet*[138] *before him.*

Albany. Ask him his purposes, why he appears
Upon this call o' th' trumpet.

Herald. What are you?
Your name, your quality,[139] and why you answer
This present summons?

Edgar. Know, my name is lost;
By treason's tooth bare-gnawn[140] and canker-bit:[141]
Yet am I noble as the adversary
I come to cope.[142]

Albany. Which is that adversary?

Edgar. What's he that speaks for Edmund, Earl of Gloucester?

Edmund. Himself: what say'st thou to him?

Edgar. Draw thy sword,
That if my speech offend a noble heart,
Thy arm may do thee justice: here is mine.
Behold it is my privilege,[143]
The privilege of mine honors,
My oath, and my profession.[144] I protest,

[137] **armed** (possibly with the visor of his helmet down, concealing his face)
[138] **trumpet** trumpeter
[139] **quality** rank
[140] **bare-gnawn** gnawed bare
[141] **canker-bit** worm-eaten
[142] **cope** encounter in combat
[143] **it is my privilege** (i.e., as a knight, to challenge a traitor to a duel, and have my challenge accepted)
[144] **honors . . . profession** (all associated with the oath he swore on being made a knight)

Maugre[145] thy strength, place, youth, and eminence,
Despite thy victor sword and fire-new[146] fortune,
Thy valor and thy heart,[147] thou art a traitor,
False to thy gods, thy brother, and thy father,
Conspirant[148] 'gainst this high illustrious prince,
And from th' extremest upward[149] of thy head
To the descent[150] and dust below thy foot,
A most toad-spotted[151] traitor. Say thou "No,"
This sword, this arm and my best spirits are bent[152]
To prove upon thy heart,[153] whereto I speak,[154]
Thou liest.

Edmund. In wisdom[155] I should ask thy name,
But since thy outside looks so fair and warlike,
And that thy tongue some say[156] of breeding
breathes,
What safe[157] and nicely[158] I might well delay[159]
By rule of knighthood, I disdain and spurn:
Back do I toss these treasons[160] to thy head;
With the hell-hated[161] lie o'erwhelm thy heart;

[145] **Maugre** in spite of

[146] **fire-new** newly forged or minted

[147] **heart** courage

[148] **Conspirant** conspiring

[149] **extremest upward** crown

[150] **descent** lowest part (i.e., the sole of his foot)

[151] **toad-spotted** stained with villainy; venomous (the spots on a toad were thought to be poisonous)

[152] **bent** directed

[153] **To . . . heart** (In trial by combat, the gods were thought to prove the verity of one's assertions by guaranteeing that the one speaking the truth would win the duel.)

[154] **whereto I speak** (That is, Edgar's words are directed at Edmund's heart.)

[155] **In wisdom** to be prudent. (He is not bound to fight an unknown adversary, nor one who may be beneath him in rank.)

[156] **say** flavor; proof ("assay")

[157] **safe** with safety (from reproach)

[158] **nicely** observing niceties

[159] **delay** postpone; refuse

[160] **treasons** charges of treason

[161] **hell-hated** hated by me as much as I hate Hell

Which[162] for[163] they yet glance by and scarcely bruise,
This sword of mine shall give them instant way,
Where[164] they shall rest for ever. Trumpets, speak!

Alarums. [*They*] *fight.* [*Edmund falls.*]

Albany. Save him,[165] save him!

Goneril. This is practice,[166] Gloucester:
By th' law of war thou wast not bound to answer
An unknown opposite;[167] thou are not vanquished,
But cozened[168] and beguiled.

Albany. Shut your mouth, dame,
Or with this paper shall I stop it. Hold, sir;[169]
Thou worse than any name, read thine own evil.
No tearing, lady; I perceive you know it.

Goneril. Say, if I do, the laws are mine, not thine:[170]
Who can arraign me for 't?[171]

Albany. Most monstrous! O!
Know'st thou this paper?

Goneril. Ask me not what I know.

Exit.

[162] **Which** (i.e., "these treasons")

[163] **for** because

[164] **Where** to the place where (i.e., Edgar's heart)

[165] **Save him** spare his life (perhaps to extract a confession)

[166] **practice** trickery; treachery

[167] **opposite** (See note at 5.3.43.)

[168] **cozened** cheated

[169] **Hold, sir** This has been variously interpreted as "Take it!" (to Edmund, of the letter); "Just a moment!"; and "Stop, sir!" (to Edgar, to prevent him from killing Edmund).

[170] **the ... thine** (Goneril is the true sovereign, Albany only her consort; Lear, however, gave his authority and power to Albany and Cornwall in Act 1 [1.1.138–41].)

[171] **Who ... for 't** (She has no peer and thus cannot be tried.)

Albany. Go after her; she's desperate; govern[172] her.

Edmund. What you have charged me with, that have
I done;
And more, much more; the time will bring it out.
'Tis past, and so am I. But what art thou
That hast this fortune on[173] me? If thou 'rt noble,
I do forgive thee.

Edgar. Let's exchange charity.[174]
I am no less in blood[175] than thou art, Edmund;
If more,[176] the more th' hast wronged me.
My name is Edgar, and thy father's son.
The gods are just, and of our pleasant vices[177]
Make instruments to plague us:[178]
The dark and vicious place[179] where thee he got[180]
Cost him his eyes.[181]

Edmund. Th' hast spoken right, 'tis true;
The wheel is come full circle; I am here.[182]

[172] **govern** restrain; keep watch over

[173] **fortune on** victory over (with the help of luck)

[174] **charity** forgiveness and love (as Edmund has forgiven Edgar for killing him. This recalls the line from the Our Father, stating, "Forgive us our debts as we forgive our debtors", and the Gospel maxim about being reconciled with your brother, before appearing before God [Mt 5:23–26].)

[175] **blood** lineage, noble parentage

[176] **more** more noble (being legitimate and of noble blood on both sides)

[177] **of our pleasant vices** out of the vices in which we take pleasure

[178] **The . . . us** (Compare Wisdom 11:16, "one is punished by the very things by which he sins", and Wisdom 12:23, "those who in folly of life lived unrighteously thou didst torment through their own abominations".)

[179] **place** (the adulterous bed)

[180] **got** begot

[181] **Cost . . . eyes** His punishment fits his crime, lust being a sin of the eyes.

[182] **wheel . . . here** (Edmund began at the bottom of Fortune's wheel, which turned for him, bringing him to the top, but has turned again, bringing him back to the bottom.)

Albany. Methought thy very gait[183] did prophesy[184]
A royal nobleness: I must embrace thee:
Let sorrow split my heart, if ever I
Did hate thee or thy father!

Edgar. Worthy[185] Prince, I know 't.

Albany. Where have you hid yourself?
How have you known the miseries of your father?

Edgar. By nursing them, my lord. List[186] a brief tale;
And when 'tis told, O, that my heart would burst!
The bloody proclamation to escape[187]
That followed me so near—O, our lives' sweetness,
That we the pain of death would hourly die
Rather than die at once!—taught me to shift
Into a madman's rags, t' assume a semblance
That very dogs disdained: and in this habit[188]
Met I my father with his bleeding rings,[189]
Their precious stones new lost; became his guide,
Led him, begged for him, saved him from despair;
Never—O fault!—revealed myself unto him,
Until some half-hour past, when I was armed,
Not sure, though hoping, of this good success,
I asked his blessing, and from first to last
Told him our pilgrimage.[190] But his flawed[191] heart—
Alack, too weak the conflict to support—

183 **gait** bearing

184 **prophesy** foreshow

185 **Worthy** noble; deserving

186 **List** listen to

187 **The . . . escape** in order to escape the death sentence against

188 **habit** apparel

189 **rings** eye-sockets

190 **our pilgrimage** of our journey together (which, like a pilgrimage, was penitential and spiritually beneficial)

191 **flawed** cracked

'Twixt[192] two extremes of passion, joy and grief,
Burst smilingly.

Edmund. This speech of yours hath moved me,
And shall perchance do good: but speak you on;
You look as you had something more to say.

Albany. If there be more, more woeful, hold it in;
For I am almost ready to dissolve,[193]
Hearing of this.

Edgar. This would have seemed a period[194]
To such as love not sorrow; but another,
To amplify too much, would make much more,
And top extremity.[195]
Whilst I was big in clamor,[196] came there in a man,
Who, having seen me in my worst estate,[197]
Shunned my abhorred society; but then, finding
Who 'twas that so endured, with his strong arms
He fastened on my neck, and bellowed out
As he'd burst heaven; threw him on my father;
Told the most piteous tale of Lear and him
That ever ear received: which in recounting
His grief grew puissant,[198] and the strings of life[199]
Began to crack: twice then the trumpets sounded,
And there I left him tranced.[200]

Albany. But who was this?

[192] **'Twixt** Between

[193] **dissolve** (i.e., dissolve in tears)

[194] **period** highest point

[195] **but . . . extremity** Even one more sorrow, if told in detail, would exceed the limit.

[196] **big in clamor** loudly lamenting (Gloucester's death)

[197] **estate** condition

[198] **puissant** powerful; overpowering

[199] **strings of life** heart-strings

[200] **tranced** dazed; stupefied

Edgar. Kent, sir, the banished Kent; who in disguise
Followed his enemy[201] king, and did him service
Improper for a slave.

Enter a Gentleman, with a bloody knife.

Gentleman. Help, help, O, help!

Edgar. What kind of help?

Albany. Speak, man.

Edgar. What means this bloody knife?

Gentleman. 'Tis hot, it smokes;[202]
It came even from the heart of—O, she's dead!

Albany. Who dead? Speak, man.

Gentleman. Your lady, sir, your lady: and her sister
By her is poisoned; she confesses it.

Edmund. I was contracted[203] to them both: all three
Now marry[204] in an instant.

Edgar. Here comes Kent.

Albany. Produce the bodies, be they alive or dead.

[*Exit Gentleman.*]

This judgment of the heavens,[205] that makes us tremble,
Touches us not with pity.

Enter Kent.

[201] **enemy** hostile

[202] **smokes** steams

[203] **contracted** promised; pledged

[204] **marry** (i.e., in death. Recall Edmund's words to Goneril [4.2.25], "Yours in the ranks of death".)

[205] **judgment of the heavens** (Albany, like Edgar, sees divine intervention in these events.)

O, is this he?
The time will not allow the compliment[206]
Which very manners[207] urges.

Kent. I am come
To bid my king and master aye[208] good night:
Is he not here?

Albany. Great thing of[209] us forgot!
Speak, Edmund, where's the King? and where's Cordelia?
Seest thou this object,[210] Kent?
The bodies of Goneril and Regan are brought in.

Kent. Alack, why thus?

Edmund. Yet Edmund was beloved:[211]
The one the other poisoned for my sake,
And after slew herself.

Albany. Even so. Cover their faces.

Edmund. I pant for life: some good I mean to do,
Despite of mine own nature.[212] Quickly send,
Be brief in it, to th' castle; for my writ[213]
Is on the life of Lear and on Cordelia:
Nay, send in time.

Albany. Run, run, O, run!

[206] **compliment** ceremonious greeting
[207] **very manners** even common courtesy
[208] **aye** forever (Kent is dying)
[209] **of** by
[210] **object** spectacle (indicating what has distracted him: the dying Edmund and the bodies of Goneril and Regan)
[211] **Yet . . . beloved** (Not a few critics have taken this line as an indicator of the motives for Edmund's evil actions: he felt unloved.)
[212] **Despite . . . nature** (Edmund defies his supposed nature not as in Act 1, sc. 2, by scoffing at its being fixed by the stars, but in attempting to do good despite it.)
[213] **writ** warrant for execution

Edgar. To who, my lord? Who has the office?[214] Send
Thy token of reprieve.

Edmund. Well thought on: take my sword,
Give it the captain.

Edgar. Haste thee, for thy life.

[*Exit Messenger*.]

Edmund. He hath commission from thy wife and me
To hang Cordelia in the prison, and
To lay the blame upon her own despair,
That she fordid[215] herself.

Albany. The gods defend her! Bear him hence awhile.

[*Edmund is borne off*.]

Enter Lear, with Cordelia in his arms [*Gentleman, and others following*].

Lear. Howl, howl, howl, howl! O, you are men of stones:
Had I your tongues and eyes, I'd use them so
That heaven's vault should crack. She's gone for ever.
I know when one is dead and when one lives;
She's dead as earth. Lend me a looking-glass;
If that her breath will mist or stain the stone,[216]
Why, then she lives.

Kent. Is this the promised end?[217]

Edgar. Or image[218] of that horror?

[214] **office** authority (That is, how will the soldier Edmund sent to do the killing be persuaded not to carry out his order?)
[215] **fordid** killed
[216] **stone** mirror of polished stone
[217] **promised end** i.e., of the world
[218] **image** mirror image

Albany. Fall and cease.[219]

Lear. This feather stirs; she lives. If it be so,
It is a chance which does redeem[220] all sorrows
That ever I have felt.

Kent. O my good master.

Lear. Prithee, away.

Edgar. 'Tis noble Kent, your friend.

Lear. A plague upon you, murderers, traitors all!
I might have saved her; now she's gone for ever.
Cordelia, Cordelia, stay a little. Ha,
What is 't thou say'st? Her voice was ever soft,
Gentle and low, an excellent thing in woman.
I killed the slave that was a-hanging thee.

Gentleman: 'Tis true, my lords, he did.

Lear. Did I not, fellow?
I have seen the day, with my good biting falchion[221]
I would have made them skip: I am old now,
And these same crosses[222] spoil me.[223] Who are you?
Mine eyes are not o' th' best: I'll tell[224] you straight.[225]

Kent. If Fortune brag of two she loved and hated,
One of them[226] we behold.

[219] **Fall and cease** (referring to the heavens and the earth)

[220] **redeem** buy back; make amends for; atone for; bring into some former condition or state; set right again. There are echoes here of Christ's redemptive sacrifice on the Cross.

[221] **falchion** light sword that was slightly curved

[222] **crosses** troubles

[223] **spoil me** (That is, they spoil his swordsmanship.)

[224] **tell** recognize

[225] **straight** at once

[226] **One of them** (That is, Lear is the one she most hated; the other is hypothetical. However, some critics suppose the passage to refer to two men *both* loved *and* hated by Fortune, Lear being one of them. Finally, some editions reading "one of them ye [i.e., you] behold", it is possible that Kent is referring to himself.)

Lear. This is a dull sight.[227] Are you not Kent?

Kent. The same,
Your servant Kent. Where is your servant Caius?[228]

Lear. He's a good fellow, I can tell you that;
He'll strike, and quickly too: he's dead and rotten.

Kent. No, my good lord; I am the very man.

Lear. I'll see that straight.[229]

Kent. That from your first[230] of difference and decay[231]
Have followed your sad steps.

Lear. You are welcome hither.

Kent. Nor no man else:[232] all's cheerless, dark and deadly
Your eldest daughters have fordone[233] themselves,
And desperately[234] are dead.

Lear. Ay, so I think.

Albany. He knows not what he says, and vain is it
That we present us[235] to him.

Edgar. Very bootless.[236]

Enter a Messenger.

Messenger. Edmund is dead, my lord.

[227] **dull sight** failing eyesight; gloomy scene

[228] **Caius** the name Kent went by while disguised

[229] **see that straight** attend to (or, possibly, "comprehend") that in a moment

[230] **first** (i.e., first moments)

[231] **difference and decay** change in and decline of your fortunes

[232] **Nor no man else** unclear. The likeliest reading seems to be "neither I nor anyone else is welcome"; other possible readings are "I am the very man and no one else", and "no one else is worthy of your welcome if I am not".

[233] **fordone** (See note at 5.3.257.)

[234] **desperately** from despair

[235] **us** ourselves

[236] **bootless** useless

Albany. That's but a trifle here.
You lords and noble friends, know our intent.
What comfort to this great decay may come[237]
Shall be applied. For us, we[238] will resign,
During the life of this old majesty,
To him our absolute power: [*To Edgar and Kent*] you, to your rights;
With boot,[239] and such addition[240] as your honors
Have more than merited. All friends shall taste
The wages of their virtue, and all foes
The cup of their deservings. O, see, see!

Lear. And my poor fool[241] is hanged: no, no, no life?
Why should a dog, a horse, a rat, have life,
And thou no breath at all? Thou'lt come no more,
Never, never, never, never, never.
Pray you, undo this button.[242] Thank you, sir.
Do you see this? Look on her. Look, her lips,
Look there, look there.[243]

He dies.

Edgar. He faints. My lord, my lord!

Kent. Break, heart;[244] I prithee, break.

[237] **What . . . come** whatever comfort it is possible to bring to this great ruined piece of nature (i.e., Lear)

[238] **we** (the royal "we")

[239] **boot** more besides

[240] **addition** added titles and distinctions

[241] **fool** (term of endearment. Here it is most likely referring to Cordelia, since the rest of the lines refer to her; though in his mental confusion she may be merging in his mind with his Fool [whose disappearance is unexplained]. The two characters both offered him truth and loyalty and can be seen as figurative personifications of his heart or conscience.)

[242] **undo this button** (He is feeling suffocated.)

[243] **Look . . . there** (indicting that Lear believes that Cordelia lives after all, and thus he dies happy)

[244] **Break, heart** (addressing either his own or Lear's, that his suffering might end)

Edgar. Look up, my lord.

Kent. Vex not his ghost:[245] O, let him pass! He hates him
That would upon the rack[246] of this tough world
Stretch him out longer.[247]

Edgar. He is gone indeed.

Kent. The wonder is he hath endured so long:
He but usurped[248] his life.

Albany. Bear them from hence. Our present business
Is general woe. [*To Kent and Edgar*] Friends of my soul, you twain,[249]
Rule in this realm and the gored[250] state sustain.

Kent. I have a journey,[251] sir, shortly to go;
My master calls me, I must not say no.

Edgar. The weight of this sad time we must obey,[252]
Speak what we feel, not what we ought to say.
The oldest hath borne most: we that are young
Shall never see so much, nor live so long.

Exeunt, with a dead march.[253]

FINIS

[245] **ghost** departing soul
[246] **rack** instrument of torture stretching the victim's joints by the turning of rollers to which his wrists and ankles were tied
[247] **longer** (here refers both to Lear's body and to time)
[248] **usurped** held unlawful possession of (i.e., beyond his limit or term)
[249] **twain** two
[250] **gored** deeply wounded
[251] **journey** (i.e., out of this life)
[252] **obey** accept
[253] **dead march** a march suitable for a funeral

Classic Criticism

On Sitting Down to Read *King Lear* Once Again

John Keats

O Golden-tongued Romance, with serene Lute!
   Fair plumed Syren, Queen of far-away!
   Leave melodizing on this wintry day
Shut up thine olden Pages, and be mute,
Adieu! for, once again, the fierce dispute,
   Betwixt Damnation and impassion'd clay
   Must I burn through; once more humbly assay
The bitter-sweet of this Shakespearean fruit.
Chief Poet! and ye Clouds of Albion,
   Begetters of our deep eternal theme!
When through the old oak forest I am gone,
   Let me not wander in a barren dream:
But, when I am consumed in the fire,
Give me new Phoenix Wings to fly at my desire.

Preface to Shakespeare

Samuel Johnson
From *Preface to Shakespeare* and "King Lear"

Nothing can please many, and please long, but just representations of general nature. Particular manners can be known to few, and therefore few only can judge how nearly they are copied. The irregular combinations of fanciful invention may delight awhile, by that novelty of which the common satiety of life sends us all in quest; but the pleasures of sudden wonder are soon exhausted, and the mind can only repose on the stability of truth.

Shakespeare is above all writers, at least above all modern writers, the poet of nature; the poet that holds up to his readers a faithful mirror of manners and of life. His characters are not modified by the customs of particular places, unpracticed by the rest of the world; by the peculiarities of studies or professions, which can operate but upon small numbers; or by the accidents of transient fashions or temporary opinions: they are the genuine progeny of common humanity, such as the world will always supply, and observation will always find. His persons act and speak by the influence of those general passions and principles by which all minds are agitated, and the whole system of life is continued in motion. In the writings of other poets a character is too often an individual; in those of Shakespeare it is commonly a species.

It is from this wide extension of design that so much instruction is derived. It is this which fills the plays of Shakespeare with practical axioms and domestic wisdom. It was said of Euripides, that every verse was a precept; and it may be said of Shakespeare, that from his works may be collected a system of civil and economical prudence. Yet his real power is not shown in the splendor of particular passages, but by the progress of his fable, and the tenor of his dialogue; and he that tries to recommend him by select quotations, will succeed like the pedant in *Hierocles*, who, when he offered his house to sale, carried a brick in his pocket as a specimen....

Other dramatists can only gain attention by hyperbolical or aggravated characters, by fabulous and unexampled excellence or depravity, as the writers of barbarous romances invigorated the reader by a giant and a dwarf; and he that should form his expectations of human affairs from the play, or from the tale, would be equally deceived. Shakespeare has no heroes; his scenes are occupied only by men who act and speak as the reader thinks that he should himself have spoken or acted on the same occasion: Even where the agency is supernatural the dialogue is level with life. Other writers disguise the most natural passions and most frequent incidents; so that he who contemplates them in the book will not know them in the world: Shakespeare approximates the remote, and familiarizes the wonderful; the event which he represents will not happen, but if it were possible, its effects would be probably such as he has assigned; and it may be said, that he has not only shown human nature as it acts in real exigencies, but as it would be found in trials, to which it cannot be exposed.

This therefore is the praise of Shakespeare, that his drama is the mirror of life; that he who has mazed his imagination, in following the phantoms which other writers raise up before him, may here be cured of his delirious ecstasies, by reading human sentiments in human language; by scenes from which a hermit may estimate the transactions of the world, and a confessor predict the progress of the passions....

The censure which he has incurred by mixing comic and tragic scenes, as it extends to all his works, deserves more consideration. Let the fact be first stated, and then examined.

Shakespeare's plays are not in the rigorous and critical sense either tragedies or comedies, but compositions of a distinct kind; exhibiting the real state of sublunary nature, which partakes of good and evil, joy and sorrow, mingled with endless variety of proportion and innumerable modes of combination; and expressing the course of the world, in which the loss of one is the gain of another; in which, at the same time, the reveler is hasting to wine, and the mourner burying his friend; in which the malignity of one is sometimes defeated by the frolic of another; and many mischiefs and many benefits are done and hindered without design.

Out of the chaos of mingled purposes and casualities the ancient poets, according to the laws which custom had prescribed, selected some the crimes of men, and some their absurdities; some the momentous vicissitudes of life, and some the lighter occurrences; some the terrors of distress, and some the gaieties of prosperity. Thus rose the two modes of imitation, known by the names of *tragedy* and *comedy*, compositions intended to promote different ends by contrary means, and considered as so little allied, that I do not recollect among the Greeks or Romans a single writer who attempted both.

Shakespeare has united the powers of exciting laughter and sorrow not only in one mind but in one composition. Almost all his plays are divided between serious and ludicrous characters, and, in the successive evolutions of design, sometimes produce seriousness and sorrow, and sometimes levity and laughter.

That this is a practice contrary to the rules of criticism will be readily allowed; but there is always an appeal open from criticism to nature. The end of writing is to instruct; the end of poetry is to instruct by pleasing. That the mingled drama may convey all the instruction of tragedy or comedy cannot be denied, because it includes both in its alternations of exhibition, and approaches nearer than either to the appearance of life, by showing how great machinations and slender designs may promote or obviate one another, and the high and the low cooperate in the general system by unavoidable concatenation.

It is objected, that by this change of scenes the passions are interrupted in their progression, and that the principal event, being not advanced by a due gradation of preparatory incidents, wants at last the power to move, which constitutes the perfection of dramatic poetry. This reasoning is so specious, that it is received as true even by those who in daily experience feel it to be false. The interchanges of mingled scenes seldom fail to produce the intended vicissitudes of passion. Fiction cannot move so much, but that the attention may be easily transferred; and though it must be allowed that pleasing melancholy be sometimes interrupted by unwelcome levity, yet let it be considered likewise, that melancholy is often not pleasing, and that the disturbance of one man may be the relief of another; that different auditors have different habitudes; and that, upon the whole, all pleasure consists in variety....

Shakespeare engaged in dramatic poetry with the world open before him; the rules of the ancients were yet known to few; the public judgment was unformed; he had no example of such fame as might force him upon imitation, nor critics of such authority as might restrain his extravagance: He therefore indulged his natural disposition, and his disposition, as Rymer has remarked, led him to comedy. In tragedy he often writes with great appearance of toil and study, what is written at last with little felicity; but in his comic scenes, he seems to produce without labor, what no labor can improve. In tragedy he is always struggling after some occasion to be comic, but in comedy he seems to repose, or to luxuriate as in a mode of thinking congenial to his nature. In his tragic scenes there is always something wanting, but his comedy often surpasses expectation or desire. His comedy pleases by the thoughts and the language, and his tragedy for the greater part by incident and action. His tragedy seems to be skill, his comedy to be instinct.

The force of his comic scenes has suffered little diminution from the changes made by a century and a half, in manners or in words. As his personages act upon principles arising from genuine passion, very little modified by particular forms, their pleasure and vexations are communicable to all times and to all places; they are natural, and therefore durable; the adventitious peculiarities of personal habits are only superficial dyes, bright and pleasing for a little while, yet soon fading to a dim tinct, without any remains of former luster; but the discriminations of true passion are the colors of nature; they pervade the whole mass, and can only perish with the body that exhibits them. The accidental compositions of heterogeneous modes are dissolved by the chance which combined them; but the uniform simplicity of primitive qualities neither admits increase, nor suffers decay. The sand heaped by one flood is scattered by another, but the rock always continues in its place. The stream of time, which is continually washing the dissoluble fabrics of other poets, passes without injury by the adamant of Shakespeare.

If there be, what I believe there is, in every nation, a style which never becomes obsolete, a certain mode of phraseology so consonant and congenial to the analogy and principles of its respective language as to remain settled and unaltered; this style is probably to be sought in the common intercourse of life, among those who speak only to be understood, without ambition of elegance. The polite are always catching modish innovations, and the learned depart from established forms of speech, in hope of finding or making better; those who wish for distinction forsake the vulgar, when the vulgar is right; but there is a conversation above grossness and below refinement, where propriety resides, and where this poet seems to have gathered his comic dialogue. He is therefore more agreeable to the ears of the present age than any other author equally remote, and among his other excellencies deserves to be studied as one of the original masters of our language. . . .

Shakespeare with his excellencies has likewise faults, and faults sufficient to obscure and overwhelm any other merit. I shall show them in the proportion in which they appear to me, without envious malignity or superstitious veneration. No question can be more innocently discussed than a dead poet's pretensions to renown; and little regard is due to that bigotry which sets candor higher than truth.

His first defect is that to which may be imputed most of the evil in books or in men. He sacrifices virtue to convenience, and is so much more careful to please than to instruct, that he seems to write without any moral purpose. From his writings indeed a system of social duty may be selected, for he that thinks reasonably must think morally; but his precepts and axioms drop casually from him; he makes no just distribution of good or evil, nor is always careful to show in the virtuous a disapprobation of the wicked; he carries his persons indifferently through right and wrong, and at the close dismisses them without further care, and leaves their examples to operate by chance. This fault the barbarity of his age cannot extenuate for it is always a writer's duty to make the world better, and justice is a virtue independent on time or place.

The plots are often so loosely formed, that a very slight consideration may improve them, and so carelessly pursued, that he seems not always fully to comprehend his own design. He omits opportunities of instructing or delighting which the train of his story seems to force upon him, and apparently rejects those exhibitions which would be more affecting, for the sake of those which are more easy.

It may be observed, that in many of his plays the latter part is evidently neglected. When he found himself near the end of his work, and in view of his reward, he shortened the labor, to snatch the profit. He therefore remits his efforts where he should most vigorously exert them, and his catastrophe is improbably produced or imperfectly represented.

He had no regard to distinction of time or place, but gives to one age or nation, without scruple, the customs, institutions, and opinions of another, at the expense not only of likelihood, but of possibility. . . .

In tragedy his performance seems constantly to be worse, as his labor is more. The effusions of passion which exigence forces out are for the most part striking and energetic; but whenever he solicits his invention, or strains his faculties, the offspring of his throes is tumor, meanness, tediousness, and obscurity.

In narration he affects a disproportionate pomp of diction and a wearisome train of circumlocution, and he tells the incident imperfectly in many words, which might have been more plainly delivered in few. Narration in dramatic poetry is naturally tedious, as it is unanimated and inactive, and obstructs the progress of the action; it should therefore always be rapid, and enlivened by frequent interruption. Shakespeare found it an encumbrance, and instead of lightening it by brevity, endeavored to recommend it by dignity and splendor.

His declamations or set speeches are commonly cold and weak, for his power was the power of nature; when he endeavored, like other tragic writers, to catch opportunities of amplification, and instead of inquiring what the occasion demanded, to show how much his stores of knowledge could supply, he seldom escapes without the pity or resentment of his reader.

It is incident to him to be now and then entangled with an unwieldy sentiment, which he cannot well express, and will not reject; he struggles with it a while, and if it continues stubborn, comprises it in words such as occur, and leaves it to be disentangled and evolved by those who have more leisure to bestow upon it.

Not that always where the language is intricate the thought is subtle, or the image always great where the line is bulky; the equality of words to things is very often neglected and trivial sentiments and vulgar ideas disappoint the attention, to which they are recommended by sonorous epithets and swelling figures.

But the admirers of this great poet have never less reason to indulge their hopes of supreme excellence, than when he seems fully resolved to sink them in dejection, and mollify them with tender emotions by the fall of greatness, the danger of innocence, or the crosses of love. He is not long soft and pathetic without some idle conceit, or contemptible equivocation. He no sooner begins to move, than he counteracts himself; and terror and pity, as they are rising in the mind, are checked and blasted by sudden frigidity.

A quibble is to Shakespeare, what luminous vapors are to the traveler; he follows it at all adventures, it is sure to lead him out of his way, and sure to engulf him in the mire. It has some malignant power over his mind, and its fascinations are irresistible. Whatever be the dignity or profundity of his disquisition, whether he be enlarging knowledge or exalting affection, whether he be amusing attention with incidents, or enchaining it in suspense, let but a quibble spring up before him, and he leaves his work unfinished. A quibble is the golden apple for which he will always turn aside from his career, or stoop from his elevation. A quibble, poor and barren as it is, gave him such delight, that he was content to purchase it, by the sacrifice of reason, propriety, and truth. A quibble was to him the fatal Cleopatra for which he lost the world, and was content to lose it.

It will be thought strange, that, in enumerating the defects of this writer, I have not yet mentioned his neglect of the unities; his violation of those laws which have been instituted and established by the joining authority of poets and critics.

For his other deviations from the art of writing I resign him to critical justice, without making any other demand in his favor, than that which must be indulged to all human excellence; that his virtues be rated with his failings: But, from the censure which this irregularity may bring upon him, I shall, with due reverence to that learning which I must oppose, adventure to try how I can defend him.

His histories, being neither tragedies nor comedies, are not subject to any of their laws; nothing more is necessary to all the praise which they expect, than that the changes of action be so prepared as to be understood, that the incidents be various and affecting, and the characters consistent, natural, and distinct. No other unity is intended, and therefore none is to be sought.

In his other works he has well enough preserved the unity of action. He has not, indeed, an intrigue regularly perplexed and regularly unraveled; he does not endeavor to hide his design only to discover it, for this is seldom the order of real events and Shakespeare is the poet of nature: But his plan has commonly what Aristotle requires, a beginning, a middle, and an end; one event is concatenated with another, and the conclusion follows by easy consequence. There are perhaps some incidents that might be spared, as in other poets there is much talk that only fills up time upon the stage; but the general system makes gradual advances, and the end of the play is the end of expectation.

To the unities of time and place he has shown no regard, and perhaps a nearer view of the principles on which they stand will diminish their value, and withdraw from them the veneration which, from the time of Corneille, they have very generally received by discovering that they have given more trouble to the poet, than pleasure to the auditor.

The necessity of observing the unities of time and place arises from the supposed necessity of making the drama credible. The critics hold it impossible, that an action of months or years can be possibly believed to pass in three hours; or that the spectator can suppose himself to sit in the theater, while ambassadors go and return between distant kings, while armies are levied and towns besieged, while an exile wanders and returns, or till he whom they saw courting his mistress, shall lament the untimely fall of his son. The mind revolts from evident falsehood, and fiction loses its force when it departs from the resemblance of reality.

From the narrow limitation of time necessarily arises the contraction of place. The spectator, who knows that he saw the first act at Alexandria, cannot suppose that he sees the next at Rome, at a distance to which not the dragons of Medea could, in so short a time, have transported him; he knows with certainty that he has not changed his place; and he knows that place cannot change itself; that what was a house cannot become a plain; that what was Thebes can never be Persepolis.

Such is the triumphant language with which a critic exults over the misery of an irregular poet, and exults commonly without resistance or reply. It is time therefore to tell him by the authority of Shakespeare, that he assumes, as an unquestionable principle, a position, which, while his breath is forming it into words, his understanding pronounces to be false. . . .

There is no reason why a mind thus wandering in ecstasy should count the clock, or why an hour should not be a century in that calenture of the brains that can make the stage a field.

The truth is, that the spectators are always in their senses, and know, from the first act to the last, that the stage is only a stage, and that the players are only players. They came to hear a certain number of lines recited with just gesture and elegant modulation. The lines relate to some action, and an action must be in some place; but the different actions that complete a story may be in places very remote from each other. . . .

Time is, of all modes of existence, most obsequious to the imagination; a lapse of years is as easily conceived as a passage of hours. In contemplation we easily contract the time of real actions, and therefore willingly permit it to be contracted when we only see their imitation.

It will be asked, how the drama moves, if it is not credited. It is credited with all the credit due to a drama. It is credited, whenever it moves, as a just picture of a real original; as representing to the auditor what he would himself feel, if he were to do or suffer what is there feigned to be suffered or to be done. The reflection that strikes the heart is not, that the evils before us are real evils, but that they are evils to which we ourselves may be exposed. If there be any fallacy it is not that we fancy the players, but that we fancy ourselves unhappy for a moment; but we rather lament the possibility than suppose the presence of misery, as a mother weeps over her babe, when she remembers that death may take it from her. The delight of tragedy proceeds from our consciousness of fiction; if we thought murders and treasons real, they would please no more. . . .

[Shakespeare's] plots, whether historical or fabulous, are always crowded with incidents, by which the attention of a rude people was more easily caught than by sentiment or argumentation; and such is the power of the marvelous even over those who despise it, that every man finds his mind more strongly seized by the tragedies of Shakespeare than of any other writer; others please us by particular speeches, but he always makes us anxious for the event, and has perhaps excelled all but Homer in securing the first purpose of a writer, by exciting restless and unquenchable curiosity and compelling him that reads his work to read it through.

The shows and bustle with which his plays abound have the same original. As knowledge advances, pleasure passes from the eye to the ear, but returns, as it declines, from the ear to the eye. Those to whom our author's labors were exhibited had more skill in pomps or processions than in poetical language, and perhaps wanted some visible and discriminated events, as comments on the dialogue. He knew how he should most please; and whether his practice is more agreeable to nature, or whether his example has prejudiced the nation, we still find that on our stage something must be done as well as said, and inactive declamation is very coldly heard, however musical or elegant, passionate or sublime....

"King Lear"

The tragedy of *Lear* is deservedly celebrated among the dramas of Shakespeare. There is perhaps no play which keeps the attention so strongly fixed; which so much agitates our passions and interests our curiosity. The artful involutions of distinct interests, the striking opposition of contrary characters, the sudden changes of fortune, and the quick succession of events, fill the mind with a perpetual tumult of indignation, pity, and hope. There is no scene which does not contribute to the aggravation of the distress or conduct of the action, and scarce a line which does not conduce to the progress of the scene. So powerful is the current of the poet's imagination, that the mind, which once ventures within it, is hurried irresistibly along.

On the seeming improbability of Lear's conduct, it may be observed that he is represented according to histories at that time vulgarly received as true. And perhaps if we turn our thoughts upon the barbarity and ignorance of the age to which this story is referred, it will appear not so unlikely as while we estimate Lear's manners by our own. Such preference of one daughter to another, or resignation of dominion on such conditions, would be yet credible, if told of a petty prince of Guinea or Madagascar. Shakespeare, indeed, by the mention of his Earls and Dukes, has given us the idea of times more civilized, and of life regulated by softer manners; and the truth is, that though he so nicely discriminates, and so minutely describes the characters of men, he commonly neglects and confounds the characters of age, by mingling customs ancient and modern, English and foreign.

My learned friend Mr. Warton, who has in the *Adventurer* very minutely criticized this play, remarks, that the instances of cruelty are too savage and shocking, and that the intervention of Edmund destroys the simplicity of the story. These objections may, I think, be answered, by repeating, that the cruelty of the daughters is an historical fact, to which the poet has added little, having only drawn it into a series by dialogue and action. But I am not able to apologize with equal plausibility for the extrusion of Gloucester's eyes, which seems an act too horrid to be endured in dramatic exhibition, and such as must always compel the mind to relieve its distress by incredulity. Yet let it be remembered that our author well knew what would please the audience for which he wrote.

The injury done by Edmund to the simplicity of the action is abundantly recompensed by the addition of variety, by the art with which he is made to cooperate with the chief design, and the opportunity which he gives the poet of combining perfidy with perfidy, and connecting the wicked son with the wicked daughters, to impress this important moral, that villainy is never a stop, that crimes lead to crimes, and at last terminate in ruin.

But though this moral be incidentally enforced, Shakespeare has suffered the virtue of Cordelia to perish in a just cause, contrary to the natural ideas of justice, to the hope of the reader, and what is yet more strange, to the faith of chronicles. Yet this conduct is justified by the Spectator, who blames Tate for giving Cordelia success and happiness in his alteration, and declares, that in his opinion, *the tragedy has lost half its* beauty. Dennis has remarked, whether justly or not, that to secure the favorable reception of *Cato, the town was poisoned with much false and abominable criticism*, and that endeavors had been used to discredit and decry poetical justice. A play in which the wicked prosper, and the virtuous miscarry, may doubtless be good, because it is a just representation of the common events in human life: but since all reasonable beings naturally love justice, I cannot easily be persuaded, that the observation of justice makes a play worse; or, that if other excellencies are equal, the audience will not always rise better pleased from the final triumph of persecuted virtue.

In the present case the public has decided. Cordelia, from the time of Tate, has always retired with victory and felicity. And, if my sensations could add anything to the general suffrage, I might relate, that I was many years ago so shocked by Cordelia's death, that I know not whether I ever endured to read again the last scenes of the play till I undertook to revise them as an editor.

From *Shakespearean Tragedy*

A.C. Bradley

... [The] chief value [of the double action in *King Lear*] is not merely dramatic. It lies in the fact—in Shakespeare without a parallel—that the subplot simply repeats the theme of the main story. Here, as there, we see an old man "with a white beard". He, like Lear, is affectionate, unsuspicious, foolish, and self-willed. He, too, wrongs deeply a child who loves him not less for the wrong. He, too, meets with monstrous ingratitude from the child whom he favors, and is tortured and driven to death. This repetition does not simply double the pain with which the tragedy is witnessed: it startles and terrifies by suggesting that the folly of Lear and the ingratitude of his daughters are no accidents or merely individual aberrations, but that in the dark cold world some fateful malignant influence is abroad, turning the hearts of fathers against their children and of the children against their fathers, smiting the earth with a curse, so that the brother gives the brother to death and the father the son, blinding the eyes, maddening the brain, freezing the springs of pity, numbing all powers except the nerves of anguish and the dull lust of life.

Hence too, as well as from other sources, comes that feeling which haunts us in *King Lear*, as though we were witnessing something universal—a conflict not so much of particular persons as of the powers of good and evil in the world. And the treatment of many of the characters confirms this feeling. Considered simply as psychological studies few of them, surely, are of the highest interest. Fine and subtle touches could not be absent from a work of Shakespeare's maturity; but, with the possible exception of Lear himself, no one of the characters strikes us as psychologically a *wonderful* creation, like Hamlet or Iago or even Macbeth; one or two seem even to be somewhat faint and thin. And, what is more significant, it is not quite natural to us to regard them from this point of view at all. Rather we observe a most unusual circumstance. If Lear, Gloster, and Albany are set apart, the rest fall into two distinct groups, which are strongly, even violently, contrasted: Cordelia, Kent, Edgar, the Fool on one side, Goneril, Regan, Edmund, Cornwall, Oswald on the other. These characters are in various degrees individualized, most of them completely so; but still in each group there is a quality common to all the members, or one spirit breathing through them all. Here we have unselfish and devoted love, there hard self-seeking. On both sides, further, the common quality takes an extreme form; the love is incapable of being chilled by injury, the selfishness of being softened by pity; and, it may be added, this tendency to extremes is found again in the characters of Lear and Gloster, and is the main source of the accusations of improbability directed against their conduct at certain points. Hence the members of each group tend to appear, at least in part, as varieties of one species; the radical differences of the two species are emphasized in broad, hard strokes; and the two are set in conflict, almost as if Shakespeare, like Empedocles, were regarding Love and Hate as two ultimate forces in the universe.

The presence in *King Lear* of so large a number of characters in whom love or self-seeking is so extreme has another effect. They do not merely inspire in us emotions of unusual strength, but they also stir the intellect to wonder and speculation. How can there be such men and women? we ask ourselves. How comes it that humanity can take such absolutely opposite forms? And, in particular, to what omission of elements which should be present in human nature, or, if there is no omission, to what distortion of these elements is it due that such beings as some of these come to exist? This is a question which Iago (and perhaps no previous creation of Shakespeare's) forces us to perhaps ask, but in *King Lear* it is provoked again and again. And more, it seems to us that the author himself is asking this question: "Then let them anatomize Regan, see what breeds about her heart. Is there any cause in nature that makes these hard hearts?"—the strain of thought which appears here seems to be present to some degree throughout the play. We seem to trace the tendency which, a few years later, produced Ariel and Caliban, the tendency of imagination to analyze and abstract, to decompose human nature into its constituent factors, and then to construct beings in whom one or more of these factors is absent or atrophied or only incipient. This, of course, is a tendency which produces symbols, allegories, personifications of qualities, and abstract ideas; and we are accustomed to think it quite foreign to Shakespeare's genius, which was in the highest degree concrete. No doubt in the main we are right here; but it is hazardous to set limits to that genius. The Sonnets, if nothing else, may show us how easy it was to Shakespeare's mind to move in a world of "Platonic" ideas; and while it would be going too far to suggest that he was employing conscious symbolism or allegory in *King Lear*, it does appear to disclose a mode of imagination not so very far removed from the mode with which, we must remember, Shakespeare was perfectly familiar in Morality plays and in the *Fairy Queen*.

This same tendency shows itself in *King Lear* in other forms. To it is due the idea of monstrosity—of beings, actions, states of mind, which appear not only abnormal but absolutely contrary to nature; an idea, which, of course, is common enough in Shakespeare, but appears with unusual frequency in *King Lear*, for instance in the lines:

> Ingratitude, thou marble-hearted fiend,
> More hideous when thou show'st thee in a child
> Than a sea-monster! (1.4.267–68)

Or in the exclamation,

> Filial ingratitude!
> Is it not as this mouth should tear this hand
> For lifting food to't? (3.4.14–16)

It appears in another shape in that most vivid passage where Albany, as he looks at the face which had bewitched him, now distorted with dreadful passions, suddenly sees it in a new light and exclaims in horror:

Thou changed and self-cover'd thing, for shame,
Bemonster not thy feature. Were't my fitness
To let these hands obey my blood,
They are apt enough to dislocate and tear
Thy flesh and bones: howe'er thou art a fiend,
A woman's shape doth shield thee. (4.2.62–67)

It appears once more in that exclamation of Kent's, as he listens to the description of Cordelia's grief:

It is the stars,
The stars above us, govern our conditions;
Else one self mate and mate could not beget
Such different issues. (4.3.33–36)

(This is not the only sign that Shakespeare had been musing over heredity, and wondering how it comes about that the composition of two strains of blood or two parent souls can produce such astonishingly different products.)

This mode of thought is responsible, lastly, for a very striking characteristic of *King Lear*—one in which it has no parallel except *Timon*—the incessant references to the lower animals and man's likeness to them. These references are scattered broadcast through the whole play as though Shakespeare's mind were so busy with the subject that he could hardly write a page without some allusion to it. The dog, the horse, the cow, the sheep, the hog, the lion, the bear, the wolf, the fox, the monkey, the polecat, the civet cat, the pelican, the owl, the crow, the chough, the wren, the fly, the butterfly, the rat, the mouse, the frog, the tadpole, the wall newt, the water newt, the worm—I am sure I cannot have completed the list, and some of them are mentioned again and again. Often, of course, and especially in the talk of Edgar as the Bedlam, they have no symbolical meaning; but not seldom, even in his talk, they are expressly referred to for their typical qualities—"hog in sloth, fox in stealth, wolf in greediness, dog in madness, lion in prey." "The fitchew nor the soiled horse goes to't with a more riotous appetite." Sometimes a person in the drama is compared, openly or implicitly, with one of them. Goneril is a kite: her ingratitude has a serpent's tooth: she has struck her father most serpentlike upon the very heart: her visage is wolfish: she has tied sharp-toothed unkindness like a vulture on her father's breast: for her husband she is a gilded serpent: to Gloster her cruelty seems to have the fangs of a boar. She and Regan are dog-hearted: they are tigers, not daughters: each is an adder to the other: the flesh of each is covered with the fell of a beast. Oswald is a mongrel, and the son and heir of a mongrel: duckling to everyone in power, he is a wagtail: white with fear, he is a goose. Gloster, for Regan, is an ingrateful fox: Albany, for his wife, has a cowish spirit and is milk-liver'd: when Edgar as the Bedlam first appeared to Lear he made him think a man a worm. As we read, the souls of all the beasts in turn seem to us to have entered the bodies of these mortals; horrible in their venom, savagery, lust, deceitfulness, sloth, cruelty, filthiness; miserable in their feebleness, nakedness, defenselessness, blindness; and man, "consider him well" is even what they are. Shakespeare, to whom the idea of the transmigration of souls was familiar and had once been material for jest,[1] seems to have been brooding on humanity, in the light of it. It is remarkable,

[1] E.g., in *As You Like It*, 3.2.187: "I was never so berhymed since Pythagoras' time, that I was an Irish rat, which I can hardly remember"; *Twelfth Night*, 4.2.55: "*Clown*. What is the opinion of Pythagoras concerning wild fowl? *Mal*. That the soul of our grandam might haply inhabit a bird. *Clown*. What thinkest thou of his opinion? *Mal*. I think nobly of the soul, and no way approve his opinion." But earlier comes a passage that reminds us of *King Lear*, *Merchant of Venice*, 4.1.128:

> O be thou damn'd, inexecrable dog!
> And for thy life let justice be accused.
> Thou almost makest me waver in my faith
> To hold opinion with Pythagoras,
> That souls of animals infuse themselves
> Into the trunks of men: thy currish spirit
> Govern'd a wolf, who, hang'd for human slaughter,
> Even from the gallows did his fell soul fleet,
> And, whilst thou lay'st in thy unhallow'd dam,
> Infused itself in thee; for thy desires
> Are wolvish, bloody, starv'd and ravenous.

and somewhat sad, that he seems to find none of man's better qualities in the world of the brutes (though he might well have found the prototype of the selfless love of Kent and Cordelia in the dog whom he so habitually maligns); but he seems to have been asking himself whether that which he loathes in man may not be due to some strange wrenching of this frame of things, through which the lower animals' souls have found a lodgment in human forms, and there found—to the horror and confusion of the thinking mind—brains to forge, tongues to speak, and hands to act, enormities which no mere brute can conceive or execute. He shows us in *King Lear* these terrible forces bursting into monstrous life and flinging themselves upon those human beings who are weak and defenseless, partly from old age, but partly because they *are* human and lack the dreadful undivided energy of the beast. And the only comfort he might seem to hold out to us is the prospect that at least this bestial race, strong only where it is vile, cannot endure: though stars and gods are powerless, or careless, or empty dreams, yet there must be an end of this horrible world:

> It will come;
> Humanity must perforce prey on itself
> Like monsters of the deep. (4.2.48–50)

The influence of all this on imagination as we read *King Lear* is very great; and it combines with other influences to convey to us, not in the form of distinct ideas but in the manner proper to poetry, the wider or universal significance of the spectacle presented to the inward eye. But the effect of theatrical exhibition is precisely the reverse. There the poetic atmosphere is dissipated; the meaning of the very words which create it passes half-realized; in obedience to the tyranny of the eye we conceive the characters as mere particular men and women; and all that mass of vague suggestion, if it enters the mind at all, appears in the shape of an allegory which we immediately reject. A similar conflict between imagination and sense will be found if we consider the dramatic center of the whole tragedy, the Storm-scenes. The temptation of Othello and the scene of Duncan's murder may lose upon the stage, but they do not lose their essence, and they gain as well as lose. The Storm-scenes in *King Lear* gain nothing and their very essence is destroyed. It is comparatively a small thing that the theatrical storm, not to drown the dialogue, must be silent whenever a human being wishes to speak, and is wretchedly inferior to many a storm we have witnessed. Nor is it simply that, as Lamb observed, the corporal presence of Lear, "an old man tottering about the stage with a walking stick", disturbs and depresses that sense of the greatness of his mind which fills the imagination. There is further reason, which is not expressed, but still emerges, in these words of Lamb's: "the explosions of his passion are terrible as a volcano: they are storms turning up and disclosing to the bottom that sea, his mind, with all its vast riches." Yes, "they are *storms*." For imagination, that is to say, the explosions of Lear's passion, and the bursts of rain and thunder, are not, what for the senses they must be, two things, but manifestations of one thing. It is the powers of the tormented soul that we hear and see in the "groans of roaring wind and rain" and the "sheets of fire"; and they that, at intervals almost more overwhelming, sink back into darkness and silence. Nor yet is even this all; but, as those incessant references to wolf and tiger made us see humanity "reeling back into the beast" and ravening against itself, so in the storm we seem to see Nature herself convulsed by the same horrible passions; the "common mother",

> Whose womb unmeasureable and infinite breast
> Teems and feeds all; (*Timon of Athens*, 4.3.179–80)

turning on her children to complete the ruin they have wrought upon themselves. Surely something not less, but much more, than these helpless words convey is what comes to us in these astounding scenes; and if, translated thus into the language of prose, it becomes confused and inconsistent, the reason is simply that it itself is poetry, and such poetry as cannot be transferred to the space behind the footlights, but has its being only in imagination. Here then is Shakespeare at his very greatest, but not the mere dramatist Shakespeare.

And now we may say this also of the catastrophe, which we found questionable from the strictly dramatic point of view. Its purpose is not merely dramatic. This sudden blow out of the darkness, which seems so far from inevitable, and which strikes down our reviving hopes for the victims of so much cruelty, seems now only what we might have expected in a world so wild and monstrous. It is as if Shakespeare said to us: "Did you think weakness and innocence have any chance here? Were you beginning to dream that? I will show you it is not so."

I come to a last point. As we contemplate this world, the question presses on us, What can be the ultimate power that moves it, that excites that gigantic war and waste, or, perhaps, that suffers them and overrules them? And in *King Lear* this question is not left to *us* to ask, it is raised by the characters themselves. References to religious or irreligious beliefs and feelings are more frequent than is usual in Shakespeare's tragedies, as frequent perhaps as in his final plays. He introduces characteristic differences in the language of the different persons about fortune or the stars or the gods, and shows how the question What rules the world? is forced upon their minds. They answer it in their turn: Kent, for instance:

> It is the stars,
> The stars above us, govern our condition: (4.3.33–34)

Edmund:

> Thou, nature, art my goddess; to thy law
> My services are bound: (1.2.1–2)

and again,

> This is the excellent foppery of the world, that, when we are sick in fortune—often the surfeits of our own behavior—we make guilty of our disasters the sun, the moon and the stars; as if we were villains by necessity, fools by heavenly compulsion,

... and all that we are evil in by a divine thrusting on: (128–136)

Gloster:

> As flies to wanton boys, are we to the gods,
> They kill us for their sport; (4.1.36–37)

Edgar:

> Think that the clearest gods, who make them honours
> Of men's impossibilities, have preserved thee. (4.6.73–74)

Here we have four distinct theories of the nature of the ruling power. And besides this, in such of the characters as have any belief in gods who love good and hate evil, the spectacle of triumphant injustice or cruelty provokes questionings like those of Job, or else the thought, often repeated, of divine retribution. To Lear at one moment the storm seems the messenger of heaven:

> Let the great gods,
> That keep this dreadful pother o'er our heads,
> Find out their enemies now. Tremble, thou wretch,
> That hast within thee undivulged crimes.... (3.2.49–52)

At another moment those habitual miseries of the poor, of which he has taken too little account, seem to him to accuse the gods of injustice:

> Take physic, pomp;
> Expose thyself to feel what wretches feel,
> That though mayst shake the superflux to them
> And show the heavens more just; (3.4.33–36)

and Gloster has almost the same thought (4.1.67 ff.). Gloster again, thinking of the cruelty of Lear's daughters, breaks out,

> but I shall see
> The winged vengeance overtake such children. (3.7.66–67)

The servants who have witnessed the blinding of Gloster by Cornwall and Regan, cannot believe that cruelty so atrocious will pass unpunished. One cries,

> I'll never care what wickedness I do,
> If this man come to good; (100–101)

and another,

> if she live long,
> And in the end meet the old course of death,
> Women will all turn monsters. (101–103)

Albany greets the news of Cornwall's death with the exclamation,

> This shows you are above,
> You justicers, that these our nether crimes
> So speedily can venge; (4.2.78–80)

and the news of the deaths of the sisters with the words,

> This judgment of the heavens, that makes us tremble,
> Touches us not with pity. (5.3.233–34)

Edgar, speaking to Edmund of their father, declares

> The gods are just, and of our pleasant vices
> Make instruments to plague us, (173–74)

and Edmund himself assents. Almost throughout the latter half of the drama we note in most of the better characters a preoccupation with the question of the ultimate power, and a passionate need to explain by reference to it what otherwise would drive them to despair. And the influence of this preoccupation and need joins with other influences in affecting the imagination, and in causing it to receive from *King Lear* an impression which is at least as near of kin to the *Divine Comedy* as to *Othello*.

For Dante that which is recorded in the *Divine Comedy* was the justice and love of God. What did *King Lear* record for Shakespeare? Something, it would seem, very different. This is certainly the most terrible picture that Shakespeare painted of the world. In no other of his tragedies does humanity appear more pitiably infirm or more hopelessly bad. What is Iago's malignity against an envied stranger compared with the cruelty of the son of Gloster and the daughters of Lear? What are the sufferings of a strong man like Othello to those of helpless age? Much too that we have already observed—the repetition of the main theme in that of the underplot, the comparisons of man with the most wretched and the most horrible of the beasts, the impression of Nature's hostility to him, the irony of the unexpected catastrophe—these, with much else, seem even to indicate an intention to show things at their worst, and to return the sternest of replies to that question of the ultimate power and those appeals for retribution. Is it an accident, for example, that Lear's first appeal to something beyond the earth,

> O heavens,
> If you do love old men, if your sweet sway
> Allow obedience, if yourselves are old,
> Make it your cause: (2.4.188–91)

is immediately answered by the iron voices of his daughters, raising by turns the condition on which they will give him a humiliating harborage; or that his second appeal, heart-rending in its piteousness,

> You see me here, you gods, a poor old man,
> As full of grief as age; wretched in both: (271–72)

is immediately answered from the heavens by the sound of the breaking storm? Albany and Edgar may moralize the divine justice as they will, but how, in the face of all that we see, shall we believe that they speak Shakespeare's mind? Is not his mind rather expressed in the bitter contrast between their faith and the events we witness, or in the scornful rebuke of those who take upon them the mystery of things as if they were God's spies? Is it not Shakespeare's judgment on his kind that we hear in Lear's appeal,

And thou, all-shaking thunder,
Smite flat the thick rotundity o' the world!
Crack nature's moulds, all germens spill at once,
That make ingrateful man! (3.2.6–9)

and Shakespeare's judgment on the worth of existence that we hear in Lear's agonized cry, "No, no, no life!"?

Beyond doubt, I think, some such feelings as these possess us, and, if we follow Shakespeare, ought to possess us, from time to time as we read *King Lear*. And some readers will go further and maintain that this is also the ultimate and total impression left by the tragedy. *King Lear* has been held to be profoundly "pessimistic" in the full meaning of that word—the record of a time when contempt and loathing for his kind had overmastered the poet's soul, and in despair he pronounced man's life to be simply hateful and hideous. And if we exclude the biographical part of this view, the rest may claim some support even from the greatest of Shakespearean critics since the days of Coleridge, Hazlitt, and Lamb. Mr. Swinburne, after observing that *King Lear* is "by far the most Aeschylean" of Shakespeare's works, proceeds thus:

"But in one main point it differs radically from the work and the spirit of Aeschylus. Its fatalism is of a darker and harder nature. To Prometheus the fetters of the lord and enemy of mankind were bitter; upon Orestes the hand of heaven was laid too heavily to bear; yet in the not utterly infinite or everlasting distance we see beyond them the promise of the morning on which mystery and justice shall be made one; when righteousness and omnipotence at last shall kiss each other. But on the horizon of Shakespeare's tragic fatalism we see no such twilight of atonement, such pledge of reconciliation as this. Requital, redemption, amends, equity, explanation, pity and mercy, are words without a meaning here.

As flies to wanton boys are we to the gods;
They kill us for their sport. (4.1.36–37)

Here is no need of the Eumenides, children of Night everlasting; for here is very Night herself.

"The words just cited are not casual or episodical; they strike the keynote of the whole poem, lay the keystone of the whole arch of thought. There is no contest of conflicting forces, no judgment so much as by casting of lots: far less is there any light of heavenly harmony or of heavenly wisdom, of Apollo or Athene from above. We have heard much and often from theologians of the light of revelation: and some such thing indeed we find in Aeschylus; but the darkness of revelation is here."[2]

It is hard to refuse assent to these eloquent words, for they express in the language of a poet what we feel at times in reading *King Lear* but cannot express. But do they represent the total and final impression produced by the play? If they do, this impression, so far as the substance of the drama is concerned (and nothing else is in question here), must, it would seem, be one composed almost wholly of painful feelings—utter depression, or indignant rebellion, or appalled despair. And that would surely be strange. For *King Lear* is admittedly one of the world's greatest poems, and yet there is surely no other of these poems which produces on the whole this effect, and we regard it as a very serious flaw in any considerable work of art that this should be its ultimate effect. So that Mr. Swinburne's description, if taken as a final, and any description of *King Lear* as "pessimistic" in the proper sense of that word, would imply a criticism which is not intended, and which would make it difficult to leave the work in the position almost universally assigned to it.

But in fact these descriptions, like most of the remarks made on *King Lear* in the present lecture, emphasize only certain aspects of the play and certain elements in the total impression; and in that impression the effect of these aspects, though far from being lost, is modified by that of others. I do not mean that the final effect resembles that of the *Divine Comedy* or

[2] *A Study of Shakespeare* (1880), pp. 171, 172.

the *Oresteia:* how should it, when the first of these can be called by its author a "Comedy", and when the second, ending (as doubtless the *Prometheus* trilogy also ended) with a solution, is not in the Shakespearean sense a tragedy at all? Nor do I mean that *King Lear* contains a revelation of righteous omnipotence or heavenly harmony, or even a promise of the reconciliation of mystery and justice. But then, as we saw, neither do Shakespeare's other tragedies contain these things. Any theological interpretation of the world on the author's part is excluded from them, and their effect would be disordered or destroyed equally by the ideas of righteous or of unrighteous omnipotence. Nor, in reading them, do we think of "justice" or "equity" in the sense of a strict requital or such an adjustment of merit and prosperity as our moral sense is said to demand; and there never was vainer labor than that of critics who try to make out that the persons in these dramas meet with "justice" or their "deserts". But, on the other hand, man is not represented in these tragedies as the mere plaything of a blind or capricious power, suffering woes which have no relation to his character and actions; nor is the world represented as given over to darkness. And in these respects *King Lear*, though the most terrible of these works, does not differ in essence from the rest. Its keynote is surely to be heard neither in the words wrung from Gloster in his anguish, nor in Edgar's words "the gods are just". Its final and total result is one in which pity and terror, carried perhaps to the extreme limits of art, are so blended with a sense of law and beauty that we feel at last, not depression and much less despair, but a consciousness of greatness in pain, and of solemnity in the mystery we cannot fathom. . . .

But there is another aspect of Lear's story, the influence of which modifies, in a way quite different and more peculiar to this tragedy, the impressions called pessimistic and even this impression of law. There is nothing more noble and beautiful in literature than Shakespeare's exposition of the effect of suffering in reviving the greatness and eliciting the sweetness of Lear's nature. The occasional recurrence, during his madness, of autocratic impatience or of desire for revenge serves only to heighten this effect, and the moments when his insanity becomes merely infinitely piteous do not weaken it. The old King who in pleading with his daughters feels so intensely his own humiliation and their horrible ingratitude, and who yet, at fourscore and upward, constrains himself to practice a self-control and patience so many years disused; who out of old affection for his Fool, and in repentance for his injustice to the Fool's beloved mistress, tolerates incessant and cutting reminders of his own folly and wrong; in whom the rage of the storm awakes a power and a poetic grandeur surpassing even that of Othello's anguish; who comes in his affliction to think of others first, and to seek, in tender solicitude for his poor boy, the shelter he scorns for his own bare head; who learns to feel and to pray for the miserable and houseless poor, to discern the falseness of flattery and the brutality of authority, and to pierce below the differences of rank and raiment to the common humanity beneath; whose sight is so purged by scalding tears that it sees at last how power and place and all things in the world are vanity except love; who tastes in his last hours the extremes both of love's rapture and of its agony, but could never, if he lived on or lived again, care a jot for aught beside—there is no figure, surely, in the world of poetry at once so grand, so pathetic, and so beautiful as his. Well, but Lear owes the whole of this to those sufferings which made us doubt whether life were not simply evil, and men like the flies which wanton boys torture for their sport. Should we not be at least as near the truth if we called this poem *The Redemption of King Lear*, and declared that the business of "the gods" with him was neither to torment him, nor to teach him a "noble anger", but to lead him to attain through apparently hopeless failure the very end and aim of life? One can believe that Shakespeare had been tempted at times to feel misanthropy and despair, but it is quite impossible that he can have been mastered by such feelings at the time when he produced this conception....

... Lear's insanity, which destroys the coherence, also reduces the poetry of his imagination. What it stimulates is that power of moral perception and reflection which had already been quickened by his sufferings. This, however partial and however disconnectedly used, first appears, quite soon after the insanity has declared itself, in the idea that the naked beggar represents truth and reality, in contrast with those conventions, flatteries, and corruptions of the great world, by which Lear has so long been deceived and will never be deceived again....

... *King Lear* ... is the tragedy in which evil is shown in the greatest abundance; and the evil characters are peculiarly repellent from their hard savagery and because so little good is mingled with their evil. The effect is therefore more startling than elsewhere; it is even appalling. But in substance it is the same as elsewhere....

On the one hand we see a world which generates terrible evil in profusion. Further, the beings in whom this evil appears at its strongest are able, to a certain extent, to thrive. They are not unhappy, and they have power to spread misery and destruction around them. All this is undeniable fact.

On the other hand this evil is *merely* destructive: it founds nothing, and seems capable of existing only on foundations laid by its opposite. It is also self-destructive.... These ... are undeniable facts; and in face of them, it seems odd to describe *King Lear* as "a play in which the wicked prosper" (Johnson).

Thus the world in which evil appears seems to be at heart unfriendly to it. And this impression is confirmed by the fact that the convulsion of this world is due to evil, mainly in the worst forms here considered, partly in the milder forms which we call the errors or defects of the better characters. Good, in the wildest sense, seems thus to be the principle of life and health in the world; evil, at least in these worst forms, to be a poison. The world reacts against it violently, and, in the struggle to expel it, is driven to devastate itself.

If we ask why the world should generate that which convulses and wastes it, the tragedy gives no answer, and we are trying to go beyond tragedy in seeking one. But the world, in this tragic picture, *is* convulsed by evil, and rejects it.

. . . I might almost say that the "moral" of *King Lear* is presented in the irony of this collocation:

> *Albany*. The gods defend her!
> *Enter Lear with Cordelia dead in his arms*. (5.3.258)

The "gods", it seems, do *not* show their approval by "defending" their own from adversity or death, or by giving them power and prosperity. These, on the contrary, are worthless, or worse; it is not on them, but on the renunciation of them, that the gods throw incense. They breed lust, pride, hardness of heart, the insolence of office, cruelty, scorn, hypocrisy, contention, war, murder, self-destruction. The whole story beats this indictment of prosperity into the brain. Lear's great speeches in his madness proclaim it like the curses of Timon on life and man. But here, as in *Timon*, the poor and humble are, almost without exception, sound and sweet at heart, faithful and pitiful. And here adversity, to the blessed spirit, is blessed. It wins fragrance from the crushed flower. It melts in aged hearts sympathies which prosperity had frozen. It purges the soul's sight by blinding that of the eyes.[3] Throughout that stupendous Third Act the good are seen growing better through suffering, and the bad worse through success. The warm castle is a room in hell, the storm-swept heath a sanctuary. The judgment of this world is a lie; its goods, which we covet, corrupt us; its ills, which break our bodies, set our souls free;

> Our means secure us, and our mere defects
> Prove our commodities. (4.1.20–21)

Let us renounce the world, hate it, and lose it gladly. The only real thing in it is the soul, with its courage, patience, devotion. And nothing outward can touch that.

This, if we like to use the word, is Shakespeare's "pessimism" in *King Lear*. . . .

[3] "I stumbled when I saw", says Gloster.

Contemporary Criticism

King Lear on Film

James Bemis
California Political Review

Shakespeare's plays, it should be noted, were written to be seen and heard. Thus, it is important for students of Shakespeare not only to read these great plays, but also to see them performed. Fortunately, the performances of some of our greatest actors are on film. Their interpretation of Shakespeare's characters can reveal a great deal to the discerning student, deepening their enjoyment of any play.

When reading, our perception of the story's elements—plot, dialogue, characters, theme, etc.—is limited by our own imagination and experience. On the other hand, seeing a play performed well can increase our enjoyment and understanding of the story and characters because both become less abstract and more tangible—more lifelike, if you will—making it easier for the mind to perceive and comprehend. Viewing a performance adds an important physical dimension to a dramatic work.

Each actor and actress brings a unique set of physical and mental attributes to a role. If an actor is young and athletic, for example, these qualities are manifest in the character portrayed. This may improve or, perhaps, detract from one's appreciation of the role. Conversely, a more mature actor brings different physical characteristics and, again, this may either enhance or diminish the performance. The point is obvious: when you see a play performed, part of your perception of the characters is influenced by the abilities and physical qualities of the actors or actresses in the performance. This is one of the primary differences between viewing and reading a play.

Thus, an actor can bring out illuminating nuances easily overlooked by the casual reader. For example, when the great Laurence Olivier performed *King Lear* in 1984, he was ill with cancer.

Filming was halted on several occasions while he recuperated. Consequently, his Lear is an old, feeble, and yet expressive king, as Olivier's great acting vividly, some say exaggeratedly, portrayed the weakness and suffering endured by his character.

Conversely, Orson Welles was a young, vibrant thirty-eight-year-old actor when performing *King Lear* on television in 1953. Welles' Lear, then, is an energetic, proud, and forceful king, regal in bearing. That works fine for the first two acts when Lear exhibits these traits. Later in the play, though, Welles is less than credible as a frail, bewildered old man, traits that Olivier brought to the screen in abundance.

So, by studying different film versions of Shakespeare's plays, students can find distinction, depth, and richness in the manner actors and actresses approach their characters. Often, then, a greater understanding of Shakespeare's stories and characters results when seeing a play acted, particularly by an accomplished performer. This is not to denigrate the importance of reading these great works—reading can develop an ear for the poetry and familiarity with the stories, both supreme virtues in Shakespearean studies. But to achieve a fuller appreciation of the Bard, it is vital to see the plays performed also. Film is a marvelous means of doing this, although live performances remain more compelling and authentic than film.

Key Scenes in Understanding *Lear*

At its core, *King Lear* is a story about pride and redemptive suffering. As the play begins, the king has decided to abdicate his throne, preferring an "unburdened crawl toward death" to shouldering his royal duties. Splitting his kingdom in thirds, he intends giving one section to each of his daughters. First, though, each sibling must proclaim her love in a contest of extravagant flattery.

Lear's vanity proves to be his unraveling. Two insincere daughters, Goneril and Regan, compete to exalt the old man. Cordelia, his loyal and most beloved daughter, refuses to play along, saying she simply loves him according to "her bond", the natural love that a daughter owes her father, and when she marries, she'll give half her love to her husband. Enraged by her frankness, Lear disowns Cordelia. When his old friend the Earl of Kent protests, Lear banishes him from the kingdom upon pain of death. Thus, in one furious action, Lear casts out the two most loyal to him.

For the next four acts, Lear suffers humiliation, rejection, deprivation, madness, and great sorrow. Not until the play's final act does Lear find both happiness and wisdom, as he first reunites with, and then loses, his beloved Cordelia. In a magnificent soliloquy in Act 5, scene 3, a happy and humble Lear learns to endure, telling Cordelia, "Let's away to prison [and] ... sing like birds i' th' cage" (lines 8, 9). Thus, only after a great fall and tremendous suffering, the old man finally obtains wisdom and insight. Meanwhile, because of his irresponsible abdication, his kingdom descended from order into chaos, finally restoring order again under the virtuous Edgar, but only at great cost to the king's friends and subjects.

Shakespeare's Lear is a Promethean figure and is actually many characters in one: proud Lear, fierce Lear, bewildered Lear, mad Lear, sad Lear, feeble Lear, wise Lear, joyful Lear. In giving a complete performance, an actor must tackle all these Lears. Consequently, this is one of the theater's most demanding roles. In fact, few actors are capable of depicting all these Lears in a single staging.

Five scenes are critical in understanding Lear and are keys to evaluating any performance:

First, Act 1's opening scene, when Lear abdicates and splits his kingdom (the proud, arrogant Lear). Here, the king irresponsibly shirks his duties "intent / to shake all cares and business from our age, / Conferring them on younger strengths" (1.1.40–42). The haughty old fool lashes out at Cordelia and Kent for daring to tell the truth. In this scene, Lear is forceful, vain, and hot-tempered.

Second, the scenes on the heath in Act 3, scenes 2 and 4, when Lear rages and fantasizes (the mad Lear). The king, after being humiliated by Goneril and Regan in Act 2, is in "high rage" (2.4.294). Blustering against a wild storm, the king is like a mythic figure, challenging the gods of nature to do their worst: "Blow, winds, and crack your cheeks!" (3.2.1). At the same time, he is a pitiful, disgraced old man, "more sinned against than sinning" (3.2.59). But he has not entirely taken leave of his senses: he still recognizes his shivering, wet Fool and pulls him under his royal cloak, asking, "How dost, my boy? Art cold?" (3.2.68). The fires of charity are beginning to burn in the old king.

Third, the reconciliation scene in Act 4, scene 7, with Cordelia (the sad, contrite Lear) is one of the most moving moments in all literature, ranking with *The Iliad*'s great scene of Priam begging for the return of his son Hector's dead body from Achilles. In a tent, Lear, waking from a deep sleep, at first thinks he's in Purgatory.

> I am bound
> Upon a wheel of fire, that mine own tears
> Do scald like molten lead
> (4.7.46–48)

Slowly, he realizes where he is and, purged of his rage and bitterness, sorrowfully begs Cordelia's forgiveness.

Fourth, the scene where a captured Lear (the joyful Lear) and Cordelia are about to be imprisoned in Act 5, scene 3 is full of irony: although captured by the enemy, the king is content simply to be with his beloved daughter. To Cordelia's compassionate "For thee, oppressèd King, I am cast down" (5.3.5) Lear responds that no, they will go away to prison:

> So we'll live,
> And pray, and sing, and tell old tales, and laugh
> At gilded butterflies, and hear poor rogues
> Talk of court news; and we'll talk with them too,
> Who loses and who wins; who's in, who's out;
> And take upon's the mystery of things,
> As if we were God's spies.
> (lines 11–17)

In the unlikeliest of circumstances, Lear, enlightened by his travails, has finally found happiness.

Fifth, the final scene in Act 5, scene 3, when Lear enters, bearing Cordelia in his arms (the chastened, wiser Lear), is an incredibly difficult scene for both actors and audience. The great writer and Shakespearean critic Samuel Johnson was so shocked by Cordelia's death that for many years, "I know not whether I ever endured to read again the last scenes of the play till I undertook to revise them as editor." Lear's speeches here are incredibly emotional—"Howl, howl, howl, howl! (line 259), "Never, never, never, never, never" (line 310)—and there is every opportunity for overacting.

But the performance should temper Lear's obvious grief with the insight that he has finally, through his suffering, become wiser. He now values Cordelia more than himself, even his suffering (the chance that she might live after all "is a chance which does redeem all sorrows / That ever I have felt"—line 268), and recognizes and welcomes his loyal Kent ("Are you not Kent? ... You are welcome hither"—lines 284, 291). In many ways, this is one of theater's most demanding moments, and only the most skilled manage to perform it with suitable nuance.

Lear on Film—Six Performances

Fortunately, a number of great (and not so great) filmed performances of *King Lear* are easily available. Let's look at how the five key scenes in establishing Lear's character are handled in six films.

1. In 1953, the *Omnibus* television program broadcast a live performance of *King Lear*, starring Orson Welles, one of the most prodigious talents ever to work in Hollywood. Welles led the Mercury Theatre's famous 1938 broadcast version of "The War of the Worlds", which caused a nationwide panic. His first film, *Citizen Kane* (1941), is regarded by many as the best movie ever made.

Along the way, he directed and starred in films of a number of Shakespeare's plays, including *Macbeth*, *Othello*, *Chimes at*

Midnight (based on the *Henry IV* plays), and *Lear*. Welles appeared in the top-rated picture for both the American Film Institute (*Citizen Kane*) and British Film Institute (*The Third Man*). In 1975, he received the American Film Institute's Lifetime Achievement Award, and in 1984 the Directors Guild of America awarded him the D. W. Griffith Award, its highest honor.

When evaluating a live telecast, certain latitude must be given in recognition of the difficulties involved in both production and acting. Not surprisingly, then, by today's standards the *Omnibus* broadcast appears primitive and some of the staging crude. (For example, when Lear enters in the final scene bearing Cordelia's lifeless body, Welles appears to be dragging a giant rag doll.) Nevertheless, Welles' stature in the industry makes this a *Lear* that must be seen.

In the opening of Act 1, scene 1, Welles makes a vibrant, forceful Lear appear arrogant and brash. The unbridled pride leading to Lear's downfall is prominent here. Welles' magnificent voice and clear enunciation of Shakespeare's lines creates a scene that is a pleasure to watch. Unfortunately, to shorten the play, the important subplot featuring the Duke of Gloucester's sons, Edmund and Edgar, is eliminated. This has catastrophic consequences.

In Act 3, Welles' raging against the storm is the film's highlight. Welles' gargantuan figure dwarfs the other characters, and his Lear turns into the mythic figure Shakespeare intended, a lone man raging wildly against the overwhelming forces of nature.

Throughout his career, Welles, though extraordinarily gifted, often exhibited a tendency to overact. (In short, he was a ham.) This dooms his scenes in Acts 4 and 5. The reconciliation scene with Cordelia is not convincing, and Welles appears entirely too robust to be an old man "fourscore and upward" (4.7.61) for which the scene calls.

Likewise, the imprisonment scene with Cordelia strains credibility as Welles' overplaying steals Shakespeare's thunder. In the final scene, many of the best lines are edited out, and the staging is dreadful. As mentioned, when he enters bearing Cordelia, Welles appears to be dragging a giant rag doll. Furthermore, the deletion of the subplot lead to the wrong characters saying some of the play's most crucial lines. For instance, the mature Albany, rather than the heroic Edgar, says the play's final lines—"We that are young / Shall never see so much, nor live so long" (5.3.327–28)—although Shakespeare clearly intended this to spoken by someone in his youth.

2. Peter Brook's 1971 film version of *Lear* features the great English actor Paul Scofield, who played a legendary Lear in a long-running Broadway production. However, Brook turns *King Lear* into an existentialist drama, without an ounce of real humanity. In Brook's *Lear*, filmed in the cold, barren Danish landscape, Scofield is a frozen-faced, animal-like king. Actors move as if catatonic, and the film's 132 minutes seem more like 132 hours.

Perhaps existentialism was trendy in the early 1970s, but nowadays Brook's approach seems silly. Interestingly, this perspective on Lear was suggested by *Shakespeare, Our Contemporary*, a controversial book by Jan Kott. Kott puts forth the inane proposition that Shakespeare was one of us—not one of those backward medievals, but a real modern guy. Hence, Brook's version of *Lear* has fashionable roots. In keeping with this "progressive" theme, Scofield's portrayal of Lear is monotone, bleak, and exhausted. Unfortunately, staging the play as an existentialist drama ignores its obvious redemptive elements. So while this may be Brook's *Lear*, it certainly is not Shakespeare's.

A sense of coldness and savagery runs through the film, personified by Scofield's sometimes indecipherable voice, more like a brute's growl than human expression. The camera work tries to be impressionistic and symbolic, but instead only distracts and confuses. For example, when Lear is raging against the storm, the focus is blurred and the figures so obscure that much of the scene's great pathos is lost.

In Act 1, Lear barely seems awake and the rest of the cast seems comatose. In the claustrophobic hut serving as the king's court not a hint of order or majesty exists, although the scene is written to take place in a palace and the stage direction calls for sennets, coronets, and flourishes, indicating the presence of some sort of grandeur. It is difficult to recognize that anything momentous is happening as the king abdicates. Thus, Lear's ruin seems less the fall of a great man than the knocking over of a mumbling bully. From the outset, we feel no connection with any of the characters.

Act 3's scene on the heath is poorly staged and, with the intentionally blurred camera work, at times one cannot tell which characters are speaking. For all we know, it could be the Fool raging against the storm and taunting the gods, and not Lear. The difference is not trivial.

In perhaps the film's greatest flaw, Scofield's inexpressive countenance fails to convey Lear's progression from pride to madness, sorrow to joy, then wisdom. Because of this detachment, Lear's Act 4 reconciliation with Cordelia is emotionless, with no apparent bond created between Lear and his beloved daughter.

Consistent with the director's vision, during Act 5's imprisonment scene, when a joyful Lear and Cordelia go off to prison, the poignancy is missing. Next, a jarring scene of Cordelia being hanged is both graphic and gratuitous, undercutting the intended shock of Lear's final entrance, carrying "my poor fool". Lear's death scene here is heavily edited, difficult to understand, and utterly unconvincing. Rather than ending with Edgar's address to the next generation, the film concludes with a final shot of Lear's white head dissolving into nothingness. Brook's existentialism diminishes the emotional wallop of the final scene.

The essence of *King Lear* is simple: pride cometh before a fall, and it is through suffering that we gain wisdom, understanding, and, finally, hope. But in this film, Lear seems to have realized nothing from his tribulations. Without Lear learning from the misery, the play loses its core. Since the essence of existentialism is that life has no meaning anyway, its philosophy is entirely at odds with the story Shakespeare wrote.

As Lear says, "Nothing will come of nothing." And nothing is what Brook's film delivers.

3. In Joseph Papp's New York Shakespeare Festival 1974 performance of *King Lear*, James Earl Jones plays the king. Jones is an actor of extraordinary gifts: witness his powerful speech to Goneril in Act 1, in which he exclaims,

> How sharper than a serpent's tooth it is
> To have a thankless child.
> (1.4.295–96)

Filmed live, like Welles' *Lear*, the production is limited in its staging, most noticeably in the storm scene when the audience must imagine the howling wind and rain. A bigger drawback is a relatively weak cast—Rene Auberjonois is woefully miscast as Edgar, and Rosalind Cash and Ellen Holly, playing Goneril and Regan, seem far too amiable to be capable of committing the evil later performed by their characters.

In Act 1's opening scene, Jones portrays the arrogant and brash Lear with tremendous force. "Nothing. I have sworn. I am firm" (line 247), he bellows at Burgundy, and we believe him. He continues his strong performance through Act 2 and is at his enraged best when crossed by his two thankless daughters:

> No, you unnatural hags!
> I will have such revenge on you both.
> (2.4.277–78)

Act 3's scene on the heath is another tour de force for Jones as his great physical presence dominates the stage. Jones' powerful voice and commanding authority overcome the natural limitations of live performance, giving us a sense of how far this great king has fallen:

> O Regan, Goneril,
> Your old kind father, whose frank heart gave you all—
> O, that way madness lies; let me shun that.
> No more of that.
> (3.4.19–21)

But what about the feeble Lear, the weak Lear, the chastened Lear? Here Jones' enormous strength works against him. In Act 4's reconciliation scene, Jones is too robust to be credible as a "foolish, fond old man" (4.7.60). He still looks like he could wipe the floor with any of the younger actors. In Act 5's imprisonment scene, his joyous Lear works fine, although a stronger Cordelia would have improved the effectiveness. Jones' overacting (too much power, not enough poignancy) slightly undercuts Lear's death scene, but overall this solid production is carried off nicely upon Jones' sturdy back.

4. In the 1983 BBC/Time-Life Films version of *King Lear*, directed by Jonathan Miller, Michael Hordern makes a reliable, workmanlike Lear. He is forceful when he should be forceful, compassionate when he should be compassionate, sorrowful when he should be sorrowful. Hordern plays the king straight up, with no gloss. If his performance lacks the glorious high points of, say, Olivier's, this is as steady as it gets. For example, Olivier's Lear turns soft after the first act, while Hordern's Lear remains suitably fierce throughout the first and second acts until madness overtakes him at the beginning of Act 3. (Recall that through the second scene, the king is vibrant enough to hunt and ride with his knightly friends.)

In Act 1, Hordern is credible as a proud, arrogant king who decides to abdicate the throne but wants to keep the trappings of office. His anger at Cordelia's truthfulness is palpable. He growls persuasively,

> Better thou
> Hadst not been born than not t' have pleased me better.
> (1.1.235–36)

In Act 3's scene on the heath, though, Hordern's Lear lacks the required fierceness and misses the mythic quality evident with some of the bigger names.

Act 4's reconciliation scene and Act 5's imprisonment scene, the emotional touchstones of any performance, work fine in Hordern's experienced hands, with the reconciliation scene particularly moving. In the imprisonment scene, this production's dull Cordelia undercuts the mood a bit, but Hordern's woozy but happy Lear helps keep things together.

The final heart-wrenching scene of Lear entering with Cordelia in his arms is a high point, with Hordern's simple but effective depiction of a father's sorrow at the loss of a child. One complaint about this production is that Hordern lacks the majesty of a truly great King Lear. His Lear is all too human, more crusty than upper crust. But compared to the much larger flaws in other productions, this is a rather minor criticism. Overall, the BBC/Time Life rendering is a very solid effort.

5. Sir Laurence Olivier's superb performance as Lear in Michael Elliott's 1984 Emmy award-winning production ranks as the standard by which all others are judged. As mentioned, during filming, Olivier was suffering with cancer. In fact, work halted several times because the load proved too much for the great actor. A taxing role under the best of conditions, Olivier's illness nearly made the picture impossible to complete. Finally, the movie was shot in pieces over two months, providing Olivier time to recuperate between scenes.

Nevertheless, Olivier's performance is magnificent. A great physical actor, Olivier implies more by arching his eyebrows than most can say in an entire soliloquy. Olivier's illness meant his Lear accentuated, by necessity, the aged and feeble nature of the king. But there was just enough fire left in the old master's belly that he captured all the Lears in his last—and perhaps most glorious—film performance.

Olivier's reading was augmented by an excellent cast, including Diana Rigg as Regan, Dorothy Tutin as Goneril, Leo McKern as Gloucester, and, perhaps most memorably, John Hurt as the Fool. While many productions eliminate the Fool, director Elliott wisely not only preserves the role, but emphasizes this wonderful character. Hurt is marvelous, expertly rendering both the Fool's sarcasm and great love for his fallen sovereign and friend.

Colin Blakely, playing the Earl of Kent, deserves special mention. Kent is one of the great characters in all of literature: steadfastly loyal, plain-speaking, and courageous. Blakely plays Kent as straightforwardly and honorably as Shakespeare wrote the character, bringing an earthiness and doggedness to the role. These only add to Kent's already numerous virtues.

In Act 1's opening, Olivier's Lear lacks the arrogance and forcefulness one expects. However, the king's foolish pride is well conveyed. As mentioned, one criticism of Olivier's performance is that his Lear is feeble by Act 2, when the king is still capable of hunting and carousing with his rowdy knights, much to Goneril's chagrin. In Act 3, scenes 2 and 3, Lear's raging against the storm is muted as Olivier's strength seems to have run low.

But the later action in the hovel, when Lear is mad, is outstanding. The scene of the king praying for his lowly subjects, the "poor naked wretches, wheresoe'er you are / That bide the pelting of this pitiless storm. . . . O, I have ta'en / Too little care of this!" (3.4.28–29, 32–33) is played to perfection. Here, when the king has suffered sufficiently to empathize with the pain of others, is a glimpse that Lear's tribulations are having a redemptive effect.

In Act 4's reconciliation scene, Elliott's direction is as magnificent and touching as Olivier's great skills and emotional range are awe-inspiring. Further, Anna Calder-Marshall's Cordelia is wonderful, adding greatly to the pathos of the scene. When, to Lear's insistence that she, unlike her sisters, has reason to hate him, she answers, "No cause, no cause" (4.7.75), only true hearts of stone can remain unmoved.

Act 5's two crucial scenes are wonderfully performed. The imprisonment is set up beautifully, as the affection the audience has developed for both the king and Cordelia enhances the drama. Lear's death scene is glorious—Shakespearean acting at its best. The masterful Olivier, white-haired and frail, yet finally cognizant of his folly, is simply splendid, bringing the film to a magnificent climax.

6. The Royal National Theater's 1998 production of *King Lear* starring Ian Holm cannot quite make up its mind what it wants to be. Although characters charge around with swords, the action takes place mainly in the dark corridors of anonymous corporate offices, with the cast wearing space-age clothing. Apparently, this is an attempt to make the play seem

timeless. Instead, without grounding in time or place, it appears rootless, although Shakespeare took great pains to locate the play in pre-Christian Britain. Thus, director Richard Eyre betrays the author's intent from the very beginning. Further, the cast looks oh-so-modern. Lear's three daughters are nearly laughable in their smart pantsuit outfits, and Goneril and Regan look more like soccer moms than fiends from the deep.

Ian Holm is a fine actor, having given many wonderful performances in his long and distinguished career. But he plays Lear in perpetual anger, which is not called for by Shakespeare at all. Additionally, he lacks the stature to be a credible Lear, commanding more like a pit bull rather than a Great Dane. This shortcoming (no pun intended) makes Lear's fall something less than tragic. To paraphrase, the smaller they are, the softer they fall.

For instance, in Act 1's opening, Holm lacks the regal bearing necessary to carry off this important scene. His abdication seems forced, and the rest of the cast appears more interested in how they look than whether the old boy has finally lost it. On the other hand, in Act 3's scene on the heath, Holm is wonderful, brilliantly conveying Lear's madness and anger at the vile treatment at the hands of his daughters. Unfortunately, Michael Bryant's Fool seems older than Lear, thus undercutting the pathos of the scenes between them, particularly when the king recognizes the suffering of his "boy" and tries to comfort him from the stormy wind and rain.

In Act 4's reconciliation scene, it is essential that the audience feel affection for both Lear and Cordelia. However, Victoria Hamilton is a petulant, unlikable Cordelia, severely impacting the scene's effectiveness. Thus, instead of a touching father-daughter reunion, there is a sense of rivalry between two arrogant, headstrong characters.

Neither of the two critical Act 5 scenes works here, either. In the imprisonment scene, Lear and Cordelia are coldly distant toward each other, less like father and child than estranged spouses. What's worse, Holm's Lear doesn't seem to have learned anything through his suffering. In his death scene, several weird touches prove distracting. In Paul Rhys' hands, a wimpy Edgar—supposedly one of the play's heroes—is sneakier and more unlikable than the diabolical Edmund. (One almost roots for Edmund to win when the brothers duel.)

In a particularly unnerving moment, the dead bodies of Regan, Goneril, and Edmund are piled on a cart. When Lear enters, he is wearing bedroom slippers and pulling Cordelia's body on another cart (perhaps because the actress playing Cordelia is larger than Holm), looking like a crying brat pulling his Red Flyer instead of a king carrying his fallen offspring. What should be moving is instead confusing, and the audience, rather than feeling relief that order has been restored, is left wondering if normal life can ever be regained in a land of such strange creatures.

King Lear and "The Mystery of Things"

As mentioned, Lear's role is extremely demanding: it is not enough to be a strong presence like Welles or Jones, nor an elderly one like Scofield or Hordern, nor a forceful one like Holm. No, it takes all of these traits and more to play a complete Lear, virtuosity beyond the capability of nearly any actor, living or dead. Perhaps the closest we'll ever come to seeing a perfect performance of Lear is the one delivered by the great Sir Laurence Olivier in 1984—and even his was flawed.

Nevertheless, *King Lear* is one of Western civilization's greatest creations, a play so rich, so deep, and so profound that it comes closer than almost any other work to explaining the meaning of our existence. Although no one truly can do the play justice, actors will perform—and audiences will enjoy—this magnificent play, so long as minds can wonder, like Lear and Cordelia, about "the mystery of things".

The wise student, seeking to know himself and his world, can do no better than to drink deeply from Shakespeare's life-giving spring, experiencing his great artistry in forums as frequently and varied as possible. As Samuel Johnson said, "The man who knows his Shakespeare will find few surprises in this crowded world."

King Lear on Film—Six Performances

Year Produced	1953	1971	1974	1983	1984	1998
Director	Andrew McCullough	Peter Brook	Joseph Papp	Jonathan Miller	Michael Elliott	Richard Eyre
Lear	Orson Welles	Paul Scofield	James Earl Jones	Michael Hordern	Laurence Olivier	Ian Holm
Act 1, sc.1: Opening	Vibrant, forceful	Barely awake; cast seems catatonic	Jones plays with tremendous force	Solid, workmanlike	Olivier's Lear lacks arrogance and forcefulness but does convey foolish pride	Lack of regal bearing makes scene seem forced
Act 3, sc. 1 and 2: On the Heath	Welles' raging against the storm is film's highlight	Poorly staged; hard to make out which characters talking	Another tour de force, Jones commanding	Horden's Lear lacks fierceness of others'	Lear's raging is muted, but mad hovel scenes are outstanding	Film's best scene; Holm is wonderful here
Act 4, sc. 7: Reconciliation	Not credible; too robust	Emotionless; no connection between Lear and Cordelia	Lear too robust	Works fine; lacks brilliance but is moving	Magnificent, touching; Olivier's great skills played to perfection	Poor performance by actress playing Cordelia undercuts scene
Act 5, sc. 3: Imprisonment	Not convincing; Welles' overacting steals thunder	Difficult to hear; heavily edited	Jones fine, but Cordelia weak	Dull Cordelia undercuts scene slightly, but Horden's woozy Lear is fine	Set up beautifully; audience's love for both characters carries scene	None of characters likeable; Holm's Lear doesn't seem to have learned anything
Act 5, sc. 3: Lear's Death	Poorly staged; best lines edited out; Welles appears to be dragging a huge rag doll; deletion of subplot means wrong characters saying lines	Film's existentialism undercuts emotional wallop of final scene; view of Cordelia hanging is gratuitous	Jones overacts, but production solid	Excellent heart-wrenching scene of Lear, holding dead Cordelia	Glorious; Shakespearean acting at its best	Weird touches distract viewers: dead bodies on cart, Lear in slippers, unlikable Edgar
Overall Grade	C+	F	B–	B	A–	D+

Nature and Convention in *King Lear*[1]

Paul A. Cantor
University of Virginia

i

At the center of *King Lear*, the mad king has an extraordinary vision. Staring at the near-naked beggar, Tom o' Bedlam, in the midst of a raging storm, Lear sees all of humanity reduced to this bare level:

> Is man no more than this? Consider him well. Thou ow'st the worm no silk, the beast no hide, the sheep no wool, the cat no perfume. Ha! here's three on's are sophisticated. Thou art the thing itself: unaccommodated man is no more but such a poor, bare, forked animal as thou art. Off, off, you lendings! Come, unbutton here.
> (3.4.105–11)

Lear thinks that the way to get at man's essence is to reduce him to some kind of lowest common denominator, in particular, to strip away his clothing, symbolic of all the additions with which civilization tries to raise human beings above the level of beasts. Having undergone a profoundly disillusioning experience with his cruel daughters, Lear has learned to see through the appearances on which human beings conventionally pride themselves. Accordingly, he starts to divest himself of his clothing, to cast aside the customary trappings of his kingly status and thereby bring himself in line with the diminished image of humanity he sees embodied in Poor Tom. In an eerie anticipation of Rousseau, Lear believes that to uncover

[1] This essay was originally published under the same title in *Poets, Princes, & Private Citizens*, ed. Joseph M. Knippenberg and Peter Augustine Lawler (Lanham, Md.: Rowman and Littlefield, 1996), 213–33. For further development of my thoughts on *King Lear*, see my essay "*King Lear*: The Tragic Disjunction of Wisdom and Power", in *Shakespeare's Political Pageant: Essays in Politics & Literature*, ed. Joseph Alulis and Vickie Sullivan (Lanham, Md.: Rowman and Littlefield, 1996), 189–207.

human nature, one has to go back to man's origins; one arrives at a definition of man by finding the bare minimum one can still call human, and in that state a man is virtually indistinguishable from a beast.

Most modern interpretations of *King Lear* quote this passage, and many view it as expressing the deepest wisdom of the play. Lear's vision of the emptiness of human pretensions evidently strikes a responsive chord in our time. From the 1960s on, existentialist and absurdist productions of the play have stressed the reductive element in its vision. Hearing the word *nothing* echo throughout the early scenes, critics have interpreted the play as nihilistic, revealing the hollowness of human values, as if it were a kind of seventeenth-century *Waiting for Godot*.[2] Interpreters have assumed that Lear somehow speaks directly for Shakespeare in the passage about "unaccommodated man". The tough-mindedness of this vision serves to validate it for our iconoclastic age, raising Shakespeare in our esteem for the way he seems to share our ability to stare into an existential abyss without flinching.

Lear's vision of Poor Tom does seem to be a remarkable anticipation of modern ideas, and it is difficult not to give this passage a prominent place in any interpretation of the play. But before getting carried away by Lear's eloquence here, it is well to remember the at least equally moving words he later speaks over Cordelia's dead body:

> Why should a dog, a horse, a rat, have life,
> And thou no breath at all?
> (5.3.308–9)

Here Lear heartbreakingly insists on the difference between a human being and an animal, reminding us that Cordelia was once living proof that humanity can rise above the level of

[2] The classic absurdist interpretation of *King Lear* is Jan Kott's 1964 essay "King Lear or Endgame", in his *Shakespeare Our Contemporary*, trans. Boleslaw Taborski (Garden City, N.Y.: Anchor Books, 1966), 127–68. That this mode of interpretation is still in vogue is evidenced by Jagannath Chakravorty, *King Lear: Shakespeare's Existentialist Hero* (Calcutta: Avantgarde Press, 1990).

the beasts. In light of this later passage, Lear's vision of Poor Tom as the "thing itself" cannot represent the teaching of the play as a whole.

In fact, moments after viewing Tom as "unaccommodated man", Lear changes his mind about the figure. Asked to withdraw from the storm, Lear keeps insisting on consulting with Tom, only he now starts to refer to him in elevated terms as his "philosopher", and more specifically as a "learnèd Theban" and a "good Athenian" (3.4.157, 160, 183). From embodying the lowest in humanity, Tom suddenly comes to represent for Lear its highest potential. It says something about critics of *King Lear* that, drawn as they are to Lear's vision of man as beast, they almost entirely neglect his collateral vision in the very same scene of man as philosopher. It is in fact remarkable that critics almost all speak as if Lear had a single vision in this scene, confronting only the "forked animal" in man but not his capacity for wisdom. But in Act 3, scene 4, Shakespeare does not simply anticipate modern philosophy in its attempt to define man in terms of his origins; he also harks back to ancient philosophy, and, in particular, to Plato and Aristotle in their idea that the nature of a thing is revealed not in its lowest form, but in its perfection, in what it tends toward in its fullest development. That is why to define the nature of humanity, Plato and Aristotle always take into account our highest potential, above all, our capacity to philosophize.

Indeed, in a moment of imaginative daring that is remarkable even by his own sublime standards, in Act 3, scene 4 of *King Lear* Shakespeare stages a scene Plato presents as the highest achievement of humanity, the union of a philosopher and a king.[3] On the brink of madness, and hence free from customary ways of thinking, Lear seeks the advice of a man he views as some form of Greek sage:

> *Lear*. First let me talk with this philosopher.
> What is the cause of thunder?

[3] See Plato, *Republic*, 473d–e.

Kent. Good my lord, take his offer; go into th' house.
Lear. I'll talk a word with this same learnèd Theban.
What is your study?
Edgar How to prevent the fiend, and to kill vermin.
Lear. Let me ask you one word in private.
(3.4.157–63)

The stage is thus set for what might well be the most profound dialogue in all of Shakespeare's plays, a king and a philosopher enquiring into the principles that govern nature and into how those principles might be related to the curing of human ills. But Shakespeare tantalizingly denies us access to the most profound conversation in the central scene of his greatest play. Lear and his philosopher drift away from center stage, and whatever words they exchange are drowned out by the noise of the storm and Gloucester's conventional observations to the disguised Kent. Nevertheless, the very fact of their meeting points to a larger question raised by the play as a whole: What is the relation of wisdom and political power? Perhaps *King Lear* as a whole offers what 3.4 seems to deny us: a dialogue about philosophy and kingship.

The key to understanding 3.4 is thus to recognize the dual character of Lear's vision; he sees the disguised Edgar not just as Tom o' Bedlam but as the learnèd Theban as well. This pattern is repeated in Act 4. When the mad Lear encounters Gloucester, he once again articulates a vision of the bestial side of human nature, dwelling obsessively and almost pathologically on female sexuality and its corrupting tendencies. Critics often cite these passages as examples of the fullness of the wisdom Lear learns from his devastating experience. But they tend to forget that in the very next scene (4.7), Lear moves from his vision of the female body as a form of corruption to his transcendent vision of Cordelia as a spirit in all her purifying and redemptive power. Neither vision can by itself be taken as Shakespeare's last word on the question of human potential; interpreting the view of humanity articulated in *King*

Lear seems to require us to integrate the visions that remain fragmented in Lear's eyes.

As difficult as that task may be, I would like to make a start on such an interpretation by calling attention to Edgar, who seems to encapsulate in a single enigmatic figure the extremes of human possibility *King Lear* explores. Edgar begins the play as a conventional man, blind, for example, to the evil in his half-brother Edmund and unaware of his father's limitations. Throughout the play, Edgar is given to pious moralizing and platitudes and seems to represent a man firmly anchored in society and its customary opinions. Yet, forced, like Kent, into a kind of internal exile, Edgar miraculously bifurcates in Lear's vision into Poor Tom and the learnèd Theban, thereby revealing both the animal side of human nature and man's capacity to transcend the limits of his body in thought. What is torn asunder in Lear's mad imagination is somehow united in the strange figure of Edgar as both Tom o' Bedlam and the learnèd Theban. The complex figure of Edgar poses the fundamental question of *King Lear*: How can humanity encompass the range of possibilities from the "bare, forked animal" to the "noble philosopher"? In her own vulgar way, Goneril manages to state the central issue of *King Lear*: "O, the difference of man and man!" (4.2.26). I want to analyze how *King Lear* explores the mystery of human difference, to show how at first human differences are obscured and occluded in the play, and then how human differences become revealed and clarified.

ii

King Lear begins with the kingdom in a relatively settled state, with Lear firmly in control and presenting a plan to prevent future turmoil. Under these stable political conditions, the extreme differences among human beings have tended to be obscured or even suppressed. To be sure, it is not a matter of no differences whatsoever among human beings being evident. Some critics talk about Lear as if he were simply a senile old man at the beginning of the play, blind to the difference between Cordelia on the one hand and Goneril and Regan on the other.[4] In fact, Lear is reasonably clear-headed about the contrasting natures of his daughters. Shakespeare supplies several indications that Lear clearly prefers Cordelia to his other daughters and has in fact pinned his hopes for a secure future on his being allied with her.[5] But if Lear is aware of something wrong in Goneril and Regan, he is certainly blind to the depths of evil lurking in their souls. Indeed, up to this point, he evidently has no reason to suspect how evil they are. As long as Lear rules securely, he keeps the evil forces in his kingdom in check; they are unwilling to show their true faces out of fear of his power to punish them. The successful political regime tends to have a moderating effect, concentrating on the middle range of humanity and leveling out the extremes. The regime works to suppress the animal urges in humanity and to keep evil impulses in check (it also, as we shall see, works to limit the higher impulses). It is important to realize that the obscuring of the differences among human beings is somehow endemic to political life as presented in the play and is not just the result of faulty vision on the part of individual characters.

The political neglect of differences is illustrated in the opening lines of the play:

> *Kent.* I thought the King had more affected the Duke of Albany than Cornwall.
> *Gloucester.* It did always seem so to us; but now, in the division of the kingdom, it appears not which of the dukes he values most, for equalities are so weighed that curiosity in neither can make choice of either's moiety.
> (1.1.1–7)

Here we see that Lear was not blind to the difference between the Duke of Albany and the Duke of Cornwall, and, as events

[4] Kott makes explicit what many critics assume when he says of Lear: "He does not see or understand anything. . . . Lear is ridiculous, naive and stupid" (Kott, *Shakespeare*, p. 130).

[5] See, for example, 1.1.82–86, 123–24, 194–97, 213–16, 242–44.

prove, he was quite right to prefer the former to the latter. But there are times in public life when a ruler must, for valid political reasons, put personal preferences aside and treat people equally. As quickly as these opening lines go by, they are crucial to understanding the play. Most critics assume that Lear is guilty of acting according to whim in the opening scene, of placing his private preferences above the public good. But Shakespeare supplies the brief opening conversation between Kent and Gloucester to indicate that just the opposite is the case. Though in the first scene Lear ends up on the spur of the moment improvising an ill-conceived plan for dividing the kingdom, he enters the scene with a plan all drawn up, the details of which are known to his closest advisors, who do not seem to object to it, as well as to other concerned parties, such as the Duke of Burgundy.[6] And what strikes Kent and Gloucester is precisely the evenhandedness of the plan, the fact that Lear has ignored his personal preferences, presumably for the sake of achieving some form of balance of power between the dukes.

The opening lines of *King Lear* point to the pattern that develops in the play as a whole. The king's plan initially obscures his longstanding awareness of the difference between

[6] For an imaginative attempt to tease out the details of Lear's original plan, see Harry V. Jaffa, "The Limits of Politics: *King Lear*, Act I, scene i", in Allan Bloom, *Shakespeare's Politics* (New York: Basic Books, 1964), pp. 113–45. Briefly stated, Jaffa's thesis is that the intent of Lear's original plan was to give Cordelia the bulk of his kingdom (the middle portion), while giving Goneril the extreme northern and Regan the extreme southern portion, regions their husbands already controlled as feudal lords. Lear intends to marry Cordelia to the Duke of Burgundy, a foreign power strong enough to give her support but not strong enough to conquer and absorb Britain (as the King of France might). Jaffa is the only critic of the play to have worked out the details of Lear's original plan, but he was not the first to note that Lear enters 1.1 with a division of the kingdom already worked out (after all, maps have been drawn up). See Samuel Taylor Coleridge, *Shakespearean Criticism*, ed. Thomas Middleton Raysor (London: J. M. Dent, 1960), pp. 49–50; A. C. Bradley, *Shakespearean Tragedy* (1904; repr., New York: Meridian Books, 1955), pp. 202–3; and Kenneth Muir, *Shakespeare: King Lear* (Harmondsworth: Penguin, 1986), 32, 55. For a further elaboration of Jaffa's analysis of Lear's plan, see David Lowenthal, "*King Lear*", *Interpretation* 21 (1994): 393–96.

Albany and Cornwall, but the action of the play works to bring out how deep the difference between the two dukes really is. Once Lear's hold on power is loosened, the evil nature of Cornwall is free to emerge. In Lear's treatment of the two dukes, we begin to see how the conventional order tends to obscure the natural order; conventional political considerations may sometimes dictate that a king ignore his knowledge of his subjects' differing natures. Indeed, the problem of nature and convention is at the heart of *King Lear*.

Lear's central problem is that he cannot distinguish what is natural from what is conventional in his rule. In the course of his many years as king, Lear has come to take his power for granted and to assume that he rules simply by nature and not at all by an element of convention. He believes that his rule is as natural as the movement of the heavenly bodies. Hence, when he banishes Cordelia, he swears by the natural order:

> For, by the sacred radiance of the sun,
> The mysteries of Hecate and the night,
> By all the operation of the orbs,
> From whom we do exist and cease to be.
> (1.1.111–14)

For much of the play, Lear characteristically assumes that nature will back up his decrees as king. He invokes the goddess Nature when he curses Goneril ("Hear, Nature, hear; dear Goddess, hear" [1.4.283]), expecting that the natural order will help him accomplish his revenge. This attitude culminates in the moment in the storm in Act 3 when, as Lear approaches madness, he believes that he can command the elements to strike down his enemies.

It would be easy to dismiss Lear's tendency to identify his commands with the dictates of nature as the exaggerated self-conception of a megalomaniac, compounded by the effects of senility and/or madness. But Shakespeare depicts Lear's confusion of nature and convention more as a kind of occupational hazard of his kingship than as the peculiar failing of a particular man. Lear is a tragic figure, and not a pathetically confused old man, precisely because Shakespeare shows that his tendency to identify his will with that of nature is intimately bound up with his success in the role of king. For others to believe in Lear, he must first believe in himself, and indeed his ability to project the aura of command so effectively is linked to his titanic self-image, which makes him assume that his word is not just law, but a law of nature. As he himself eventually learns, Lear is wrong that nature underwrites his kingship, but his power to a great extent rests on his belief in his bond with the natural order, which gives him the self-confidence that inspires confidence in others in his fitness to rule. *King Lear* provides the fullest development of a theme Shakespeare explores throughout his history plays, that the power of the king is in large part an illusion, though a politically necessary one. A king's subjects, and the king himself, must to a great extent be blind to his limitations as a man in order for him to seem sufficiently raised above the ordinary run of humanity to command their respect and obedience.

Thus *King Lear* offers Shakespeare's profoundest treatment of the disjunction of wisdom and power in human existence. What makes political life fundamentally tragic for Shakespeare is the fact that, by the very nature of political power, the ruler is cut off from the kind of wisdom he needs to rule justly in the fullest sense of the term. Lear is undeniably a great king, ruling effectively over a wide realm and earning his subjects' obedience and loyalty. But precisely because of his success as a ruler, the Lear we see at the beginning of the play has begun to lose touch with reality. From the opening scene of the play, Shakespeare focuses on the problem of flattery, and how it interferes with the knowledge—and especially the self-knowledge—a ruler needs. As the unfolding of Lear's love test reveals, the inevitable tendency of people is to tell a king what he wants to hear, because of his ability to reward them if they do and to punish them if they do not. As Shakespeare shows in many different contexts in his plays, it is very difficult for a ruler to know if anyone genuinely loves him, because it is not easy to separate sincere statements of love from those made merely to curry favor. In Lear's case, despite his basic grasp of the difference between his good daughter and her sisters, he allows himself to take the side of Goneril and Regan against Cordelia, because they flatter his illusions about his preeminence and she refuses to. When Kent tries to make the king aware of his folly, Lear banishes him, thus compounding the problem by denying himself the honest advice of his most trusted counselor. The opening scene of *King Lear* reveals a tragic pattern of political life: those who flatter the artificially puffed-up self-image of the king are rewarded, while those who try to speak the truth to him and call attention to his limitations are not just punished but banished from his presence.

Thus precisely because Lear is such a great king, he is blind to certain truths about his own nature and situation. In particular, his position as king causes him to overestimate his power as a father disastrously, leading him into the great blunder in the way he treats his daughters. Lear is confident that even after he relinquishes much if not all of his political power to his daughters and his sons-in-law, he will be able to keep them in line by virtue of his authority as their father. This assumption turns out, of course, to be a fatal error. When political and paternal power clash, the former will tend to prevail. The reason is that political power is more fundamental than paternal, as shown by the fact that the power of the law is necessary to champion the rights of fathers. Fathers expect their children to obey them, but if their children rebel against them, they must appeal to a higher political authority to enforce their paternal authority.

Why does Lear overestimate his authority as a father, thinking of paternal authority as somehow more fundamental than political? The answer is that there is one person in a regime who is not in a position to understand the need of fathers to appeal to political authority to enforce their rights, and that is the person who sits atop the regime, the king. At the beginning of the play, Lear is in a uniquely commanding position as a father: every order he gives as a father is automatically backed up by his authority as king; hence for him it becomes difficult to separate paternal from political authority, or to judge their relative strength. Lear's commands as king were ordinarily obeyed in his kingdom; we can imagine that his orders as a father were even more readily followed. His children had no way of appealing his decisions to an authority outside or above their family. It is no wonder then that Lear, used to being obeyed as a king, had no doubts whatsoever about his authority as a father. This is a perfect illustration of the problematic nature of kingship. In order to be able to enforce the rights of fathers, a king must be elevated above the usual need of fathers to rely on outside help to support their authority. A king thus becomes the only parent not aware of the limitation of the power of fathers. As we have seen, Lear assumes that his power as king is somehow rooted in the natural order; he is even more tempted to regard his power as a father as a natural fact and to ignore the ways in which paternal authority is established by the conventions of a given regime and even made a matter of law. Lear regards Goneril and Regan as behaving *unnaturally* when they disobey him (see, for example, 2.4.278). That is perhaps the crucial respect in which he confuses nature and convention.

iii

We have seen that at the beginning of the play Lear's regime is obscuring important differences. Precisely because Lear is securely in command, his regime tends to cover over the evil dwelling in his realm. But Lear's regime also tends to suppress the highest tendencies among his subjects. As Kent, Cordelia, and the Fool learn, the unfettered pursuit of truth is not rewarded under Lear's rule and may in fact be punished. Above all, Cordelia learns that true love must be silent in a court in which it is all too easily confused with self-serving and hypocritical professions of devotion. Thus the failure of Lear's hastily improvised plan for dividing the kingdom, though obviously a political and personal disaster, has unintended good consequences. To be sure, it sets free the evil in his kingdom and brings out the beast in Goneril, Regan, and Cornwall. But it also brings out the best in Cordelia, Kent, and the Fool and eventually allows Lear to learn the truth about himself, as well as to achieve a pure form of love with his good daughter. In short, the political storm Lear unleashes has the effect of stripping away the conventional appearances people maintain in society and getting them to reveal their true natures.

When Lear is securely in power, his enemies conceal their hostility from him; only when he loses his power does he learn who they are. The same process is evident in Lear's achieving self-knowledge. To be a successful king, he has to think of himself as almost a god; only when he loses his power does he begin to understand his limitations as a human being:

> I stand . . .
> A poor, infirm, weak, and despised old man.
> (3.2.19–20)

As a reigning monarch, Lear was flattered into self-delusion, but, once out of power, he begins to see the truth about himself, and how his servile followers used to deceive him:

> They flattered me like a dog, and told me I had the white hairs in my beard ere the black ones were there. . . . When the rain came to wet me once, and the wind to make me chatter; when the thunder would not peace at my bidding; there I found 'em, there I smelt 'em out. Go to, they are not men o' their words: they told me I was everything. 'Tis a lie, I am not ague-proof.
>
> (4.6.97–106)

Lear focuses on his bodily experience in this speech, especially the way he learned to feel the cold. No matter how elevated his social status may be, his body is fundamentally no different from that of other human beings, and thus it teaches him a lesson in common humanity and humility. Moreover, Lear is finally learning to distinguish between nature and convention; his ingrained belief that nature would support his commands as king has been put to a test in the storm and been proven false. In general, Lear's loss of power forces him to think about issues he had glossed over all his life, and he begins to distinguish what had been confused in his mind. Now that he no longer conjoins both paternal and political power in his single person, the roles of father and king begin to separate in his eyes:

> The King would speak with Cornwall. The dear father
> Would with his daughter speak.
> (2.4.99–100)

Once Lear turns over political power to his children, he loses the privileged position that made him think of himself as omnipotent as a father, and he learns the truth that is clear to all ordinary fathers, that command of an army conveys more authority than command of a household.

The story of Edmund's plot against his brother and his father embodies the same pattern of initial confusion and gradual clarification we have seen in the story of Lear and his daughters. At the beginning of the play the distinction between Gloucester's legitimate son, Edgar, and his illegitimate son, Edmund, has been effaced. In the relaxed moral atmosphere created by Lear's secure regime, Gloucester jokes about Edmund's dubious origins and reveals that he treats his sons as equally as Lear apparently is treating Albany and Cornwall: "I have a son, sir, by order of law, some year elder than this, who yet is no dearer in my account" (1.1.19–21). Like Lear, Gloucester will learn to his sorrow what comes from not sufficiently distinguishing between one human being and another. In the dissolving political order that results from Lear's ill-considered division of the kingdom, Edmund is free to set his plot in motion. As a bastard, a natural child, Edmund views himself as a partisan of nature against convention:

> Thou, Nature, art my goddess, to thy law
> My services are bound. Wherefore should I
> Stand in the plague of custom, and permit
> The curiosity of nations to deprive me,
> For that I am some twelve or fourteen moonshines
> Lag of a brother? Why bastard? Wherefore base?

When my dimensions are as well compact,
My mind as generous, and my shape as true,
As honest madam's issue? Why brand they us
With base? With baseness? Bastardy? Base, Base?
Who, in the lusty stealth of nature, take
More composition, and fierce quality
Than doth, within a dull, stale, tired bed,
Go to th' creating a whole tribe of fops
Got 'tween asleep and wake?
(1.2.1–15)

Like Lear, Edmund addresses nature as a goddess, but his view of nature, and especially its relation to convention, is completely different from the king's. While Lear's curse on Goneril assumes a harmony between what nature and convention dictate, for Edmund, convention has no basis whatsoever in nature; convention is purely arbitrary, "the plague of custom", "the curiosity of nations". For Edmund, convention is a mere matter of words, like "base" and "bastardy", falsely imposed by society. He contrasts the words by which society labels him with the physical fact of his body; the words are ugly but his body is beautiful. Edmund takes his bearings from the human body; if his body looks as good as that of legitimate issue, then society has no right to belittle him with its conventional categories. He reveals his position most clearly when he speaks of "the lusty stealth of nature". For Edmund, nature most fundamentally manifests itself in the fact of human lust, an impulse human beings share with animals. He thinks that one gets at human nature by rejecting everything that society tries to add to the bare origins of humanity in the sexual act.[7]

The consequence of Edmund's doctrine of nature is to set loose his desires and justify any action he takes to further his

[7] In this respect, Edmund's speech resembles Lear's later view of nature, in his first vision of Poor Tom as the "bare, fork'd animal", as well as the king's obsessive speeches on female sexuality in Act 4, scene 6. The fact that the villain Edmund first articulates this view of nature in the play is another sign that it cannot simply be identified as Shakespeare's.

own interest. Edmund claims that "nature" provides "the law" to which "his services are bound", but his speech involves a sophistical redefinition of such terms as "law" and "bound". In fact, Edmund's doctrine of nature is nothing but a mask for his complete devotion to his self-interest; his only law is the law of his own advancement, and that is not really a law at all. In his total egotism, Edmund reveals the practical consequences of equating the animal in man with the natural. One should never underestimate the explosive potential of trying to distinguish between the natural and the conventional. As Lear's regime shows, any social order to some degree rests upon a confusion of the natural and the conventional. For a community to function smoothly, its citizens must become naturalized to the conventions by which it operates. Hence, rejecting convention in the name of nature always has a profoundly unsettling if not subversive effect on a community.

iv

Nature and convention are thus the poles between which *King Lear* moves, providing the structuring principle of the play. Firmly anchored in the world of convention, the first scene takes place in a highly ceremonial court, with the characters playing out their customary roles of king and subject, father and child (only Cordelia refuses to play along). Act 1, scene 1 is a grand public scene, with lots of ritual and highly artificial modes of address; except for Cordelia, all the characters speak with an eye toward the public effect of their words. The elaborate costuming of the characters, richly decked out for a state occasion, contributes to the atmosphere of conventionality; as mentioned above, in this play, clothing is the chief symbol of the conventional element in human life.[8] But as we quickly learn, these conventional appearances hide a deeper reality. And the action that Lear's division of the kingdom sets in motion throughout the rest of Acts 1 and 2 progressively

[8] On the significance of clothing, see Lowenthal, "*King Lear*", p. 403.

weakens the hold convention has on the kingdom and sets the characters free to be more "natural", in a variety of senses of the word, some of them good, some of them evil.

By the time we reach Act 3, the distance the play has traveled in moving from the conventional to the natural is remarkable. The principal setting of Act 3 is a barren heath; instead of being in the safe confines of Lear's castle, the characters are exposed to nature at its most violent in the form of the storm. All the details contribute to making the contrast between a conventional and a natural setting as sharp as possible. In Act 3 the characters no longer have on their ceremonial costumes from Act 1, scene 1. The clothing of Lear and the Fool is barely adequate to the weather, and Edgar disguised as Tom is almost naked. Though Lear's scenes on the heath take place out in the open, they are not public in the way Act 1, scene 1 is. Lear begins to drop his guard, and we are suddenly privy to his innermost thoughts, thoughts that break out in titanic rages, alternating with calm reflections. Most of what appears to be dialogue in these scenes actually has some of the effect of soliloquy, as Lear finally pours out what most deeply disturbs him without regard to who may be listening. Indeed, at the center of the play, with Lear going mad, Edgar feigning madness, and the Fool spouting his usual nonsense, any conventional sense of dramatic dialogue breaks down. The characters frequently talk past each other, each wrapped up in the world of his private torments and obsessions, whether real or imagined.

Act 3 as a whole shows us what happens when the conventional order gives way to the natural. In the ensuing chaos, both the highest and the lowest impulses in humanity are free to emerge. The scenes of Act 3 alternate between Lear's party and his antagonists, all the evil characters who have leagued against him, including Goneril, Regan, Cornwall, and Edmund. In Lear's scenes we see the mad king groping toward the truth about himself, his political role, and the world of nature. By pairing Lear with his learnèd Theban, Shakespeare explicitly portrays the king moving toward philosophy and thus rising above the conventional limits of his earlier regime in thought. In their own way, Lear's antagonists act just as unconventionally, banding together to violate all law and morality as they plot against both Lear and Gloucester. In Act 3, Lear and his "noble philosopher" rise above the normal level of humanity; Goneril, Regan, Cornwall, and Edmund sink below it, descending to the level of beasts.[9] Act 3 builds up to two highly unconventional acts of justice: Lear's arraignment of his two evil daughters and the trial of Gloucester by Regan and Cornwall. Shakespeare brilliantly juxtaposes these two scenes, each in its own peculiar way an example of "natural" justice. As two extremes they help define the conventional middle ground of political justice.

Act 1, scene 1 provides a paradigm of customary political justice, which is usually an uneasy and haphazard mixture of the natural and the conventional. In disposing of his kingdom, if Lear went strictly by the nature of his daughters, Cordelia, as he seems to be aware, ought to get the bulk if not the whole of his realm. But primogeniture is presumably the law of the land, and thus convention dictates that Goneril, as his eldest daughter, ought to inherit Lear's kingdom.[10] Lear's original plan apparently attempted to blend natural and conventional justice in a delicate, and, as it proves, unstable compromise. In acknowledgment of her superior nature, Cordelia was supposed to get "a third more opulent" (1.1.88) than her sister's portions, but in a bow to convention, Goneril and Regan were each to get something. But as often happens with political compromises, Lear's plan ends up pleasing none of the parties involved. Goneril would have every reason to feel deprived of her birthright and Cordelia baulks at the love test Lear devises, evidently

[9] This contrast is not absolute, since, as we have seen, Lear has a double vision of the nature of humanity, which incorporates a perception of the animal side of man.

[10] The fact that Lear lacks sons makes the issue of the succession murky, but willing the kingdom to his eldest daughter would certainly have been more conventional than what Lear ends up doing.

with the hope of giving a respectable cover to his uneven disposition of his kingdom. She cannot abide a scheme that at least on the surface equates her with her sisters (even though the point of the elaborate charade is to display Lear's greater love for her). If anything, Lear's behavior in the opening scene shades toward a conception of natural justice; in his original plan for disposing of the kingdom, he is clearly attempting something very unconventional in the hope of securing the bulk of his kingdom for the best of his daughters. Nevertheless, or perhaps precisely because of the unconventionality of his plan, Lear does everything he can in the first scene to cloak his actions in ceremony and to get the power of convention on his side, especially by getting his daughters to agree to the plan in public (which in turn is precisely what alienates Cordelia). Lear's plan in Act 1, scene 1 is emblematic of how political justice normally operates. Sometimes it succeeds and sometimes it fails, but in any event political justice always occupies a kind of middle ground, trying to effect a compromise between what nature and convention may differently dictate.

The two trials that take place in Act 3 provide contrasting examples of natural justice in all its uncompromising character. As extreme forms of justice, these trials turn out to be in some ways superior to normal political justice, in some ways inferior. The way Regan and Cornwall put Gloucester on trial in Act 3, scene 7 is what we would call a mockery of justice, as Cornwall freely admits:

> Though well we may not pass upon his life
> Without the form of justice, yet our power
> Shall do a court'sy to our wrath, which men
> May blame, but not control.
> (3.7.25–28)

Cornwall here articulates one view of natural justice, the idea that right makes right. As long as his party has the superior power, Cornwall believes that they may execute any judgment they wish, and if they bow to any higher standard of justice, it is only for the sake of appearances.[11] For Cornwall, justice is in fact only a sham, a disguise that superior power may adopt for merely prudential reasons. This view of justice, which might well be characterized as the law of the jungle, appropriately corresponds to the animal view of human nature Edmund articulates in his defense of bastards. Like Edmund, Cornwall rejects what he regards as the false idealism of conventional views of justice and concentrates on what he regards as the "thing itself"—the naked truth of power. Yet even Cornwall recognizes the need to observe "the form of justice" in disposing of Gloucester. Cornwall and Regan may be utterly devoid of moral scruples, but even they must bow to certain basic legal principles: they produce evidence against Gloucester, interrogate him, and allow him to speak in his own defense.

Thus even the evil characters in *King Lear* are forced to practice a kind of rough justice. No one would claim that they give Gloucester a fair trial; yet the fact is that in a certain real sense he *is* guilty of the crimes of which he stands accused. The evasiveness of his initial answers betrays his consciousness that he has been conspiring against Cornwall and his party. Since this course of action has involved him in dealing at least indirectly with the French forces invading England, one might even say that Gloucester is toying with being a traitor to his native land, however high-minded and defensible his motives may be in doing so. In that sense, Cornwall and Regan do have a "case" against Gloucester, and, however bestial their conduct toward him, in some respects they avoid the genuine defects of conventional political justice. They act swiftly and decisively, and above all they cut through all Gloucester's evasions to get at the truth of what he has done. Unlike Lear in the first scene, they are not taken in by appearances. Their justice is natural in the sense that it is primitive, barbaric, and savage.

As such, their form of justice, however repellant, at least serves as a reminder of certain aspects of the phenomenon that

[11] Goneril later articulates the same view of justice at 5.3.159–60.

are easy to lose sight of in the midst of civilized life. At the beginning of the play, Lear has become so used to dictating justice unopposed that he forgets that ultimately his right to do so rests on his power to back up his decisions by the force of arms. This consideration explains his fundamental error in disposing of his kingdom, his mistaken assumption that he can in effect transfer military power to his children and still command their obedience. The cruelty with which Regan and Cornwall treat Gloucester is a good reminder of why we need the procedural safeguards embodied in conventional political justice, but it also calls attention to one essential but often obscured aspect of the nature of justice: that the right to make a judgment can never stray too far from the power to enforce it.

Lear's trial of Goneril and Regan in Act 3, scene 6 provides a more complex example of natural justice.[12] In a sense this trial represents the purest form of justice, since in effect it takes place entirely within Lear's mind, thus eliminating all the constraints that ordinarily compromise conventional courtroom procedures. Yet in another sense, Lear's legal proceedings against Goneril and Regan are another mockery of justice. By this point in the play, we are so sympathetic to Lear that it may seem mean-spirited to suggest the ways in which he violates customary legal principles in his conduct of their trial, but it is worth doing so to sharpen our sense of the contrast between what I have been calling natural and conventional justice. Lear attempts to play all the roles in this trial; he is the injured party, the principal witness, the prosecutor, and the presiding officer of the court. He takes it upon himself to appoint the judges, and an impartial observer would have to raise some questions concerning the qualifications of the Fool and Poor Tom to sit on the bench, not to mention concerning their sanity (as well as Lear's). Goneril and Regan are tried *in absentia*,

[12] The fact that this trial is omitted in the Folio version of the play is a good indication of why neither the Folio nor the Quarto versions are wholly adequate and why the common editorial practice of presenting a conflation of the two, though problematic, is probably the wisest procedure.

and hence, unlike even Gloucester at his trial, Lear's daughters are not allowed to speak a word in their defense. Indeed Lear appears to have decided upon their punishment before the trial begins (3.6.15–16).[13]

Having raised all these conventional legal quibbles, one must grant that Lear's case against Goneril and Regan, despite his failure to follow customary procedures, or perhaps because of it, is basically sound, and the verdict he wishes to obtain is just. Lear cuts through all the customary circumlocutions of the law and gets to the heart of the matter, stating the facts directly and unambiguously: "I here take my oath before this honorable assembly, she kicked the poor King her father" (3.6.46–48). By supervising all aspects of the trial, Lear can see to it that corruption is excluded from the courtroom (3.4.53–55). Moreover, although Lear's panel of judges may not have the composition custom would dictate, it does include two of the characters who have shown the most regard for truth and justice in the play—Kent and the Fool—as well as Edgar in his disguise as Tom, a figure who in his previous scene has been identified as a philosopher. By engaging this figure in an act of justice, Lear is in effect pursuing Plato's program of the philosopher-king. In Act 3, scene 4, Lear enters into a private conversation with what he takes to be a philosopher about nature and the curing of human ills. In his next scene, he seems to apply what he has learned from his noble philosopher to his kingly function of dictating justice. He seems in fact to recall his dialogue with the learnèd Theban about nature: "Then let them anatomize Regan. See what breeds about her heart. Is there any cause in nature that make these hard hearts?" (3.6.75–77).

Lear comes to recognize that the question of justice is profoundly linked to the question of nature, specifically the nature of human differences. He finally realizes that he must take into account how different his daughters are and that justice chiefly

[13] Regan and Goneril similarly pronounce judgment on Gloucester before his "trial" even begins (3.7.4–5).

involves "anatomizing" human beings, being able to see beneath surface appearances and thus to spy out their inner natures. The way Lear conducts the trial of Goneril and Regan may be evidence of his growing madness, but in the judgment he reaches, his madness seems a higher form of sanity, much like the behavior of the philosophers in Plato's parable of the cave, who, returning to the darkness of the cave after viewing the sun, seem to stumble about crazily in the eyes of their fellow human beings who have never seen the true light.[14] In the first scene of the play, Lear seems to be observing all the conventional forms of kingship, and he ends up being taken in by appearances and committing a monumental act of injustice. In Act 3, scene 6, he violates all customary procedures and yet achieves a higher form of justice, precisely because he finally recognizes that acting justly hinges ultimately on getting at the truth about human nature.

V

Thus freed in Act 3 from his conventional role as king, and finally capable of seeing beyond the limits of normal political justice, Lear rises to a more profound understanding of the duties of a ruler. Realizing that he shares the ordinary limitations of humanity helps teach Lear the virtue of compassion, and as he works his way out of his titanic egoism, he begins to show concern for the welfare of others, especially his Fool:

> Come on, my boy. How dost, my boy? Art cold?
> I am cold myself. Where is this straw, my fellow?
> The art of our necessities is strange,
> That can make vile things precious. Come, your hovel.
> Poor Fool and knave, I have one part in my heart
> That's sorry yet for thee.
>
> (3.2.68–73)

[14] See *Republic*, 517a.

Once again we see that it is the feelings of Lear's body that teach him what he has in common with other human beings. In one of the most moving speeches in the play, Lear openly criticizes the failings of his own regime and conventional political justice in general:

> Poor naked wretches, wheresoe'er you are,
> That bide the pelting of this pitiless storm,
> How shall your houseless heads and unfed sides,
> Your looped and windowed raggedness, defend you
> From seasons such as these? O, I have ta'en
> Too little care of this! Take physic, pomp,
> Expose thyself to feel what wretches feel,
> That thou mayst shake the superflux to them,
> And show the heavens more just.
>
> (3.4.28–36)

Rethinking both retributive and distributive justice, Lear now has a better idea of how he might use the power of a king. He finally recognizes that the throne carries with it obligations as well as privileges.

As we have repeatedly seen, at the beginning of the play Lear's success in ruling has created a kind of complacency in his kingdom and made people, including himself, lose touch with reality. Lear's plan for dividing the kingdom disastrously confuses political and familial power. In general, at the beginning of the play people in Lear's kingdom are confused about the ties that bind them together. Lear's love test highlights this confusion, revealing the mixture of motives that link one human being to another. Human beings can be bound together by both convention and nature, and, if by nature, either in a lower or a higher sense of the term. Human beings may have low motives like appetite or necessity when they league together for a common purpose. In such cases they are bound to each other by nothing more than self-interest, and their association is in principle no different from the way animals like ants work together. But human beings can also be united by their higher nature, their shared admiration for the higher things in life, such as their passion for truth. This is the way in which human association transcends the animal level. Finally, all human bonds contain a strong element of convention; people are tied together by the force of habit and by the patterns of association social custom dictates. The complexity of the motives behind human association is what frustrates Lear's attempt to elicit the truth about his daughters in Act 1, scene 1. Under the circumstances he himself creates, he has no hope of distinguishing their motives for saying what they say. Given the terms of the love test, when any daughter claims to love Lear, he cannot know if she is speaking out of self-interest, true love, or mere habit. By talking of love, Lear appears to be appealing to the higher nature of his daughters. But by offering to reward the daughter who says she loves him most, Lear has given a base, material motive for professing love, thus appealing to their lower nature.

Moreover, by staging the scene in a public forum, Lear has brought the power of convention at its strongest to bear upon his daughters. Even if they had nothing to gain, they would feel the pressure of custom to behave as good daughters in front of the whole community. In their love speeches to Lear, both Goneril and Regan are clearly playing to their audience. With their artificial and inflated rhetoric, they are acting out the conventional role of the good daughter and telling Lear exactly what he expects to hear. All these considerations help to explain why Cordelia feels frustrated under the circumstances and tries to remain silent. She does not want her true love for her father to be confused with expressions of self-interest or customary deference. Overreacting to her distasteful situation, Cordelia stresses the conventional element in her feelings:

> I love your Majesty
> According to my bond, no more nor less.
> (1.1.94–95)

In a barely veiled rebuke to her sisters, Cordelia dwells upon the material motives she has for loving her father, as well as her obedience to custom, neglecting all the higher motives that distinguish her from her sisters and make her truly love him:

> You have begot me, bred me, loved me. I
> Return those duties back as are right fit,
> Obey you, love you, and most honor you.
> Why have my sisters husbands, if they say
> They love you all?
>
> (1.1.98–102)

When Lear tragically misinterprets Cordelia's attempt to cut through the conventional rhetoric of his court and expose the flattery and hypocrisy of her sisters, he sets in motion a process that will in the end distinguish what has hitherto been confused in his kingdom.

As we have seen, in Act 3 the truth about humanity begins to clarify for Lear, as he achieves insight into the extremes of human nature. Lear finds out, not just who his true enemies are, but who his true friends are as well. Men like Kent and the Fool are finally free to demonstrate their genuine devotion to Lear, unmixed with baser or conventional motives. Serving him can no longer be said to be in their self-interest; on the contrary, material considerations would dictate their abandoning Lear's cause, as the Fool repeatedly points out. Thus, if these men remain loyal to Lear, it can only be out of true love for him, and not out of mere habit or prudential calculations. By the same token, in the alternating scenes in Act 3, involving Goneril, Regan, Cornwall, and Edmund, Shakespeare shows the lower or animal nature of human bonds distilled into its appalling essence. Blind to any higher motives, these characters are guided solely by self-interest, a combination of greed and ambition. In the process, they disregard all the conventional restraints a regime normally tries to impose on our animal instincts and impulses.

As Lear searches for truth with his learnèd Theban in Act 3, we see what it means to liberate the higher or spiritual side of human nature to go beyond conventional limits. As Goneril,

Regan, Cornwall, and Edmund pursue their advancement in Act 3, we see what it means to liberate the lower or animal side of human nature and sink beneath all conventional standards of decency. We can get a feel for the range of human nature *King Lear* explores when we realize that, in the terms of the play, both these forms of behavior are in some sense of the word "natural". It all depends on whether one adopts the modern view that man's nature is to be found in his lower origins or the ancient view that it is to be found in his higher perfection, in short, whether one takes one's bearings from man's beginning or his end (in the sense of goal or *telos*). Shakespeare shows his awareness in *King Lear* of the dark truths about human nature taught by modern thinkers like Machiavelli, the vision of the "poor, bare, forked animal"embodied in Poor Tom—that even sounds like an anticipation of Hobbes's view of the state of nature. But ultimately Shakespeare's affinities seem to lie more deeply with ancients like Plato and Aristotle, especially in his vision of the philosophic potential of humanity embodied in Lear's "learnèd Theban".

Chaos and Order in *King Lear*: Shakespeare's Organic Conceptions of Man and Nature

Robert Carballo
Millersville–University of Pennsylvania

For many of us, living as we do in postmodern times, the notion of organic ordering—or organicism—will often carry scientific rather than moral or social connotations. One thinks of organic chemistry or of human anatomy. But for the student of philosophy and literature the term "organicism" has larger, far-reaching associations. It has the force of a powerful metaphor evocative of functional and constitutional harmony and efficiency; it is the simple, yet complex, idea of all the parts of an organism—understood in its social, moral, and religious senses—working together well for a desired goal: good health and survival. It is in this philosophical sense that Shakespeare's *King Lear* can be understood as a vital dramatic statement on the nature of man and society and about the natural world where they exist temporally. More specifically, this play from Shakespeare's middle tragical period should be seen as part of the broader conception of all his tragedies: vast allegories of politico-ethical import reflective of the author's, and his culture's, preoccupation with order.[1] In Shakespeare's tragedies we always sense an uneasy concern with the frailty of civilized life, the exigencies of nature, and the ubiquitous danger of chaos when the thin veneer of civilization is corroded. Barbaric behavior, political danger, and deep personal suffering are never too distant in the world of Shakespearean tragedy; they follow when the blueprint for order in man and nature is violated.

[1] For an interesting, if somewhat idiosyncratic, study of the nexus between the high tragedies and contemporaneous political realities, see Lilian Winstanley's *Macbeth, King Lear, and Contemporary History* (Cambridge: Cambridge University Press, 1922).

It is against the background of medieval and Renaissance common assumptions of cosmic, theocentric order that man, nature, and society can be understood when reading *King Lear*. These assumptions had in Shakespeare's time a long, distinguished pedigree in Platonism and are reflected in important works of philosophy and literature of the period, even if the rise of commercialism and novel theories, such as Machiavelli's, had started to weaken the older notions of order. Sir Thomas Elyot's *The Governour*, Richard Hooker's *Of the Laws of Ecclesiastical Polity*, and Edmund Spenser's "Hymn of Heavenly Beauty" are but a few of several Renaissance works that treat the notion of order and hierarchy, its earthly manifestations as reflections of cosmic, divine order. The idea seems to have been developed first in Plato's *Timaeus*. It was further developed by Aristotle and later by the Neoplatonists and Boethius's *Consolation of Philosophy* in the Middle Ages. It was often presented through embellished metaphors, such as the great chain of being, the music of the spheres (prominently presented by Saint Isidore of Seville), or various theories of correspondences.[2] In Shakespeare himself the idea of order appears directly in many works besides *King Lear*: in the unleashing of chaos in *Othello*, *Hamlet*, and *Macbeth* after unnatural deeds have been committed; in Ulysses' speech on "degree" in *Troilus and Cressida*; in the reestablishment of order after Prospero's repentance of his hubris in *The Tempest*. Many other examples from Shakespeare could be cited, but these should suffice for an understanding of how central the notion of order and organic hierarchy is, not only for Shakespeare but for the writers of the English Renaissance in general.

The germinal disruption of order in *King Lear* would appear to be his startling declaration before most of the players in this drama of his "darker purpose" (1.1.38): the triple division of the kingdom so that he can retire. Here "darker" is

[2] Two classic studies of the conception of cosmic order and of the great chain of being that remain very useful are Arthur O. Lovejoy's *The Great Chain of Being* and E. M. W. Tillyard's *The Elizabethan World Picture*.

ambiguous, referring both to his hitherto concealed (hence in the dark) plan and unintentionally to the dark consequences that will follow this disruption of the natural hierarchy of kingship and of the integrity of the kingdom. In this, Lear anticipates the scholarly Prospero in *The Tempest*, who is at least partially culpable for his brother's usurpation of his title as Duke of Milan and for the chaotic events that follow. Prospero's love of learning, and particularly of arcane learning, is as disruptive as Lear's abdication and equally results in civil and familial discord. Both rulers put personal satisfaction above sacred and civic duty. But catalytic as the kingdom's division may be, the immediate chaotic consequences of the abdication are familial and personal and unfold as a veritable titanomachy of filial rebellion and ingratitude. Within this context Shakespeare dramatizes the pivotal role of personal responsibility so central to the Judeo-Christian ethic.

When considering Lear's culpability in the chaos that ensues after the division of the kingdom, it is important to remember that even if the act is self-indulgent his intention appears pure. He declares that he wishes to cast aside all the cares of governance and, in an ironic foreshadowing, to provide for his people so "that future strife / May be prevented now" (1.1.46–47). However, simple good intentions are not sufficient. Lear's *hamartia*[3]—his myopic vision of the future and appetite for flattery—results in dreadful personal suffering and civic strife. Cordelia, together with Kent, retains a clear sense of the balance between duty and affection. She refuses to enter a contest of verbal protestations of love with her false sisters and suffers disinheritance and banishment for simply declaring the natural order of filial affection:

> I love your Majesty
> According to my bond; no more nor less.
> (1.1.94–95)

[3] A. C. Bradley's lecture on *King Lear* contains an insightful discussion of Lear's character flaw and of other tragic elements within the larger context of the tragic genre. See Bradley's *Shakespearean Tragedy* (New York: St. Martin's Press, 1992).

Kent sees the reasonableness of Cordelia's circumspect declaration and begs Lear to "see better". France also can see what Lear cannot and "seizes" Cordelia's virtue. The question of perception is specifically tied in this play to the recognition of order that comes through reason: Cordelia's well-ordered filial affection, France's detection of a comely soul, Kent's caveat to Lear about the disorder evident in his rash judgment of his one loyal daughter, and the Fool's wisely comical admonitions.

Almost immediately the old king begins to suffer the consequences of his rashness. Goneril begins to speak of her father as an old fool who must be treated as a baby with flatteries; Regan suggests he is senile and lacks self-knowledge. The Fool, who represents ironic if somewhat irreverent wisdom, pointedly declares the reason the old king is now treated with diminished respect (Oswald refers to Lear reductively as "My lady's father"); it is the reversal of the natural order: "thou mad'st thy daughters thy mothers" (1.4.176–77). Finally, when the old king, who has abdicated rule but clings to royal dignity, is denied his retinue he loses as well his sense of identity. The Fool cruelly but realistically reminds him he is "Lear's shadow" (1.4.237), rendered thus by the "unnatural hags" (2.4.277) to whom he has given all. The loss of kingly dignity is intimately tied to Lear's loss of identity and, eventually, of reason itself when he goes mad on the heath. He must suffer and become "unaccommodated man ... a poor, bare, forked animal" (3.4.109–10) before he regains a sense of self, of reason, and of the right proportion of the affections. In other words, the old king must go through his passion, the "wheel of fire" (4.7.47), before his redemptive healing and clear recognition of Cordelia's goodness at the end of Act 4 and throughout Act 5. Natural bonds have been ruptured. In harmony with the classic Aristotelian theory of tragedy and the tragic hero, chaos in high places will affect individual persons as well as the civic order. In this play, Lear represents fatherhood and kingship, and his well-intentioned but unwise actions have a nefarious impact on both.

Parallel conventions of blindness, lost identity, disguised identity, filial ingratitude, and abiding loyalty are found in the subplot involving Gloucester and his two sons. Here, too, the natural order is reversed with dire consequences for all: the illegitimate Edmund fools his father, turns him against his legitimate and loyal son, Edgar, and the consequences that follow are both fitting and richly symbolic. Old Gloucester, like Lear, is easily fooled by Edmund, who, like Iago in *Othello*, knows "[his] price" and embodies the Renaissance concept of the Machiavellian villain. He boasts:

> Edmund the base
> Shall top th' legitimate. . . .
> Now, gods, stand up for bastards!
> (1.2.20–22)

Gloucester's gullibility in accepting Edmund's intrigues against Edgar has a symbolic retribution in his physical blindness and a correspondence in Lear's own moral blindness in rejecting Cordelia. Correspondent, too, are the following: Edgar's and Cordelia's steadfast love; Kent's and Edgar's disguised kindness toward the old, afflicted men who banished them; their adoption of necessary clever disguises; Edgar's feigned madness and Lear's real, though temporary, insanity; the purgatorial suffering Lear and Gloucester must endure before their epiphanies and before justice is restored. Through the parallel plots and close correspondences in characterization—elements of artistic order in themselves—Shakespeare creates a harrowing picture of familial discord. It is in the family—as we see in the Old Testament and in ancient Greek tragedy—that the seeds of civil and cosmic discord are sown. The strict causality of tragic events, with the family as subject and stage, evident in *King Lear* is one of the perennial qualities of tragedy, from the plays of Sophocles to those of Ibsen and O'Neill.

The inelegant squabble over Edmund between Regan and Goneril that first surfaces in Act 4 illustrates how, in the classic conception of tragedy in high places, personal and familial strife translates quickly and easily into socio-political upheavals. There is ample antecedent for this connection in ancient Greek drama, particularly in the *Oresteia* and in *Oedipus Rex*.

The two sisters, with their husbands, are, after the unhappy events of Act 1, the rulers of Britain; therefore their in-fighting bodes ill for the unity of the kingdom itself. Not only is their adulterous inclination a symptom of deeper, far-reaching corruption, but their lack of self-restraint forces questions about their suitability to rule. Neither is, like their sister Cordelia, "queen over her passion" (4.3.14–15). Their passions are disordered, and as a consequence the kingdom is vulnerable to both internal and external dangers. The latter comes mainly from France—the ancestral enemy of the English—and indeed the French invasion occurs in the last scene of Act 3. In fact, a topical interpretation of *King Lear* reads it as a subtle warning to the monarchy of the frailty of a national unity consolidated during Elizabeth's long and able (if not merciful) rule but endangered by the political and religious strife that would result in the Puritan commonwealth and the abolition of the monarchy in just a few years after the writing of *King Lear*. At the time, since the royally imposed break of England from Catholic Christianity in the previous century, the English were also particularly sensitive to real and imagined dangers from their "Papist" enemies on the continent, especially France and Spain.

The concern with the larger social and political ramifications of Lear's unwise division of the kingdom is intimately associated with Renaissance notions of kingship. One of the central concerns of the Renaissance was the question of what makes a good ruler. After the gradual break-up of medieval cohesiveness[4] in Christendom, particularly in the turbulent

[4] Several twentieth-century works substantially treat the question of *King Lear*'s relationship to the modern world that arguably began with the Renaissance. Marshall McLuhan, for example, discusses the role of the play in depicting the transition from medieval to modern society, particularly with reference to the transformation of a world of traditional roles to one of impersonal actions, in *The Guttenberg Galaxy* (Toronto: University of Toronto Press, 1962). In "*King Lear* or *Endgame*" (in *Shakespeare Our Contemporary* [Garden City, N.Y.: Doubleday, 1964]), Jan Kott maintains the thesis that the theme of *Lear* is the decay and fall of the Renaissance and modern worlds. Maynard Mack's existential study of *King Lear* remains invaluable (*King Lear in Our Time* [Berkeley: University of California Press, 1965]).

fifteenth century, thinkers and political theorists began to speculate on the nature of modern rule and the character of the ruler.[5]

In an oblique manner, *King Lear*, too, is a statement on kingship and on its organic pedigree in antiquity and the Middle Ages. The play has as its philosophical frame the ancient notion of king as father and servant to his people. Notions of absolute monarchy were not yet in vigor. We see that older and exalted notion of monarchy, for example, in *Oedipus Rex*, where Oedipus must again aid his people during the plague by finding the killer of Laius, the former king. Oedipus must serve his people and behaves paternally toward them—in fact, he addresses them as "my children" in the opening lines of the play. Moreover, the paternalistic monarchy is a historical reality of the European Middle Ages. Lear departs from this older tradition by seeking a carefree retirement, and in doing so disrupts the organic bond between a king and his people. The first to suffer the dreadful consequences of this "unnatural" act is the old king himself, soon after bereft of his dignity as king by the "marble-hearted fiend" (1.5.266) of filial ingratitude. The abdication of his authority—coming, as it does in the Christian understanding of authority, from God primarily and secondarily from natural relations, from ancestry, and from virtuous application of skill and power—issues into the crass exercise of raw power. Regan and Goneril's power soon devolves into the despotic treatment of their father, the strife between Cornwall and Albany, and the unjustified violence against Gloucester. In a scene reminiscent of the violation in *Macbeth* of one of the more sacred traditions of the West, that of hospitality, Regan, Goneril, and Cornwall abuse and blind old Gloucester on the scurrilous accusations of treason. Only

[5] Numerous Renaissance works of literature and political theory can be consulted for contemporaneous theses concerning the character of government and rulers. Among these are Sackville's *The Mirror for Magistrates*; Spenser's *The Faerie Queene*; Sidney's *Arcadia*; Castiglione's *Il Cortegiano*; Machiavelli's *The Prince*; Shakespeare's own *Henry* plays; the plays of Marlowe, Chapman, and Jonson; and the direct literary ancestor of *King Lear*, Norton and Sackville's *Gorboduc*.

Albany is absent from this barbaric and chaotic scene. This is fitting, as he is to become a force in the restoration of order and justice after his denunciation of the evil sisters, the arrest of Edmund for capital treason, and his handing the rule of the kingdom to Kent and Edgar. But before this restoration personal relationships, civilized institutions, and the governance of the nation unravel in riotous chaos. To use a Yeatsean term, "the center cannot hold", and nature itself must reflect the fruits of human folly.[6] In important ways, *King Lear* is a plaintive anthem about postlapsarian man and his wounded nature. As a dramatic theodicy, it nurtures no Pelagian illusions about the human condition. It offers a poetic correspondence between acts of defective human will and the natural world in a sustained conceit of chaos and order.

The organic conception of life in *King Lear*, however disrupted it becomes throughout the play, recognizes a bond that binds human beings—and all human activity—with the world of nature and with the Creator of man and nature, God himself. While the references to divinity in the play are subdued and mostly to pagan "gods", probably to reflect the pre-Christian world the characters inhabit, the ethical underpinning of the play is informed by a sense of divine purpose and design. Gloucester appeals to the "kind gods" (3.7.36) when he discovers Edgar was calumniated and repents of his attempted suicide to the "ever-gentle gods" (4.6.220); Albany appeals to the "justicers" (4.2.79) that are above when he learns of Gloucester's abuse and murder; Lear, on his way to prison with Cordelia, tries to console her by suggesting the philosophical vocation of becoming "God's spies" (5.13.17) in order to decipher "the mystery of things" (5.3.16); and Edgar, in his majestic final confrontation with Edmund where he asserts the primacy of legitimacy and virtue, declares "the gods are just" (5.3.172). There are others, but these should suffice to establish the importance of the notion

[6] A judicious study of the comic or absurd elements that underscore *King Lear* can be found in G. Wilson Knight's *The Wheel of Fire* (London: Methuen and Company, 1930), where he argues the affinity between the play and the comedy of the grotesque.

of divine presence and justice in the play. Moreover, *King Lear* posits the physical world around us and human nature as the great reflections of divine, cosmic order. For the Renaissance, the ultimate evil is the chaos engendered by violations of the natural order; conversely, civilization comes from nature tamed and guided by God's law. As Thomas Wilson puts it, in a paraphrase from Cicero, the wisdom of princes is:

> to allowe things confirmed by nature, and to bear with old custome, or els they should not onely suffer in body temporall punishment, but also lose their soules for euer [for] Nature is a right that phantasie hath not framed, but God had graffed and giuen man power thereunto.[7]

In the opening scene of *King Lear* we immediately sense the ominous consequences that will come from violations of nature's order. Gloucester declares to Kent his equal affection for the legitimate Edgar and Edmund, the "whoreson [that] must be acknowledged" (1.1.24–25). Edmund is present during this conversation and in the next scene acts according to his father's unnatural equal regard for his two sons (one should remember that to the Renaissance mind, unaffected by modern sentimentality, this equal recognition was both unjust and unnatural). He pronounces nature—that is, chaotic, untamed nature—his goddess and declares his Machiavellian purpose:

> Edmund the base
> Shall top th' legitimate.
> (1.2.20–21)

Ironically, Gloucester himself, believing Edmund's lies against Edgar, discourses eloquently about the chaos in nature correspondent to the rupture of the natural human bonds:

> These late eclipses in the sun and moon portend no good to us. Though the wisdom of Nature can reason it thus and thus, yet Nature finds itself scourged by the sequent effects. Love

[7] Thomas Wilson, *The Arte of Rhetorique*, ed. G.H. Mair (Oxford: Clarendon Press, 1909), p. 32.

> cools, friendship falls off, brothers divide. In cities, mutinies; in countries, discord; in palaces, treason; and the bond cracked 'twixt son and father. This villain of mine comes under the prediction, there's son against father; the King falls from bias of nature, there's father against child ... machinations ... treachery, and all ruinous disorders follow us disquietly to our graves. (1.2.112–24)

This passage is both prophecy and a veritable syllabus of chaotic nature mirroring, in a causal relationship, the violation of natural affection.

As mentioned before, the Gloucester subplot has a close parallel to the events surrounding Lear. Like Gloucester, Lear has listened to his opportunistic daughters at the expense of his loyal, truthful child. Like Gloucester, he will pay the high price of his folly. By the end of Act 1, Lear is already cursing Goneril with barrenness, and, like Edmund, evokes nature as his goddess to effect the "disnatured torment" that would match her unnatural ingratitude. When he next appeals to Regan to observe "the offices of nature, bond of childhood ... [and] dues of gratitude" (2.4.177–78), the old king again encounters the sharp tooth of filial ingratitude. Like Gloucester, Lear must suffer the effects of mental and spiritual torment. The famous scene of the storm on the heath that opens Act 3 is a powerful metaphor for the storm in Lear's mind and soul. It is fitting, then, that the entire act should be punctuated by dramatic references to chaotic, raging nature. When the grieving Lear exclaims, "Blow, winds, and crack your cheeks.... You cataracts and hurricanoes, spout" (3.2.1–2), the correspondence between "winds" and sorrowful sighs and between "cataracts" and tears suggests itself. At this point in Lear's passion—where "man's life [seems] as cheap as beast's" (2.4.266)—begins the *anagnorisis* that will lead to his epiphany in Act 5. His passion consists in hard lessons about ingratitude (he wonders whether there is "any cause in nature" for "these hard hearts" [3.6.76–77]), the frailty of man, the thin veneer of civilization, the need for the trappings of civilized customs in order to stave off barbarism, and his own humble recognition of his essential humanity. Lear ostensibly goes mad on the heath, but in his declaration to Kent, "I am a man / More sinned against than sinning" (3.2.58–59), we remark the beginning of this progress toward wisdom—the just appreciation of oneself, of nature, and of others—and the ephemerality of his grief-induced insanity. In a further instance of poetic correspondence, the tempest in nature will pass just as surely as the one in Lear's mind will. Edgar, who with Kent and Cordelia exemplifies wisdom and virtue, detects "reason in madness" (4.6.177) in the old king in the poignant scene where he, Gloucester, and Lear come together (4.6). They may all be, in Gloucester's pathos-filled words, "ruin'd pieces of nature", but the theistic conception of the universe that informs this play cannot allow for utter and final pessimism. If nature's order has been disrupted it can also be restored—and the restoration must begin, in yet another correspondence, where chaos began: at the personal and familial levels.

The reunion of Lear and Cordelia in the French camp at the end of Act 4 signals the restoration of familial and moral order.[8] It is also the occasion of the old king's epiphany as he sees, with moral vision, his foolishness and the enormous suffering it has caused. His recognition is double: "I am a very foolish fond old man" (4.7.60) and "For, as I am a man, I think this lady / To be my child Cordelia" (4.7.69–70). From here to the end of the play the motif of recognition is sustained: Edgar throws off his disguise and confronts Edmund and his villainy; Albany arrests Edmund and discovers the identities of the disguised Kent and Edgar; Lear recognizes Kent for his faithful companion; Cordelia learns the revealing lesson that injustice toward the good somehow mysteriously coexists with the general harmony evident in nature. All these revelations, and perhaps wisdom itself, come at the price of much suffering and are requisite for the regaining of lost harmony. For this reason *King Lear* can be seen as a theodicy, an anatomy of the causes

[8] Harold Skulsky offers a lucid discussion of the symbolic role of Cordelia, as a Christlike character, in the restoration of order in this play, and specifically in Lear's epiphany. See "*King Lear* and the Meaning of Chaos", *Shakespeare Quarterly*, Winter 1966, pp. 6–17.

for the existence of evil and the analysis of its purpose in the human economy. Perhaps more importantly, the play is in a sense a parable of love and redemption, for, as often happens in Shakespearean tragedy, personal, social, and natural order is usually restored—but only after the purgation that the old, unsettled king calls "a wheel of fire".

The quick reestablishment of political order in the last scene, when Albany hands over the rule of the realm to Kent and Edgar, is accompanied by the death of Cordelia and of Lear as he holds her body. Nature—in the amplest understanding of the word—once disrupted exacts a sacrifice, a holocaust, where the good will suffer. The correspondence of life and death here is clear. Furthermore, parallels with Christian notions of suffering and redemption are inevitable but elegantly subtle. For these reasons the 1681 emendation by Nahum Tate—where Cordelia is revived and Lear is restored to the throne—appears not only absurd, as it did to the Romantic essayist Charles Lamb, but unnatural as well. In the words of the wise Kent:

> Vex not his ghost: O, let him pass! He hates him
> That would upon the rack of this tough world
> Stretch him out longer. (5.3.315–17)

Nothing indeed was left for the old, wounded man but to leave this world. The expiation dramatized in the closing scenes of *King Lear* is indispensable for a restored order and for personal and social peace.

It is not, however, until the period of the romances that Shakespeare's insight into cosmic order, the immanent rightness of what is, comes to full philosophical maturation. The notions and metaphors for the inherent harmony of creation, so grandly reflected in the microcosm of *King Lear*, will receive a lyrical exposition in his last plays, especially in *The Tempest*. Yet the calmer, sublime vision of God, man, and nature of these plays might not have been possible, one can speculate, without the harrowing portrayals of the high tragedies. Among these, *King Lear* offers perhaps the most cogent and sublime vision of the beauty and fragility of the created order.

Looking There: The Literary and the Dialectical in a Class on *King Lear*

Scott F. Crider
University of Dallas

> What is mere talk, nothing but talk, can, however untrustworthy it may be, still bring about understanding among human beings—which is to say that it can still make human beings human.
>
> —Hans-Georg Gadamer[1]

Allow me to provide the class from which I first began to consider the relationship between literature and dialectic.

I

"Professor Crider, how do we know that he doesn't see something?"

The student's polite question during our last meeting on Shakespeare's *King Lear* was, and is, a good one. We had been reading the play for Tragedy and Comedy—the third of four literature courses required of all of our undergraduates—and I had provided them with both the Quarto (Q) and the Folio (F) versions of Cordelia's death and Lear's end. I explained the hypothesis that Shakespeare revised his plays: In Act 5 scene 3, Lear dies differently in Q than in F, and this may indicate Shakespearean revision.[2] In Q, having asked someone, perhaps Kent, to undo his button, he thanks him and

[1] Hans-Georg Gadamer, *Dialogue and Dialectic*, trans. P. Christopher Smith (New Haven, Conn.: Yale University Press, 1980), p. 123.

[2] The literature on Shakespearean revision is now vast. I have found highly useful *The Division of the Kingdoms: Shakespeare's Two Versions of* King Lear, ed. Gary Taylor and Michael Warren (Oxford: Oxford University Press, 1983), esp. "'Is this the promis'd end?': Revision and the Role of the King", pp. 121–41. See esp. pp. 131–37 for his discussion of the moment I emphasized in class.

expires: "O, o, o, o."[3] In F, however, there is no *exclamatio*; instead, Lear regains power to say,

> Do you see this? Look on her: look, her lips,
> Look there, look there!
> (lines 312–13)

These lines are famously ambiguous. I asked my students a two-part question: "What are the differences between Q and F, and why might Shakespeare have revised the play?" After I listed the differences on the board as students contributed them, we concluded that the fundamental difference between Q and F is that in Q, he simply dies, but in F, he sees something before dying. There was no doubt that most of the students, three-fourths of whom are Catholic, preferred F because, in the consensual reading that was developing, Lear has had a vision. I began to interrogate the consensus:

"What does he have a vision of? 'Do you see *this*?' What's the antecedent to the demonstrative pronoun 'this'? The next line may help some: 'Look on *her*: look, her *lips*, / *Look there*, look *there*!' At first, it looks like he is indicating Cordelia's body, her face, her lips, but what do you do with 'there'? Look where? At what?"

It was quiet, and I was tempted, as I always am when my questions bring only silence, to start answering them, but this time I didn't submit to my own impatience. The silence was meditative.

"He doesn't see anything. She's dead, and he can't handle it. He's deluded." The student was pleased with himself because he knew that many of his colleagues would not agree. I was pleased because someone *else* had offered a skeptical reading.

[3] Cited from *The Norton Shakespeare*, ed. Stephen Greenblatt, et al. (New York: W.W. Norton, 1997), which offers both Q and F on opposite pages for easy comparison. R.A. Foakes' 3rd Arden ed. of the play (Surrey: Arden, 1997) provides a conflated text that does, however, provide a key to Q/F differences. His introduction examines several of those textual moments that would enable lively discussion (128–46).

"How do you know that?" asked another student. "Maybe he sees her soul. Hamlet saw his father's ghost. Maybe Lear sees Cordelia's ghost, her soul."

There it was, the topic: the immortality of the soul.

"No one else sees it. Edgar just says, 'He faints: my lord, my lord!'" returned our skeptic.

Our pious reader wouldn't let it go.

"Hamlet's mother didn't see the ghost, but Hamlet did. At the end, Lear is having a vision, which he's trying to share with those present: 'Look there', he's saying, all of our suffering has some purpose."

"It doesn't have any purpose in the play. People just get hurt; then, they die."

It was time for me to paraphrase.

"Okay, now, we have two very different readings: Nicole, you're arguing that Lear has a vision of Cordelia's immortal soul ascending to judgment, in which case suffering and death in the play are not meaningless; Todd, you're arguing that he only imagines he has some vision—maybe of her coming back to mortal life, or maybe of her ascending to immortal life—but he doesn't, in which case, suffering and death are meaningless. How can we decide which interpretation is stronger? What's your evidence, Nicole, here or anywhere in the play, that Lear sees Cordelia's ghost or soul?"

"Kent tells Edgar to let Lear die: 'Vex not his ghost' (314), he says, so the characters believe in the immortal soul. You said 'ghost' means 'soul or departed spirit'. So there appears to be some communication between the living and the dead."

"What do you mean 'communication'?"

"Kent says, 'O, let him pass', which has to mean that Edgar might persuade him to return during this—I don't know what to call it—this ..."

"... this transition from the land of the living to the land of the dead."

"Yes. If Lear's 'ghost' could hear Edgar, why couldn't Lear see Cordelia's soul?"

"That's a great question. Can you answer it, Todd?"

"Edgar might be able to revive Lear before he dies. So what? That doesn't mean the soul is immortal. Besides, you told us before that Shakespeare isn't his characters: just because Kent believes in Lear's immortal soul doesn't mean Shakespeare does. He could've given us a dialogue between Lear and Cordelia's ghost—just like in *Hamlet*—but he doesn't."

"Nicole, what do you do with Todd's point about Shakespeare *not* giving us Cordelia's ghost?"

"That would be too obvious. This way, the scene tests your faith."

That was meant for Todd, but it began to answer my question—"Why has Shakespeare revised the scene?"—so I pursued it.

"What do you mean?"

"If you put a ghost in, then it's too easy, really. What Paul says is that 'we walk by faith, not by sight'." Nicole is, you should know, a theology major. "Shakespeare wants to test our faith: if you don't believe, you'll think Lear is deluded."

The class is clearly on Nicole's side, and Todd is growing sullen.

"But how would we know", I ask her, "if he's assuming the immortality of the soul or questioning it?"

"He is questioning it, but, when they look at Lear's vision, the 'faithful' will see that there is a higher order."

"So, in your reading, Shakespeare revises the scene to give Lear, and us, a vision—the suggestion of a vision—a vision of eternity which lessens the pain of human suffering and gives death meaning?"

"Yes."

Then there is a long silence, during which we all catch up with the discussion. All I have to do is ask,

"Todd?"

"Maybe the soul *is* immortal, but we're talking about what the play's doing. I think he revises the scene to get that faith going, only to crush it. It's a tragedy."

"So you agree that the language is ambiguous, but you think the ambiguity itself is skeptical?"

"Yeah, Lear says, 'thou'lt come no more', and then you get all those 'never's."

"But Nicole is saying that that's what Lear believes *before* the vision."

Nicole is pleased.

"But maybe he just knows we want Cordelia to be alive *somewhere* 'cause we can't handle the truth: when we die, we're nothing."

More silence.

"Professor Crider, how do we know that he doesn't see something?" The polite student has not been active in the discussion, but she has been listening, and we are running out of time, so I fashion a summary. This is, remember, the last day on the play, and the students will be indignant if I run past 12:20 P.M. They're hungry.

"We don't know that he doesn't, but we don't know that he does. Both Nicole and Todd have excellent readings, and they have evidence for their thoughtful interpretations. The play really does allow both readings. If that's true, the next question would be this: Why does Shakespeare revise the scene in such a way that *both* readings—of the scene and the play—work, either as tragedy or as romance? Maybe Shakespeare doesn't know. Maybe he knows, but he wants us to have this very discussion." I pause. "I don't know."

I hear paper and backpack zippers.

"Maybe he wants us to 'take upon us the mystery of things'."

Yes, I did say that. They're sophomores, and I am myself moved by the discussion and the play. Class is over.

II

Imaginative literature, by its very mimetic nature, can encourage Socratic dialectic in the classroom, and literary ambiguity, especially on central questions of human being, is a highly promising occasion for dialectic in the classroom since the centrality of the question will arouse student opinions, and the ambiguity of the representation will ensure more than one good opinion, each good one not fully adequate, though, given the plausibility of the others. (This does not at all mean that all responses are good.) If true, this would suggest both that "critical thinking" can perhaps be best taught through literary texts and that teachers of literature ought to be trained in dialectic, perhaps in graduate school, in order to avoid the twin dangers of an excessive reliance upon "lecture" and an undisciplined "discussion" of student opinion. Because literature represents human beings whose central questions both can be answered in more than one way and will remain unanswered, if by "answered" we mean finally so, then it is a discourse supremely suited to the dialectical practice of response and refinement that characterizes the best classroom discussions, both because the literature is enacting questions that are inherently interesting to students as human beings and because the best of such representations enact them in such a way that one's first response and opinion will be strongly held, yet somehow inadequate, especially in the face of other, different responses. Shakespearean ambiguity here aroused students to explore a fundamental, not simply "literary" question—Does Shakespeare believe in the immortality of the soul? Do we?—yet demanded that they do so with a care of precision that educates aroused response. Literature arouses, then, and dialectic cares for, response, thereby inventing a more mature response. Let me use my own last class on *King Lear* to examine imaginative literature first, then dialectic, though that class will limit what can be said about both since it was composed, after all, of sophomores and of an imperfect Socrates.

In an Aristotelian understanding of "imaginative literature",[4] the poet represents human action and being in order

[4] "Imaginative literature" is a term for what Aristotle would call *mimesis*. On the mimetic question in Shakespeare studies, see Brian Vickers, *Appropriating Shakespeare: Contemporary Quarrels* (New Haven, Conn.: Yale University Press, 1993), esp. pp. 129–44. For a fine examination and defense of *mimesis*, see Kendall Walton, *Mimesis as Make-Believe: On the Foundations of the Representational Arts* (Cambridge, Mass.: Harvard University Press, 1990). As well, see the following full studies of the *Poetics*: Gerald F. Else, *Aristotle's Poetics: The Argument*

to make both moving and intelligible. The *Poetics* defines poetry's essence as mimesis.[5] Imaginative literature, then, represents, and the purpose of representation is understanding:

> [P]oetry was broadly engendered by a pair of causes, both natural. For it is an instinct of human beings, from childhood, to engage in mimesis (indeed, this distinguishes them from other animals: human beings are the most mimetic of all, and it is through mimesis that they develop their earliest understanding; and equally natural that everyone enjoys mimetic objects). A common occurrence indicates this: we enjoy contemplating the most precise images of things whose actual sight is painful to us .... The explanation of this too is that understanding gives great pleasure not only to philosophers but likewise to others too, though the latter have a smaller share of it [the philosopher explains]. This is why people enjoy looking at images, because through contemplating them it comes about that they understand and infer what each element means, for instance that "this person is so-and-so." (1448b3–17)

For Aristotle, representations please because learning is pleasurable. In imaginative literature, this pleasure is experienced through plot, the mythic arrangements of fictive episodes into an intelligible order, one which operates by, yet influences our understanding of, "probability" in human action. Aristotelian universalism does not deny difference in human beings, but it

(Cambridge, Mass.: Harvard University Press, 1967); Stephen Halliwell, *Aristotle's Poetics* (London: Duckworth, 1986); Amelie Oksenberg Rorty, ed., *Essays on Aristotle's Poetics* (Princeton, N.J.: Princeton University Press, 1992); and Elizabeth Belfiore, *Tragic Pleasures: Aristotle on Plot and Emotion* (Princeton, N.J.: Princeton University Press, 1992). Paul Ricoeur has a fine discussion of *mimesis* in *Time and Narrative*, vol. 1, trans. Kathleen McLaughlin and David Pellauer (Chicago: University of Chicago Press, 1984), esp. pp. 52–87. See pp. 31–51 for his discussion of "emplottment". For his defense of the general value of Aristotelian plot, see vol. 2, pp. 7–28, as well. Ricouer's discussion provides a hermeneutical understanding that augments my examination of dialectic below, informed by it is, in part, by Gadamer.

[5] All citations from the *Poetics* are from Stephen Halliwell's Loeb edition (Cambridge, Mass.: Harvard University Press, 1995), though I have also consulted Richard Janko's edition (Indianapolis, Ind.: Hackett, 1987).

does assume that there is a human species and that our literary pleasures in response to representations of even the most apparently alien human actions are an indication that, within the mimetic experience, we are learning about ourselves. Aristotelian mimesis is philosophic precisely because its pleasures are those of learning that we might be so-and-so, and his *Poetics* helps the city and its citizens fulfill the Apollonian command of self-knowledge. When I enter the classroom, I do so confident that *King Lear* can help the students discern, within the unshaped particularities of their own lives, patterns that may help them flourish through increased understanding.

Most, however, are hoping that those patterns will answer certain questions that Shakespeare himself is famous for leaving ambiguous, yet Shakespearean ambiguity augments Aristotelian ethical poetics by moving us through mimetic moments that demand that we attend to what we do not, and perhaps finally cannot, know about ourselves. Act 5, scene 3 of *King Lear* is Shakespeare's representation of the question, Is the soul immortal?—and both Nicole and Todd recognized the question, yet answered it passionately and differently, for three reasons: (1) because it is a question that cannot leave a reflective person indifferent; (2) because each had a prejudice in favor of his own answer; and (3) because the play will allow itself to be interpreted either way. Imaginative literature, especially Shakespearean, arouses in us strong opinions because we know, even if it is unfashionable to put it thus, that these mimetic actions have something to do with us, and that literary interpretation here might be a means to self-understanding and even human flourishing, even when—maybe especially when—the enactment of the question is subtle. By placing at the end of the play a fundamental question about the consequences of Lear's error in the beginning of it—Has Lear by Act 5 scene 3 irrevocably destroyed his daughter through his earlier immaturity in Act 1 scene 1, even though he recognized that error before her destruction?—and by not answering it, Shakespeare arouses in us a desire to reflect upon a question that, even after clarification, will remain a mystery, as I pointed out rather melodramatically. Or, rather, by allowing the question to be answered in more than one way, but not fully or confidently, he demands that we refine our own prejudices, testing our own unexamined beliefs against mimetic complexity. Nicole does believe that the soul is immortal; Todd does not. The play demanded of both that they put earlier beliefs to the test of the text, and, although both did, neither came away from the discussion self-assured; both wanted the play to confirm their certainties, but it clarified and moderated them instead.

III

The play did not do this alone, however; the textual test of Folio required more than reading and performance. It required dialectic. By "dialectic", I mean Socratic.[6] For Socrates, a student's opinion must be held, then clarified and refined through a "refutation" that is ultimately, even if imperfectly, definitional. Socratic refutation, unlike sophistic eristic, leads one closer to the matter at hand, even if that matter cannot be known in and of itself. As Hans-George Gadamer explains in *Plato's Dialectical Ethics*,

> [t]he fact that failure to reach a shared understanding, even in conversations that are concerned with the facts of the matter, is sometimes interpreted in such a way that the contradiction that has emerged is taken as a positive result—that is, as showing a difference in assumption that is not open to discussion—does not cast doubt on what has been said about the guiding concern for the facts of the matter but instead confirms it. (39)

[6] The literature on Socratic dialectic is vast. For the purposes of this paper, I have used Hans-Georg Gadamer's discussions to reflect on what occurred in class. See note 1 above and *Plato's Dialectical Ethics: Phenomenological Interpretations Relating to the* Philebus, trans. Robert M. Wallace (New Haven, Conn.: Yale University Press, 1991), esp. pp. 17–65. In earlier reflections, I found Gregory Vlastos, "The Socratic Elenchus: Method is All", *Socratic Studies*, ed. Myles Burnyeat (Cambridge, Mass.: Cambridge University Press, 1994), pp. 1–29, very instructive. Plato's dialogues themselves remain an indispensable source for enactments of dialectic, as do Shakespeare's plays.

Socratic refutation provides dialogue both with energy, since the interlocutors are attached to their positions, and with purpose, since those positions should be refined through the questioning that discloses contradiction. Again, the exposure of contradiction is not mere deconstruction, but rich reconstruction, during which one grows less, not more confused. Gadamer, again: "Socrates' logical traps ... are living forms of a process of shared understanding which always has the facts of the matter themselves before it and which finds its criterion solely in its success in developing its capacity to see those facts" (58). Our last class on the play was also characterized by yet another method of invention, the rhetorical method of *contraversia*, since I was fortunate enough to have two articulate students disagree, the controversy of which allowed me to put polite pressure on each while siding with neither.[7] Because Todd observed that Shakespeare did not give us a direct representation of Cordelia's ghost, Nicole had to concede that the definition of the soul's immortality she shares with Shakespeare is based on faith; because Nicole observed that Shakespeare need not have done so, Todd had to concede that the soul's mortality is no more confirmed by the play than its immortality. Gadamer: "A dialectical contradiction is not present when one opinion is opposed to another; instead, it is constituted precisely when one and the same faculty of reason has to grant validity to both the opinion and the counter-opinion" (44). The particular form of dialectic here is, by philosophical standards, actually elementary: all they did for each other under my direction was point out that the text did not necessarily support the reading of the other, and, as a result, each subtilized an earlier position. As we interrogate texts, they interrogate us. In response to controversial dialectic, we refine ourselves in relation to others.

[7] For a fine treatment of *contraversia*, see Thomas O. Sloane, *On the Contrary: The Protocol of Traditional Rhetoric* (Washington, D.C.: Catholic University of America Press, 1997). The differences between dialectic and controversy are immaterial for my purposes here. I would argue, though, that they are two means to the same end.

Indeed, leading such dialectic requires that teachers also recognize, in an intimate yet nonetheless public space, their own limitations. If all goes well (it didn't happen that day only because I let Todd get schooled instead of me) students themselves will disclose places in the text that do not necessarily support one's reading, and, while one is looking there—there where the student interlocutor becomes the Socrates, and the Socrates the student—one refines one's interpretations. Given human limitations, we can be interrogated by the text perhaps only through other people, and, during those moments, we achieve greater understanding and are made human. Speech informs care, care of the literary matter at hand and care of one another. Looking there—at a textual representation in all its beautifully and movingly ordered plenitude—looking there together, one sees who we are, even when we cannot be certain who at the very end we will be.[8]

[8] I presented a version of this essay at the 2002 gathering of the Association of Literary Scholars and Critics in Washington, D.C., during "Humanities in the Twenty-First Century: Teaching and Literature, K–12 and College", chaired by Mark Bauerlein. I would like to thank him, Debra Baldwin, John Briggs, William Frank, Eileen Gregory, Joseph Pearce, and Gerard Wegemer for astute and prompt comments on drafts of this essay, and I would like to dedicate it to my Literary Tradition III students in Rome, 1998–2000.

King Lear: Seeing the Comedy of the Tragedy

Joseph Pearce
Ave Maria University

The story of King Lear did not originate with Shakespeare. It had been told by Geoffrey of Monmouth in the twelfth century and reemerged in Book II of Edmund Spenser's *Faerie Queene*, published in 1590, and also in Sir Philip Sidney's *Arcadia*, first published in 1590 and republished in a more complete edition in 1598. Although, no doubt, Shakespeare was aware of these versions of the story it is likely that his principal sources were the *Chronicles* of Holinshed, published in 1577, and, perhaps most influential of all, a dramatized version of the story, entitled *The True Chronicle History of King Leir and his three daughters*. This play, possibly written by George Peele, had been in the repertoire of the Queen's Men since the 1580s, though it wasn't published until late in 1605, around the time that Shakespeare is thought to have started work on his own version of the story.

It seems inescapable that Shakespeare would have known the earlier dramatized version and may even have acted in it. It is, however, a rather frivolous, whimsical work, climaxed with a happy ending, and is very different from the play that Shakespeare would write. Michael Wood, in his biography of Shakespeare, has us imagine him browsing in John Wright's shop near London's Newgate Market in the autumn of 1605: "There, in a freshly inked pile of quartos on the flap board of the shop, lay his old favourite, now available for the first time in print: 'The True Chronicle History of King Leir and his three daughters.... As it hath been divers and sundry times lately acted'. Given his long fascination with the tale, Shakespeare could not have resisted it."[1] In fact, *pace* Wood, there is no evidence

[1] Michael Wood, *Shakespeare* (New York: Basic Books, 2003), p. 274.

that the earlier "Leir" was ever a "favourite" and Shakespeare's decision to write a new version of the play as soon as he became aware of a published edition of the earlier version suggests that he was initially inspired by a desire to write something very different. It might not have been so much "fascination" with the earlier play as provocation by it. Peter Milward, in *Shakespeare's Meta-drama: Othello and King Lear*, writes that the earlier play had been "savagely torn to pieces and ... thoroughly rewritten" by Shakespeare, expurgating its "clearly Protestant, anti-Papist bias". Milward concludes that Shakespeare "was, no doubt, put off by the protestant bias of the old play, just as he had already undertaken in his play of *King John* to modify a similar bias in *The Troublesome Reign of King John*".[2]

Milward unearths further fascinating evidence to suggest a possible source for Shakespeare's inspiration for the writing of *Lear*. In 1603 Sir Brian Annesley, a knight at the court of Queen Elizabeth, died, leaving behind three daughters. Prior to his death, the two elder daughters had tried to have him certified as insane in order to profit from his estate. They were prevented in their efforts by his youngest daughter, Cordelia, who had a monument erected to her parents "against the ungrateful nature of oblivious time". Cordelia Annesley became the second wife of Sir William Harvey, almost certainly an acquaintance of Shakespeare, and it is possible that it was from Sir William that Shakespeare learned of this curious parallel to the story of Lear and his daughters. Further evidence that this might be the case is suggested by the fact that there is no mention of Lear's madness in the original tale, and also from the fact that Shakespeare uses the spelling "Cordelia" for Lear's youngest daughter, whereas it is rendered as "Cordella" in the earlier version of the play (though Spenser uses the spelling "Cordelia" in *The Fairie Queene*).

Regardless of the source of his inspiration for writing a new version of the story, or his motivation for doing so, it would

[2] Peter Milward, S.J., *Shakespeare's Meta-drama: Othello and King Lear* (Tokyo: Renaissance Institute, 2003), p. 104.

clearly be woefully inadequate to limit our discussion of the play to the likely seeds from which it grew without paying due attention to the abundant fruits of Shakespeare's own inimitable imagination. *King Lear*, possibly his greatest work, surpasses and transcends in literary quality and philosophical depth all the earlier versions of the story. The play is, in fact, not one story but two. It interweaves the story of Lear and his daughters with the parallel story of Gloucester and his sons, the latter of which is probably derived from "The Tale of the Blind King of Paphlagonia" in Sidney's *Arcadia*, in such a way that we cannot truly speak of plot and subplot, but only of co-plots woven together with majestic skill.

The co-plots parallel each other on the literal level. Lear is betrayed by the deception of his self-serving daughters, Regan and Goneril; Gloucester by the deception of his illegitimate son, Edmund. Cordelia, the loyal and faithful daughter of Lear, suffers the hardships of exile because of her father's blind arrogance; Edgar, the loyal and legitimate son of Gloucester, suffers the hardships of exile through his father's blind ignorance. Lear and Gloucester lose everything in the worldly sense but, in the process, gain the wisdom they were lacking. The overarching and most obvious moral theme resonates with the Christian paradox that one must lose one's life in order to gain it, or with the words of Christ that there is no greater love than to lay down one's life for one's friends. Lear and Gloucester embody the truth of the former, Cordelia and Edgar (and Kent) the truth of the latter.

Apart from this overarching moral dimension, which should be obvious to all, there is another dimension to Shakespeare's work, rooted in the politics of his day but relevant to the politics of all ages. This dimension, arising from the creative interaction of Shakespeare's Catholic sensibilities with an environment hostile to Catholicism, is discovered in what Peter Milward calls the *meta-drama* of the plays or what Clare Asquith has referred to as the *shadowplays* within the plays.

There has been a great deal of good historical detective work in recent years uncovering the Catholicism of Shakespeare's family and the likely Catholicism of Shakespeare himself. Although the arguments still rage, it seems very likely that Shakespeare remained, at the least, a sympathizer to Catholicism in an age when it was illegal, and probably a secretly practicing Catholic, whether as a so-called "Church Papist", i.e., one who outwardly conformed to the demands of the new Anglican church but secretly attended the Catholic sacraments, or whether as a "recusant", i.e., a defiant Catholic who refused to conform to Anglicanism. If this is so, and the evidence suggests strongly that it is, we would expect to find some form of coded or hidden reference to Catholicism in the plays. It is this coded or hidden Catholicism that can be found in the meta-drama or shadowplay of Shakespeare's work, including *King Lear*.

At this juncture, and before we proceed to look for the meta-dramatic elements in *Lear*, it is necessary to understand the nature of the Catholic dimension in the play. In essence, Shakespeare seems less concerned with the doctrinal differences between Protestants and Catholics than with the persecution of nonconformist believers, Protestant and Catholic alike, at the hands of the secular state. In Shakespeare's time, under the reign of Elizabeth and James, Catholics were the victims of Anglican conformists, not the relatively powerless Protestant nonconformists. The Church of England was neither Catholic nor Protestant but was an uneasy amalgam of both. From its very inception at the behest of Henry VIII, the Church of England was rooted in compromise between its "catholic" and "protestant" members. The former belonged to the so-called "high" church, the latter to the so-called "low" church. Although such differences were tolerated within the state-church, there was no tolerance for nonconformists who refused to join the Anglican communion. Catholics and Protestants alike were victimized for their failure to conform. Both groups were seen as dissidents. It is for this reason that Shakespeare's Catholicism manifests itself in *King Lear* as a dialectic against secularism and the secularist state more than as a dialogue with Protestantism. It is not sectarian but antisecularist. The meta-drama is not played out as Catholics versus Protestants, but as

Christian orthodoxy versus secular fundamentalism. The dynamism of the underlying dialectic, and therefore of the dialogue, is centered on the tension between Christian conscience and self-serving, cynical secularism. Whereas the heroes and heroines of Shakespearian drama are informed by an orthodox Christian understanding of virtue, the villains are normally Machiavellian practitioners of secular *real-politik*, and not Christian "heretics". In this sense, and paradoxically perhaps, the Catholic meta-drama represents one of the most "modern" aspects of Shakespearian drama in terms of its applicability to the contemporary world.

In *King Lear* the meta-drama is present from the very first scene when the king promises political power to those who "love us most". Lear, symbolic of the state, demands all. There can be no room for other loves. Immediately his self-serving daughters, Goneril and Regan, outdo each other in sycophantic promises of absolute allegiance. It is left to Cordelia, the youngest daughter, to "Love, and be silent". She loves her father but cannot "heave [her] heart into [her] mouth", uttering platitudes to curry favor beyond that which her conscience dictates is decorous. Unlike the feigned or affected affection of her sisters, her love is "more ponderous than [her] tongue"; it is genuine and will not debase itself with falsehood or flattery. She will love the king "according to [her] bond, no more nor less". She cannot offer the king (or state) any allegiance beyond that which her conscience dictates is appropriate morally. The parallels with the position that Catholics (and Protestant nonconformists) found themselves in during the reign of Henry VIII, and in Shakespeare's time under Elizabeth and James, is patently obvious. When Henry VIII declared himself supreme head of the Church of England, effectively making religion subject to the state, his subjects were forced to choose between conforming to his wishes, and thereby gaining his favor, or defying his will and incurring his wrath. Only the most courageous chose conscience before concupiscence; most chose to please the king and ignore their conscience. There are always more Gonerils and Regans than there are Cordelias.

The meta-dramatic element is made even more apparent in Cordelia's justification for her refusal to kowtow:

> Good my Lord,
> You have begot me, bred me, loved me. I
> Return those duties back as are right fit,
> Obey you, love you, and most honor you.
> Why have my sisters husbands, if they say
> They love you all? Haply, when I shall wed,
> That lord whose hand must take my plight shall carry
> Half my love with him, half my care and duty.
> Sure I shall never marry like my sisters,
> To love my father all.
> (1.1.97–106)

On the literal level Cordelia proclaims that her future husband has rights over her love that she is not at liberty, in conscience, to dispense with, even to her father. On a deeper level Shakespeare may have been employing marriage as a metaphor for the relationship of the individual believer with Christ. Catholic ecclesiology is rooted in the belief, itself rooted in Scripture, that Christ is the Bridegroom and the Church his Bride. Cordelia's "husband" is Christ and she is not at liberty to render unto Caesar that which belongs to Christ. The allegory and its applicability are clear. Catholics (and Protestants) are not permitted, in conscience, to offer all their love to their father or mother, or to their king or country. They can only love as Cordelia loves, according to their bond. Our parents and our country have begotten us, bred us, loved us, and we should "return those duties back as are right fit" in obedience, love, and honor. This is "right fit" but it goes beyond our bond, beyond the bounds of a good conscience, to obey, love, and honor father or mother, king or country, as gods. The worship of our parents or the worship of the state is a mark of disordered love that presages evil.

"But goes thy heart with this?" asks Lear, following Cordelia's sagacious discourse. "Ay, my good lord", she replies. "So young, and so untender?" says Lear. "So young, my Lord, and true", says Cordelia. The exchange is tellingly poignant. Cordelia is not merely being true to her heart, her conscience (and her God); she is being true to Lear. He is wrong and she is right to tell him so. It is for his good as much as it is for hers. It is no wonder that it has been suggested that the very name of Cordelia is a punning reference to *Coeur de Lear* (Lear's Heart) with echoes of *Coeur de Lion* (Lion Heart). Cordelia has the heart of a lion and she is the heart of Lear. When Lear loses Cordelia he loses his heart and his way.

Apart from the obvious parallels with the secular politics of Elizabethan and Jacobean England, with its persecution of Catholics and other "nonconformist" dissidents, the other major meta-dramatic element revolves around the nature and meaning of "wisdom". It is often said that the Fool can be seen as the personification of Lear's conscience, the voice of (self-) criticism that informs Lear of the folly of his actions and the seriousness of the predicament in which his folly has left him. This, however, is only half the story—and the less important half. The more important half of the story only begins once the Fool disappears without trace. It is only once Edgar takes his place as "Fool" that the deeper wisdom is revealed.

Why does the Fool disappear? Why does a character who has played such an important and integral part in the play, declaiming many of its best and wittiest lines, suddenly disappear into thin air, having declared, as an apparent riposte to Lear, that "I'll go to bed at noon"? Superficially it might appear that this is a formal faux pas on Shakespeare's part. If lesser playwrights allow characters to disappear, leaving apparent loose ends, without so much as a "by your leave", it would be seen as a fatal flaw in their literary abilities. Are we to assume, therefore, that the Fool's disappearance is evidence of a flaw in Shakespeare's literary abilities? Although we might be tempted to make such an assumption, we do so at our peril. Only the most arrogant literary critics would presume to know more about the art of playwriting than the world's greatest playwright. It is, therefore, much safer to assume that Shakespeare had some deeper meaning in mind for the Fool's sudden and unannounced departure. As already stated, it is often assumed that the Fool serves as the king's conscience. As a "fool", a character devoid of discernible family connections and without roots or destiny beyond his function within the drama, he is ideally suited for employment as a personified abstraction conveying allegorical significance. "But where's my Fool?" asks Lear. "I have not seen him this two days." We know therefore that the Fool (Lear's conscience) was significantly absent when Lear made the rash decision to hand his kingdom to Goneril and Regan (who may be said, within the context of this allegorical reading, to represent false love or secular ambition), whilst banishing Cordelia (representing true, self-sacrificial love and perhaps also, as Lear's "heart", Lear's own capacity to love truly and self-sacrificially). Equally significant is the Knight's response to Lear's complaint about the Fool's absence: "Since my young lady's going into France, sir, the Fool hath much pined away." Cordelia's banishment has led to the pining away of Lear's conscience. It can be deduced, therefore, on a psychological level, that his injustice toward Cordelia has left him feeling guilty and that the witticisms of the Fool represent the incessant nagging of the king's conscience.

The Fool first enters the play in person as Lear receives the first of the snubs from his disloyal "loving" daughters, via Oswald, Goneril's steward. As Lear begins to perceive that he might have been foolish in handing over power to his two unworthy daughters whilst banishing the worthy one, the Fool emerges for the first time to rebuke him for the foolishness of his action. When Lear threatens him with "the whip" for daring to speak so candidly, the Fool responds with words of salient and sapient indignation: "Truth's a dog must to kennel; he must be whipped out, when Lady the Brach may stand by th' fire and stink." Such words must have resonated powerfully amongst those members of Shakespeare's audience who feared being persecuted by the secular powers (Lady the Brach) for adhering to religious truths that had been made illegal. The adherents of Truth were suffering, literally left out in the cold, whilst those whose inequities stank to high heaven could warm themselves by the fire (before ultimately being cast into it!).

"Dost thou call me fool, boy?" Lear asks in response to the Fool's nagging witticisms/criticisms. "All thy other titles thou hast given away; that thou wast born with", replies the Fool. Literally the Fool is indeed calling the king a fool, and a fool he is; yet, since "foolishness" is being used as a metaphor for "conscience" and the wisdom it serves, the Fool is also saying that Lear is left with nothing but his conscience. All the other titles, all the other worldly accretions with which he had been robed, have been removed; he is left naked except for his "foolish" conscience, a metaphysical nakedness that is itself a foreshadowing of Lear's physical nakedness in the pivotal scene in Act 3.

It is, however, a common mistake to assume that the words of the Fool encompass and encapsulate the wisdom that Shakespeare wishes to convey in the play, whereas, in fact, and on the contrary, he shows that the wisdom of the Fool is insufficient. It is itself naked. Conscience can only be informed by the "wisdom" it serves, and the "wisdom" of the Fool is very much a worldly wisdom. It understands politics; it understands *real-politik*; it is Machiavellian, albeit in an apparently benign way (unlike the "wisdom" of Edmund, who epitomizes Machiavellianism at its most base and ugly). "Thou hadst little wit in thy bald crown when thou gav'st thy golden one away." This is the limit and the summit of the Fool's wisdom. The king is foolish, in the eyes of the Fool, for losing his kingdom, for losing his power, for exchanging the comforts of his crown for the discomforts of his crownlessness. The Fool would not understand the wisdom of Kent, speaking from the discomfort and humiliation of the stocks, into which he has been placed for defying the secular power, that "nothing almost sees miracles but misery." This, for the Fool, would be folly. Yet this is, for Shakespeare, as for Kent, the beginning of wisdom. The deepest insights in *King Lear* come from those who come to wisdom through suffering, who perceive, furthermore, that the *acceptance* of suffering is the beginning of wisdom. For the

Fool, who seems to believe that wisdom is connected with the pursuit of comfort, or the elimination of suffering, such words would be foolish.

Shakespeare's intention in showing the necessity of suffering to the attainment of wisdom is made manifest in his juxtaposition of Kent's words of wisdom with those of Edgar. The second scene of Act 2 ends with Kent's proclamation that "nothing almost sees miracles but misery"; scene 3 has Edgar, now an outlaw forced to adopt the guise of madness as Poor Tom, proclaiming that "Edgar I nothing am." Edgar is "nothing" in his "misery" and is fit to see miracles, or fit to be the means by which others may see them. He will "with presented nakedness outface the winds and persecutions of the sky" and, in his own nakedness, will inspire Lear to do likewise.

Edgar, disguised as Poor Tom (a "madman"), becomes the voice of sanity and wisdom in the second half of the play, in much the same way that the Fool is the voice of sanity and wisdom in the first half. The difference is that Poor Tom's wisdom is spiritual, unlike the worldliness of the Fool, and, indeed, is avowedly Christian. The Fool greets Poor Tom's arrival with fear: "Come not in here, Nuncle, here's a spirit. Help me, help me!" And again, the Fool repeats: "A spirit, a spirit. He says his name's Poor Tom." Edgar enters, reciting a line from a ballad about the Franciscans ("Through the sharp hawthorn blows the cold wind"), and bemoaning how the devil, "the foul fiend", had led him "through fire and through flame". The Franciscan connection is apposite and surely not accidental since Saint Francis was known as the *jongleur de Dieu*, God's juggler, or a "fool for Christ", who famously stripped himself naked in public and, "with presented nakedness", witnessed to his "houseless poverty". Edgar, as Poor Tom, plays the Franciscan part to perfection and begins to eclipse the Fool as the voice of sanity and to replace him in the role as Lear's conscience. Compare, for instance, the pragmatic worldliness of the Fool's "wisdom" with Poor Tom's allusion to the Ten Commandments followed by his candid confession of sin:

> *Fool*. This cold night will turn us all to fools and madmen.
> *Edgar*. Take heed o' th' foul fiend; obey thy parents; keep thy word's justice; swear not; commit not with man's sworn spouse; set not thy sweet heart on proud array. Tom's a cold.
> *Lear*. What hast thou been?
> *Edgar*. A servingman, proud in heart and mind; that curled my hair, wore gloves in my cap; served the lust of my mistress' heart, and did the act of darkness with her; swore as many oaths as I spake words, and broke them in the sweet face of heaven. One that slept in the contriving of lust, and waked to do it. Wine loved I deeply, dice dearly; and in woman out-paramoured the Turk. False of heart, light of ear, bloody of hand; hog in sloth, fox in stealth, wolf in greediness, dog in madness, lion in prey. Let not the creaking of shoes nor the rustling of silks betray thy poor heart to woman. Keep thy foot out of brothels, thy hand out of plackets, thy pen from lenders' books, and defy the foul fiend. Still through the hawthorn blows the cold wind. (3.4.79–100)

"Tom's a-cold." Sanity, seen as madness by the worldly, is out in the cold, confessing its sins, and gaining wisdom through suffering. (Meanwhile, insanity, "Lady the Brach", is in the warmth of Gloucester's castle, standing by the fire in the stench of its own iniquity, corrupted by the pursuit of comfort.) Tom repeats the refrain from the Franciscan ballad and Lear, pricked with the hawthorn of conscience more than by the cold wind, emulates Poor Tom's example, and the example of Saint Francis, by tearing off his clothes and proclaiming "off, off, you lendings!" This is the pivotal moment of the play, the point on which the drama turns, the moment when Lear finally goes "mad". It is the "madness" of religious conversion. His conscience is baptized and the Fool makes way for Edgar. From this moment the Fool fades from view (so much so that his disappearance is hardly noticed) and Edgar emerges in his place as Lear's *Christian* conscience. "The Prince of Darkness is a gentleman", Poor Tom proclaims; and, when Lear asks him, "What is your study?" he answers: "How to prevent the fiend, and to kill vermin." To Lear's unbaptized conscience, these words would have appeared foolish. He would have seen the poverty-stricken surface of the tramp and not the depths of his wisdom; he would have perceived that the vermin were fleas or lice, not sins and vice. Now, however, he refers to Poor Tom as "this philosopher" or as this "learnèd Theban", the latter reminiscent of the famous Teiresias, the blind seer of Greek legend whose eyeless vision is far better than those with eyes to see. The parallel with Poor Tom, who sees more in the "blindness" of his "madness" than the world sees in its "sanity", and who in his poverty is richer than kings, is clear enough.

Once one perceives the importance and profundity of Edgar's role and purpose, one begins to see that even his "nonsense" makes sense, albeit in the coded way in which a riddle makes sense. Take, for instance, the words with which Edgar brings this pivotal scene to a close:

> Child Rowland to the dark tower came;
> His word was still, "Fie, foh, and fum,
> I smell the blood of a British man."
> (3.4.185–87)

Rowland, the nephew of Charlemagne, the Holy Roman Emperor, and the hero of the medieval classic, *The Song of Roland*, is a symbol of Christian resistance to the infidels; he is also a symbol of Christian martyrdom, slain by the infidel hordes. The juxtaposition of Rowland with the nursery tale of Jack the Giant-Killer is intriguing. This nursery tale, a great favorite of G.K. Chesterton, who perceived it as a perennial reminder of the struggle of the righteous underdog against the encroachments of iniquitous power, appears to be an allusion to the play's own inner struggle between the Machiavellian giants of infidel iniquity and the righteous underdogs, stripped of power but gaining thereby in faith and wisdom. As with *The Song of Roland*, Shakespeare's *Lear* recounts the struggle between the Christian underdog and the infidel hordes; and, as with Jack the Giant-Killer, it is a struggle between the Giant Might of the State and the plight of powerless dissidents. The recitation of the Giant's ominous chant, "Fie, foh, and fum, I smell the blood of a British man", seems to evoke the martyrdom of Catholics in Shakespeare's own time at the hands of the giant power of the state and conjures the shadow of the looming presence of the play's own malicious giants, Goneril, Regan, and Edmund, who crave for the blood of their powerless enemies.

The use of the crime of "treason" as the justification for the persecution, and execution, of Catholics in Elizabethan and Jacobean England is evoked in the use of the charge of treason by Cornwall and Regan against the innocent Gloucester. The word "traitor" is employed no fewer than four times by Cornwall and Regan in the space of only eighteen lines, a repetition that must have resonated potently with the highly charged politics of Shakespeare's England.

Edgar's words at the beginning of Act 4, coming immediately after the horrific punishment carried out by Cornwall and Regan against the "traitor" Gloucester (Edgar's father), and immediately before he sees him in his pitiable blinded state, are particularly powerful and singularly apt:

> Yet better thus, and known to be contemned,
> Than still contemned and flattered. To be worst,
> The lowest and most dejected thing of fortune,
> Stands still in esperance, lives not in fear:
> The lamentable change is from the best,
> The worst returns to laughter.
>
> (4.1.1–6)

It is "better" to be "known to be contemned" (by the state), Edgar insists, "than still contemned [by God] and flattered". The one whose conscience is clean "stands still in esperance [hope]" (of Salvation) and "lives not in fear" (of Final Damnation). The words about the "lamentable change" being "from the best" whilst the "worst returns to laughter" reminds us of *The Consolation of Philosophy* by Boethius, as do the words of Kent from the "misery" of the stocks: "Fortune, good night; / Smile once more, turn thy wheel."

The arrival of Gloucester allows Shakespeare to play with the axiomatic paradoxes at the heart of the play: the blind seer, the wise fool, and the sane madman. "I stumbled when I saw", says Gloucester, alluding to his "blindness" (when he still had his sight) in believing the treachery of Edmund and in condemning the innocent Edgar. "Bad is the trade that must play fool to sorrow", says Edgar, possibly a coded allusion to Shakespeare's own position as a "closet dissident" daring only to speak out against the injustices of the time in the meta-dramatic language of blind-men, madmen, and fools. "'Tis the times' plague, when madmen lead the blind", says Gloucester, employing the paradox with the double-edged sharpness of the *double entendre* and with the implicit meta-dramatic indictment of the *status quo* in Jacobean England. Seeing more clearly now that he is blind, Gloucester speaks disdainfully of "the superfluous and lust-dieted man" who "will not see because he does not feel". Physical blindness is as nothing compared to the metaphysical blindness of those who succumb to the comfortable numbness of secular ambition and the materialism it serves.

The same axiomatic paradox prevails in the following scene in which Albany becomes Goneril's "fool". "My fool usurps my body", says Goneril, expressing her contempt for her husband. As ever, however, the "fool" in *Lear* is more than it seems. Though, no doubt, Goneril is referring to her husband, it is Edmund who is "usurping" her body. We have just learned of Goneril's adulterous relationship with him, or at least her adulterous intentions toward him. In this sense, Shakespeare is saying that Goneril, being a fool, sees her husband as a fool, whereas, in fact, Edmund is the fool, morally speaking, through his lack of virtue. One might even say that Goneril's own lustful passion, her sin, is the "fool" that usurps her body. Legitimacy, in the Christian understanding of marriage, is the love, conjugal and otherwise, between husband and wife; illegitimacy is lust and adultery, both of which can be said to usurp the legitimate bounds of marriage. In this context, Edmund's own illegitimacy seems to accentuate the deeper meanings of "foolishness" being presented to us.

If Albany is Goneril's "fool" we should not be surprised that he fulfills the same function as Lear's Fool and Lear's "madman",

Edgar. Throughout the scene he is the conveyer of wisdom, though Goneril, unlike Lear, is not disposed to listen to the promptings of her "conscience". "O Goneril!" Albany exclaims upon entering the scene, immediately after Goneril has proclaimed him her "fool":

> You are not worth the dust which the rude wind
> Blows in your face. I fear your disposition:
> That nature which contemns its origin
> Cannot be bordered certain in itself;
> She that herself will sliver and disbranch
> From her material sap, perforce must wither
> And come to deadly use.
>
> (4.2.30–36)

On the literal level of the drama, the virtuous Albany is warning his wife that her sinfulness and her evil disposition will have evil consequences; on the deeper level of the metadrama it is difficult to avoid the conclusion that Shakespeare, the Catholic or at least the Catholic sympathizer, is referring to the Anglican church, and its anomalous position, when he speaks of the "nature which contemns its origin cannot be bordered certain in itself" (that which breaks with tradition will not have the authority to define doctrine) and "will sliver and disbranch from her material sap" (will become separated from the living tradition and sacramental life of the Church), and thus "perforce must wither and come to deadly use". Albany's words echo the "prophecy" of the Fool in Act 3:

> When priests are more in word than matter;
> When brewers mar their malt with water;
> When nobles are their tailors' tutors,
> No heretics burned, but wenches' suitors;
> . . . .
> Then shall the realm of Albion
> Come to great confusion.
>
> (3.2.81–84, 91–92)

On the most obvious level, the reference to priests being "more in word than matter" alludes to hypocritical clergy failing to practice what they preach. Shakespeare may, however, have had more in mind than a merely Chaucerian condemnation of bad clergy. By Shakespeare's time, the speculation of many Catholics toward Anglicanism was such that it was commonly believed that the Anglican clergy was not validly ordained, and that, therefore, they were priests "more in word than matter".[3]

Goneril responds to her husband's reproach with contempt, telling him that "the text is foolish" upon which his sermon is based. Albany replies that "wisdom and goodness to the vile seem vile: Filths savor but themselves." The riposte is incisive. Goneril considers Albany's Christian approach to virtue "foolish" because her lack of virtue makes her blind to "wisdom and goodness". Albany is a "fool" to the eyes of the blind. Goneril's contempt for Christianity is made manifest when she calls her husband a "milk-livered man" who "bear'st a cheek for blows", indicating her disdain for anyone who "turns the other cheek". She, like Edmund, her partner in adultery, is a disciple of Machiavelli, not Christ.

The denouement begins in earnest when Edgar heals his father of his suicidal despair. "Why I do trifle thus with his despair is done to cure it." "Thy life's a miracle", Edgar tells Gloucester after the latter's failed "suicide" attempt, adding that the "fiend" (despair) has parted from him. Gloucester's recovery of hope is connected to his embrace and acceptance of suffering:

> henceforth I'll bear
> Affliction till it do cry out itself
> "Enough, enough," and die.
> (4.6.75–77)

[3] The invalidity of Anglican clergy was not formally promulgated by the Catholic Church until *Apostolicae Curae* in the reign of Pope Leo XIII (1878–1903), but because of the changes to the consecration of bishops in the Edwardian Ordinal, during the short reign of King Edward VI (1547–1553), speculation had already begun with regard to the validity, or otherwise, of Anglican Orders.

"Bear free and patient thoughts", counsels Edgar, reminding Gloucester that true freedom is connected to patience, particularly patience under crosses, patience in the face of adversity and suffering. He who loses such patience loses his freedom and becomes a slave to his appetites, a slave to sin.

As Edgar utters these words of perennial wisdom to his father, King Lear enters "fantastically dressed in wild flowers". It is now that Shakespeare's genius really excels. Lear, the epitome of "madness", emerges as a figure of Christ, the epitome of sanity. "No, they cannot touch me for coining", Lear proclaims; "I am the King himself." This is the first clue to the figurative appearance of Christ, though it becomes more obvious later. Lear is not a counterfeit king, he is "the King himself", the True King from whom all other kings derive their authority. Edgar alludes to the Christ connection immediately by heralding Lear's appearance with the exclamation "O thou side-piercing sight!"—a phrase that encapsulates both the tragedy and the comedy of Lear's "madness". His flower-clad appearance is side-piercingly comic, yet Edgar's words also remind us of the piercing of Christ's side after his death on the Cross. No doubt, to the eyes of the blind, the sight of the "King of the Jews" wearing a crown of thorns would have been side-piercingly comic. Lear declares that he is "cut to th' brains", referring to a presumably imaginary head wound and also to his "madness". His words remind us of the crown of thorns piercing the head of Christ. Lear's purgatorially purified imagination is now fit to receive the stigmata, the very wounds of Christ, echoing the Franciscan "madness" of Edgar (Saint Francis having famously received the stigmata). Immediately afterward we are given an even clearer indication of the juxtaposition of Lear's suffering with the suffering of Christ:

> *Lear*. No seconds? all myself?
> Why, this would make a man a man of salt,
> To use his eyes for garden water-pots,
> Ay, and laying autumn's dust.
> *Gentleman:* Good sir—

> *Lear*: I will die bravely, like a smug bridegroom.
> What!
> I will be jovial: come, come; I am a king;
> Masters, know you that?
> (4.6.196–203)

The imagery in these few lines is awash with references to the Agony in the Garden. "No seconds? all myself?" alludes to the fact that Christ is left alone in his Agony. Having beseeched his disciples, his "seconds", to stay awake, they had fallen asleep. This weakness on the part of his closest companions "would make a man a man of salt, / To use his eyes for garden water-pots". The tears of salt water fall to the ground, watering the Garden. Ultimately Christ's Passion and subsequent Resurrection ("Then there's life in 't", says Lear at the end of this Passion-coded discourse) would water "autumn's dust", the dust of the Fall. He "will die bravely" on the following day, "like a smug bridegroom". Christ, of course, referred to himself, through his parables, as the Bridegroom, and he is, of course, "a king", though many denied his Kingship and were scandalized by it: "I am a king; Masters, know you that?" The faithful know it; the infidels do not.

Why, one wonders, is Shakespeare so intent on equating Lear with Christ? He is indicating that, having shown contrition and having taken up his own cross, Lear has mystically united himself with the Suffering of Christ. In so doing, Christ's very Presence will be mystically united with the one who takes up his cross and follows him. Lear is one with Christ.

The profundities now come thick and fast. "Nature's above art in that respect", proclaims Lear, an allusion to the popular Renaissance debate concerning the relative importance of nature ("gift", talent or inspiration) and art (training). In insisting on the primacy of God-given talent and inspiration over artfulness or cunning, Lear is really encapsulating the inherent dynamic of the whole play. On one side are the "sheep" who come to an acceptance of God's grace, and the virtue that is its fruit (Lear, Cordelia, Edgar, Kent, Gloucester,

Albany); on the other are the "goats" who refuse God's grace and rely on their own artfulness and cunning (Goneril, Regan, Edmund, Cornwall).

Lear now swaps roles with Edgar, espousing seemingly delirious "reason in madness", or, rather, reason in riddles. In the sense that Edgar was a figurative representation of Lear's Christian conscience, Lear *becomes* Edgar as soon as he becomes one with his conscience. Referring to the words of flattery of Goneril and Regan, he remarks with humility that "they told me I was everything; 'tis a lie, I am not ague-proof." When Gloucester asks to kiss his hand, he responds: "Let me wipe it first; it smells of mortality." Cured of his pride, he denounces the harlotry of his daughters with the same shrill sanity that had characterized Edgar's earlier denunciation of the "fiend":

> Behold yond simp'ring dame,
> Whose face between her forks presages snow,
> That minces virtue and does shake the head
> To hear of pleasure's name.
> The fitchew, nor the soilèd horse, goes to 't
> With a more riotous appetite.
> Down from the waist they are Centaurs,
> Though women all above:
> But to the girdle do the gods inherit,
> Beneath is all the fiend's.
> There's hell, there's darkness, there is the
> sulphurous pit,
> Burning, scalding, stench, consumption; fie, fie, fie!
> (4.6.120–31)

Having regained the "madness" of humility, Lear is now ready to be reunited with Cordelia.

"Ripeness is all", Edgar reminds his father, and Lear is now ripe enough in wisdom and virtue to meet the daughter he had wronged and beg forgiveness, just as Gloucester had ripened through suffering to be reconciled with the son he had wronged. Having been reunited with his heart (*coeur de Lear*), the king is now ready to suffer whatever fortune throws at him.

Even the prospect of prison is desirable if it means being united with Cordelia.

> Come, let's away to prison:
> We two alone will sing like birds i' th' cage:
> When thou dost ask me blessing, I'll kneel down
> And ask of thee forgiveness: so we'll live,
> And pray, and sing, and tell old tales, and laugh
> At gilded butterflies, and hear poor rogues
> Talk of court news; and we'll talk with them too,
> Who loses and who wins, who's in, who's out;
> And take upon's the mystery of things,
> As if we were God's spies: and we'll wear out,
> In a walled prison, packs and sects of great ones
> That ebb and flow by th' moon.
>
> (5.3.8–19)

Lear gets his desire instantly, as Edmund orders them to be taken to prison. His response is one of joy: "Upon such sacrifices, my Cordelia, / The gods themselves throw incense." It is difficult to read these lines of Lear without the ghostly presence of martyred Catholics coming to mind. There is circumstantial evidence to suggest that the young Shakespeare had known the Jesuit martyr Edmund Campion, and even stronger evidence to suggest that he had known Robert Southwell, the Jesuit poet and martyr who had ministered secretly to London's beleaguered Catholics in the early 1590s. The Jesuits were "traitors" in the eyes of Elizabethan and Jacobean law but were "God's spies" in the eyes of England's Catholics. If caught they were imprisoned and tortured before being publicly executed. Since it seems likely that Shakespeare had known Southwell, and since it is even possible that he might have been amongst the large crowd who witnessed Southwell being executed, the words of Lear resonate with potent poignancy: "Upon such sacrifices. . . . The gods themselves throw incense." Within this context the repetition of the word "traitor" four times in only eighteen lines by Regan and Cornwall during their interrogation of Gloucester has perhaps an added significance. It is also significant perhaps that Edmund declares himself a disciple of the new secular creed of Machiavelli almost immediately after these words of Lear are spoken. "[K]now thou this, that men/Are as the time is", he declares, implicitly deriding the "madness" of Lear's faith-driven words in favor of relativism and self-serving *realpolitik*. Lear himself had criticized the Machiavellian worldliness of Edmund and his ilk in his stated desire that he and Cordelia, from the sanity and sanctity of their prison cell, should "laugh at gilded butterflies", those elaborately attired courtiers fluttering over nothing but fads and fashions, "and hear poor rogues talk of court news", in the knowledge that they as "God's spies" will outlast, even in "a walled prison", the "packs and sects of great ones" that "ebb and flow by th' moon". Fashions come and go, Lear seems to be saying, but the Truth remains. He also seems to be implying, through his reference to the moon, that it is Edmund and the play's other "gilded butterflies" and "poor rogues" who are the real lunatics, trading the promise of virtue's eternal reward for life's transient pleasures, trading sanity for the madness of Machiavelli.

Lear's "reason in madness" culminates in the enigma of his last words, uttered over the dead body of Cordelia.

> Do you see this? Look on her. Look, her lips,
> Look there, look there.
>
> (5.3.312–13)

His last vision, moments before his death, is that of Cordelia risen from the dead. He dies, therefore, deliriously happy.

Perhaps G.K. Chesterton had *King Lear* in mind when he dubbed Shakespeare "delirious" in comparing him to Chaucer:

> Chaucer was a poet who came at the end of the medieval age and order ... the final fruit and inheritor of that order.... He was much more sane and cheerful and normal than most of the later writers. He was less delirious than Shakespeare, less harsh than Milton, less fanatical than Bunyan, less embittered than Swift.

The fact is that Chaucer could condemn the corruption of his own day through the perspective of a Christian faith that he knew all his compatriots shared. Shakespeare lived at a time of philosophical and theological fragmentation in which the medieval age and order had been broken. He could not condemn the corruption of his age through the perspective of the Christian faith that he shared with Chaucer because the faith of Chaucer was now outlawed. Like Cordelia he had little option but to "love, and be silent". Shakespeare's delirium was the delirium of Lear, the delirium of Edgar. It was "reason in madness". Indeed one cannot avoid hearing the delirium of Shakespeare in the words of Edgar as he enunciates the final words of this finest of plays.

> The weight of this sad time we must obey,
> Speak what we feel, not what we ought to say.
> The oldest hath borne most: we that are young
> Shall never see so much, nor live so long.
> (5.3.325–28)

In Edgar's words we hear a lament for contemporary England, and a lament, perhaps, for Shakespeare's own recently deceased father, who had been persecuted for his Catholic faith. We hear also a lament for the loss of Catholic England and the rise of the modernism of Machiavelli. We hear a swansong for Chaucer's England. Yet there remains hope, a hope that is enshrined in the play's happy ending. "All friends shall taste the wages of their virtue," says Albany, "and all foes the cup of their deservings." Justice is done. Edmund, Goneril, Regan, and Cornwall are dead. Cordelia and Lear are also dead but there is an inkling in Lear's final vision that the lips of Cordelia, and those of Lear himself, are about to "taste the wages of their virtue". And, of course, there is sublime hope in the fact that the kingdom is left in the hands of Edgar, whose baptized Christian conscience had restored Lear to his sanity. It is the meekness of Edgar that inherits the earth, not the Machiavellian madness of Edmund or the more benign secularism of the Fool. As with the climax to all good comedies, all's well that ends well.

It is indeed ironic, and paradoxically perplexing, that this most delirious of Shakespeare's plays is usually considered a tragedy, even though, for those who see with the eyes of Lear, or Edgar, or Cordelia, it has a happy ending. Perhaps the real tragedy is that so many of those who read Shakespeare do not possess the eyes of Lear, Edgar, and Cordelia. In the infernal and purgatorial sufferings of life we lose sight of the promise of Paradise. We see only a tragedy where we should see a Divine Comedy.

Tragic Necessity and the Uncertainty of Faith in Shakespeare's *King Lear*

Jack Trotter
Trident College

In a recent article on *King Lear*[1] Shakespeare critic Linda Jacobs recounts an incident that occurred during her undergraduate days as an English major at Duke University. In the midst of a class discussion of the play Jacobs expressed the view that the final scene offers a "vision of transcendence". Her professor pounced upon this timid undergraduate affirmation with that near-hysterical tone of righteous indignation peculiar to bored middle-aged academics: "What do you mean, a 'vision of transcendence'? This play has no hope, no justice, no redemption. Cordelia's dead, Gloucester's dead, Lear's Fool is dead; nothing will save them." When Jacobs responded that Lear dies "believing [Cordelia] alive", her professor shrieked: "That's because he's crazy, insane—a nutty old man howling at the universe! It's all absolutely meaningless!" Indeed, it is not hard to imagine such scenes, if slightly less hysterical, being played out in college classrooms across the country even today, for, with a few notable exceptions, academic criticism of *King Lear* in recent decades has been and continues to be relentlessly secular in its assumptions and in its *modus operandi*.

Prior to the early 1960s, this by now reflexively secularist approach to *King Lear* was by no means the predominant one. During the first half of the twentieth century the normative critical assumption was that Shakespearean tragedy, like classical Greek tragedy, is incomprehensible unless it is imagined as unfolding against a transcendent horizon, unless the flawed

[1] Linda Jacobs, "Spies of God: *King Lear* and the Christian Mystics", *Intégrité Journal* (online), (Missouri Baptist University, 2005), http://www.mobap.edu/academics/fl/journal/3.2/jacobs.asp.

or partial ethical claims of its protagonists are judged against an ethical absolute external to the tragic "world" itself. For the most part, during those years, *King Lear* was assumed to be a Christian tragedy. And even when a specifically Christian interpretation was rejected, it was nonetheless frequently asserted, following the line taken by A. C. Bradley, that the play is marked by a "redemptive" pattern.[2] One might readily agree with some recent critics of the Christian interpretive tradition that it was sometimes guilty of an excessively dogmatic or allegorizing tendency. There remains, however, a compelling argument in favor of the view that a traditional reading of *King Lear*—one that recognizes its transcendent dimension—does greater justice to the play than more recent interpretations, most of which are perversely wedded to a postmodern and (implicitly) nihilistic cultural zeitgeist. While it may be somewhat misleading to refer to *King Lear* as a "Christian tragedy", the play is certainly suffused with powerful *intimations* of Christian hope of deliverance from a hideously fallen world.

Those who oppose a Christian reading of *King Lear* are ever at pains to point to what they perceive as the overwhelmingly pagan atmosphere of the play, which abounds with references to the gods, to Fate, and to an astral fatalism that portends, in Gloucester's lament, some great disruption of the natural order:

> In cities,
> mutinies; in countries, discord; in palaces,
> treason; and the bond cracked 'twixt son and
> father.
>
> (1.2.116–19).

But in one important respect the perceived dichotomy between the pagan and Christian worlds misconstrues the actuality. Gloucester's lament, properly understood, assumes a vision of the natural and cosmic order that was common to both pagans

[2] A. C. Bradley, *Shakespearean Tragedy*, 2nd ed. (London: Macmillan, 1926), p. 285.

and Christians. As Hans Urs von Balthasar (among others) has argued, the Christian break with the pagan world was by no means a complete rupture. Plato, Aristotle, the Stoics, Saint Augustine, Saint Thomas, Nicolas of Cusa—for all these great thinkers "the prevailing view is one of being sheltered in the all-embracing union of 'God and nature' ... (*Deus sive natura*)". Between pagan philosopher and Christian theologian there is a "family likeness". Even when God is understood to be transcendent, "he is at the same time so immanent that the world is experienced and understood as a spontaneous revelation ... since both in paganism and in Christianity the highest and noblest parts of the cosmos are thought to belong to the sphere of the divine, to the kingdom of God or to heaven".[3] More importantly, in the Christian Middle Ages and continuing into the Renaissance, an identity of nature and reason is assumed, one that "asserts the analogy between the physical and the spiritual, necessary and free, social and private; but it clearly gives the whole, the cosmos, priority over the part that is man." As a part of this "comprehensive world order", man's spiritual and intellectual aim must be to "reflect the whole in himself, while submitting to its gently compelling law in harmony with which he preserves [*synterein*] the parts given him."[4] In the dramatic world inhabited by Gloucester and Lear, the term "nature" is used predominantly to invoke that "comprehensive world order" of which von Balthasar speaks. But that same cosmic order, with all the psychic security that it offered, is already by the early seventeenth century showing signs of breaking up. What is now emergent, in von Balthasar's view, is a decisive shift away from that cosmos that "has priority over the part that is man" toward the priority of man himself, toward a desacralization of nature and cosmos. This new "demiurgic" humanity will in time assume the "power to arrange the world

[3] Hans Urs von Balthasar, *The God Question and Modern Man*, trans. Hilda Graef (New York: The Seabury Press, 1967), p. 17. Von Balthasar explores the same theme at greater length in his *Theo-Drama, Vol. II: Dramatis Personae: Man in God*, trans. Graham Harrison (San Francisco: Ignatius Press, 1990), pp. 346–64.

[4] Von Balthasar, *God Question*, p. 16.

according to his plans and calculations"[5] and is perhaps prefigured in the character of Edmund, Gloucester's bastard son, by whom such a demiurgic power is taken for granted.

In his ruthless manipulation of the lives of others, Edmund recognizes no natural or moral order, but only the autonomy of his own will. When in his first soliloquy Edmund addresses nature as a "goddess" to whom his "services are bound" (1.2.1–2), he is of course speaking with the flippant insincerity of an Iago or a Richard III; yet behind the cynically comic mask there is self-revelation as well. Opinions vary as to the provenance of that "Nature" the bastard here invokes, though there is general agreement that she is not the all-embracing and benign *natura* that Lear is thinking of when he cries out against his daughter Goneril's cruelty:

> Hear, Nature, hear; dear Goddess, hear:
> Suspend thy purpose if thou didst intend
> To make this creature fruitful.
> (1.4.282–84)

Rather, Edmund seems to pay homage to a desacralized nature that has been emptied of any immanent moral law. Brandishing the forged letter that he will use to betray his brother, Edgar, he embraces his bastardy (much as Richard III embraces his deformity) as if it were a perverse badge of honor:

> Fine word, "legitimate."
> Well, my legitimate, if this letter speed,
> And my invention thrive, Edmund the base
> Shall top th' legitimate. I grow, I prosper.
> Now, gods, stand up for bastards.
> (1.2.18–22)

Legitimacy, i.e., the moral law, is but a word; Edmund, the nominalist, worships a goddess who is little more than a projection of his own will to power.

[5] Ibid., p. 74.

If Edmund inhabits a desacralized cosmos in which man is no longer the microcosm of a greater, harmonic whole, Lear remains a man of the old order of hierarchy and degree, a patriarchal, sacralized order in which reverence for fathers by their offspring is as "natural" as the rising and the setting of the sun. Modern readers of *King Lear* frequently find it difficult—at least initially—to see why Lear's ill treatment at the hands of his elder daughters, Regan and Goneril, is so shocking. After all, the old king is domineering, self-centered, petulant, unpredictable, and possibly senile. Even worse, after making himself comfortable in Goneril's house, he demands the right to carouse at all hours with a small army of drinking companions and his "all-licensed fool" (1.4.206). Thus we are not without sympathy for Goneril when she demands:

> Be then desired . . .
> A little to disquantify your train,
> And the remainders that shall still depend,
> To be such men as may besort your age,
> Which know themselves, and you.
> (1.4.253–58)

When the enraged Lear calls his daughter a "degenerate bastard" (line 260) for what he perceives as her ingratitude, we are apt to suppose that the ingratitude is surely his! But Shakespeare's Jacobean audience, while recognizing in Lear's response the exaggerated spite of a man whose every want has always been satisfied without question, would doubtless have been disturbed by Goneril's cold and condescending tone. Indeed, many of them would have been well versed in the works of the Elizabethan moralist Richard Hooker, who succinctly states the commonplace wisdom of the age when he writes, "To fathers within their private families Nature hath given a supreme power; for which cause we see throughout the world even from the foundation thereof."[6]

[6] Richard Hooker, *Of the Laws of Ecclesiastical Polity*, 1.10.4.

When Lear seeks refuge with his second daughter, Regan, he still clings to the remnants of a naïve faith in filial devotion, but even that will shortly be stripped from him.

> Thou better know'st
> The offices of nature, bond of childhood,
> Effects of courtesy, dues of gratitude
> (2.4.176–78)

And when Regan proves as adamant in her refusal of nature's office as had Goneril before her, Lear declares his intention to "abjure all roofs, and choose / To wage against th' enmity o' th' air" (2.4.207–8). This already half-mad old king surely senses that it is more than his knights that his daughters wish to deprive him of, that what they want is that he should be "ruled" by them, yielding up the last of his royal prerogatives, and thus the only dignity that he understands. After Goneril joins her implacable sister in this scene that resembles nothing so much as a ritual humiliation, our sympathies are now wholly with this wretched old man, his heart torn between defiance and groveling submission. When Goneril questions Lear's need for even a single knight, he cries out in one of the most oft-quoted speeches of the play,

> O reason not the need! Our basest beggars
> Are in the poorest thing superfluous.
> Allow not nature more than nature needs,
> Man's life is cheap as beast's.
> (2.4.263–66)

Human nature, stripped of all but the barest necessities, is reduced to the bestial. Man is a symbolic animal; his truest needs are nonmaterial. It is not the knights themselves that Lear requires, but what they represent: the remains of his former pomp and power. This, of course, the sisters understand perfectly. To strip him of the last symbolic vestiges of royalty is to render him harmless, no longer a threat to their own ambitions.

When Lear declares himself prepared to "abjure all roofs ... and wage against the enmity of the air", he initiates the passage from cosmos to chaos. In renouncing the security of shelter, he symbolically abandons, in Mircea Eliade's words, "the universe that man constructs for himself by imitating the paradigmatic creation of the gods, the cosmogony".[7] To make such a transit is to enter "a foreign, chaotic space peopled by ghosts, demons, 'foreigners'".[8] Yet it is also here that Lear's genuine nobility of spirit becomes apparent for the first time as he confronts the tempest—the path of his errant will having become one with the pattern of tragic necessity that will drive him finally to join his beloved Cordelia in death. In defying the tempest, he calls chaos itself down upon his head:

> Rage, blow!
> You cataracts and hurricanoes, spout
> Till you have drenched our steeples, drowned the cocks.
> (3.2.1–3)

The imagery of drowning recalls, of course, the destructive power of the Flood and, perhaps, foreshadows that "promised end" of which Kent speaks in the final scene of the play (5.3.265). Certainly the concluding lines of the same speech suggest as much:

> And thou, all-shaking thunder,
> Strike flat the thick rotundity o' th' world,
> Crack nature's molds, all germains spill at once,
> That makes ingrateful man.
> (3.2.6–9)

Images of creation and annihilation are fused here in what must be one of the most frightening poetic visions in all of Western literature, but even in the midst of this apocalyptic return to chaos we note that Lear's personal grievance has

[7] Mircea Eliade, *The Sacred and the Profane: The Nature of Religion*, trans. Willard R. Trask (New York: Harvest/HBJ, 1959), pp. 56–57.

[8] Ibid., p. 29.

become—at least for the moment—universal; it is not merely ungrateful daughters that he rails against, but "ungrateful man".

Shakespeare's audience would have been acutely aware of another, equally pertinent, Old Testament parallel: the suffering of God's faithful servant in the Book of Job. Like Job, Lear has been stripped of all his worldly goods, has been shamed by his accusers, and made to wander in a wilderness of pain. Although Lear is not the "perfect and upright man" (Job 1:1)[9] that Job is, he is truly "more sinned against than sinning" (3.2.60). Just as Lear imagines the elements of the tempest as agents of divine vengeance against the wickedness of men, so also Job frequently conjures up images of storm and whirlwind as proofs of God's destruction of the wicked: "How oft is the candle of the wicked put out! And how oft cometh their destruction upon them! ... They are as stubble before the wind, and as chaff that the storm carrieth away" (Job 21:17–18). Both men, even in the depths of their suffering, remain hopeful that divine justice will in the end vindicate them. Yet in this shared hope there lies an important divergence as well. In the end, Job's repeated demand that God reveal Himself, that He provide a response to Job's apparent abandonment, is indeed answered. God speaks to him "out of the whirlwind" (38:1). But for Lear, no such answer is forthcoming. It may be argued, of course, that in the final scenes of *King Lear* the wicked receive their justice in death, but this argument is problematic, since Cordelia's life is perversely taken as well. In any event, at this juncture, Lear's cries are lifted to a deaf heaven. Neither God nor gods speak to him out of the whirlwind. His demands for justice become increasingly querulous and half-hearted, as we see for example in the "trial" scene (3.6).

If we are to discern a transcendent, redemptive horizon in *King Lear*, we must approach the problem from another direction. If in the desacralized cosmos God no longer speaks to man through nature, in that "spontaneous revelation" to which von Balthasar alludes, then it remains possible that the eye of

[9] All biblical references are taken from the King James Version, Revised.

faith may find providential care in the pattern of "blind" necessity that has driven Lear to the verge of madness. And does not Lear's recognition of a common humanity with his Fool and his apparently fortuitous encounter with Tom o' Bedlam in the midst of the tempest reveal a glimpse of such care? When Kent, now in disguise, discovers a hovel upon the heath and urges Lear to take shelter, the humiliated king shows for the first time some genuine concern for the suffering of another.

> Come on, my boy. How dost, my boy? Art cold?
> . . . .
> Poor Fool and knave, I have one part in my heart
> That's sorry yet for thee.
> (3.2.68, 72–73)

Later, standing alone outside the hovel, his concern for the Fool now embraces, universally, the wretched of the earth:

> Poor naked wretches, wheresoe'er you are,
> That bide the pelting of this pitiless storm,
> How shall your houseless heads and unfed sides,
> Your looped and windowed raggedness, defend you
> From seasons such as these? O, I have ta'en
> Too little care of this! Take physic, pomp,
> Expose thyself to feel what wretches feel,
> That thou mayst shake the superflux to them,
> And show the heavens more just.
> (3.4.28–36)

For Lear this moment amounts to the first in a series of "recognition" scenes. He is beginning to understand that a life of privilege has blinded him to the real needs of those whose "houseless heads" have been battered by the storms of an injustice that resides in the very nature (or fallen nature) of things. He reproaches himself and all those ("Take physic, pomp") who, sheltered by noble birth, have never known the terrors or the helplessness of poverty.

When Lear encounters Tom o' Bedlam (who has taken refuge in the hovel) this moment of recognition is swiftly followed by another more symbolically profound moment of affirmation of his kinship with the wretched. Tom, as we know, is the persecuted Edgar disguised as

> the basest and most poorest shape
> That ever penury, in contempt of man,
> Brought near to beast.
> (2.3.7–9)

He is not, as some have argued, an image of the "noble savage",[10] for there is nothing noble in his abject appearance or manner. Nor does his near nakedness endow him with any uncorrupted innocence. He is rather the bestial image of man reduced to primal need that Lear had invoked earlier in his protest against his daughters' ruthlessness:

> Thou art the
> thing itself; unaccommodated man is no more
> but such a poor, bare, forked animal as thou art.
> (3.4.108–10)

Indeed, the raving, tattered, incoherent Tom anticipates the image of man in what Thomas Hobbes, a few decades later, would call the "state of nature", man bereft of "commodious Building" in a condition of "continuall feare, and danger of violent death", his life "solitary, poore, nasty, brutish, and short".[11] Lear, in a frenzy of desire to rid himself of the now abhorrent vestments of a life that he perceives as false, tears off his clothes: "Off, off, you lendings!" (3.4.111). Naked in the face of the still roaring tempest, he is one with the "unaccommodated" Tom.

Only the most obtuse of readers could fail to see the strikingly Christian motif of identification with the poor and the outcast in Lear's solidarity with his Fool and in his recognition

[10] Maurice Charney, "'We Put Fresh Garments on Him': Nakedness and Clothes in *King Lear*", in *Some Facets of King Lear*, ed. Rosalie Littell Colie and F. T. Flahiff (Toronto: University of Toronto Press, 1974), p. 79.

[11] Thomas Hobbes, *Leviathan* 1.13.

of existential kinship with Tom o' Bedlam. Such is the message of the Beatitudes and, indeed, of dozens of Gospel passages. Thrust out of the all-sheltering sacralized cosmos, out of the illusion of luxury and pomp into the barren and godless heath, Lear takes his first step toward the redeeming forgiveness of Cordelia in this discovery of the universality of suffering. Within the pagan setting of the play, this is as near as we are likely to get to a Christian vision of the fathomless condition of need that is the state of man after the Fall. Lear's nakedness, in this context, is not the innocent nakedness of Adamic man, but a prophetic renunciation of the worldly corruption that his garments have come to signify. As Frank Bottomley notes, that in the Old Testament, nakedness (after the Fall) is frequently associated with "poverty, destitution, and exposure" and is most often "a metaphor for complete vulnerability".[12] It is precisely that condition of utter vulnerability that Lear ecstatically embraces.

If we are seeking to trace the path of a providential pattern in *King Lear*, then clearly that path leads from Lear's encounter on the heath with Tom o' Bedlam to his reconciliation with Cordelia. Few characters in Shakespeare's plays have been required to carry such a hermeneutical burden as Cordelia, and much of this criticism has been excessive. On the one extreme, Christian interpreters such as John Danby have used the unwieldy apparatus of medieval exegesis to show that, presumably, Shakespeare was not only a brilliant playwright but a medieval theologian as well. One might question whether it is very plausible or even useful to argue, as Danby does, that Cordelia "is a figure comparable with ... Beatrice: literally a woman; allegorically the root of individual and social sanity; tropologically Charity 'that suffereth long and is kind'; anagogically the redemptive principle itself".[13] On the other extreme, William R. Elton has claimed for Cordelia the distinction of being

[12] Frank Bottomley, *Attitudes to the Body in Western Christendom* (London: Lepus, 1979), pp. 25–26.

[13] John Danby, *Shakespeare's Doctrine of Nature: A Study of 'King Lear'* (London: Faber and Faber, 1949), p. 125.

a figure of the "*prisca theologica*"—that is, a neo-pagan image of the pre-lapsarian Wisdom passed down by Adam by way of Seth and a host of subsequent magi, including the legendary Egyptian sage Hermes Trismegistus.[14] More modestly, G. Wilson Knight has argued that Cordelia "represents the principle of love",[15] but surely this is too vaguely stated in view of the distinctly Christian allusions that cluster around her character.

For example, when Cordelia returns from France and is making preparations to restore Lear to power, she says (addressing the absent Lear), "O dear father, / It is thy business that I go about" (4.4.23–24), a passage that clearly derives from Jesus' reply to his anxious parents when they discover him conversing in the Temple with learned doctors: "How is it that ye sought me? Wist ye not that I must be about my Father's business?" (Lk 2:49). In another instance, even more suggestive, a Gentleman sent to search for the wandering Lear remarks that

> Thou hast one daughter
> Who redeems nature from the general curse
> Which twain have brought her to.
> (4.6.208–10).

Since it is Christ Himself who "redeems nature from the general curse", it is tempting to suggest that this passage definitively identifies Cordelia as a figure of Christ's redeeming grace. But we must allow for context; the Gentleman in question appears to be speaking hyperbolically of a woman he has come to love and admire, though we cannot go so far as to discard the allusion altogether. Perhaps the most plausible approach to the problem would be to focus upon Cordelia's *role* at this juncture in the play. At least from Lear's perspective, she is the bearer of the hope of forgiveness, of what is unmistakably

[14] William R. Elton, *King Lear and the Gods* (Lexington: University Press of Kentucky, 1988), pp. 38–42.

[15] G. Wilson Knight, *The Wheel of Fire: Interpretations of Shakespearean Tragedy*, 4th ed. (London: Methuen, 1949), p. 201.

Christian forgiveness amid an ostensibly pagan world and, more profoundly, a world seemingly drained of any indwelling sacred presence.

It is Cordelia's forgiveness, an unconditional Christlike forgiveness, that restores Lear to sanity. More to the point, it is Cordelia's forgiveness that heals Lear's soul of the hellish agony of guilt and recrimination into which it had been plunged. It is that same forgiveness that provides the shelter from which he had earlier been expelled, the "roof" that he had "abjured". When Lear comes to his senses in the tent that Cordelia has provided, he is suffering—so he imagines—the torments of the damned. He takes Cordelia for "a soul in bliss" and believes himself "bound / Upon a wheel of fire" (4.7.46–47). He falls to his knees as he begins to recognize Cordelia as the daughter he has wronged, imploring her,

> If you have poison for me, I will drink it.
> I know you do not love me; for your sisters
> Have, as I do remember, done me wrong.
> You have some cause, they have not.
> (4.7.72–75)

Cordelia, for her part, never speaks any explicit words of forgiveness, but in her acts, her tone, her every word, she is forgiveness itself.

In spite of what appears in *King Lear* to be a providential pattern of purgatorial suffering, followed by forgiveness, reconciliation, and spiritual restoration, criticism in recent decades has attempted radically to deny this perspective. The shift seems to have taken place in the early 1960s and very much reflects the *avant-garde* philosophical and artistic concerns of the era. For example, Jan Kott's influential reading of the play finds there not tragedy precisely, but rather a new form of tragedy in which the predominant note is the *grotesque*. Tragedy in the classical sense of the term, as Kott correctly perceives, "is a confirmation and recognition of the absolute". Tragedy brings *catharsis*, whereas the grotesque "offers no consolation whatsoever".[16] *King Lear*, in this view, offers no recognition of the absolute, no consolation. Shakespeare is "our contemporary" because, at least in *King Lear*, his sensibility is closer to that one finds in the absurdist drama of a Beckett or an Ionesco. For the Polish Kott, Lear's world is one of senseless, seemingly arbitrary cruelty, a world not unlike the Eastern Europe where he experienced at close view the cruelty of the Nazi occupation and, in its aftermath, the terror of the Soviet occupation.[17]

However personal and exaggerated Kott's reading of *King Lear* may have been, his perspective spread rapidly in academia where a somewhat domesticated variation on Kott's approach to the play remains the conventional paradigm. Also influential, and possibly more representative of contemporary views, is Nicolas Brooke's reading of the play. From Brooke's perspective, *King Lear* deliberately raises our hopes for justice and redemption, only to shatter them. He questions the traditional view that "affirmation", or even the hope of affirmation, is the proper purpose of tragedy. By this he seems to mean that tragedy requires no redemptive horizon. In *King Lear* he finds that "all moral structures, whether of the natural order or Christian redemption, are invalidated by the naked fact of experience".[18]

What Kott and Brooke and many other more recent critics have found most appalling is the injustice of Cordelia's death, and not only the injustice, but the seemingly gratuitous manner in which it is perpetrated. It must be admitted that the play appears almost perversely to raise our hopes that Cordelia will somehow survive, then seems cruelly to taunt us with the frustration of those hopes. When the dying Edgar says,

[16] Jan Kott, *Shakespeare Our Contemporary*, trans. Boleslaw Taborski (Garden City, N.J.: Doubleday, 1964), p. 104.

[17] Although Kott was a member of the Polish Communist party after the war, his views were regarded with hostility by the authorities, and he resigned his membership in the party in 1957. His analysis of *King Lear* draws heavily upon the common experiences of Poles living in a totalitarian regime.

[18] Nicolas Brooke, "The Ending of *King Lear*", in *Shakespeare 1564–1964*, ed. E. A. Bloom (Providence, R.I.: Brown University Press, 1964), pp. 59–60.

> some good I mean to do,
> Despite of my own nature. Quickly send
> .... for my writ
> Is on the life of Lear and on Cordelia,
> (5.3.245–48)

we believe that Lear's reconciliation with his beloved daughter will now be complete. That hope is painfully denied us when Lear reappears on the stage with the dead Cordelia in his arms, then is revived again when Lear, bending over her corpse, believes that he sees signs of breath in her yet:

> This feather stirs; she lives. If it be so,
> It is a chance which does redeem all sorrows
> That ever I have felt. (5.3.267–69)

Then, when our capacity for tragic pity seems stretched to the snapping point, the same expectation is aroused again:

> Why should a dog, a horse, a rat, have life,
> And thou no breath at all? ....
> Do you see this? Look on her. Look, her lips,
> Look there, look there. (5.3.308–9, 312–13)

Thus Lear dies, by all appearances believing that Cordelia lives.

Those critics are simply misguided who argue that Lear's dying belief that Cordelia lives is a figural representation of the Christian hope of resurrection.[19] Moreover, this is a dangerous position, since Lear's belief is clearly an illusion—and thus, by extension (it might be argued) so also is the promise of resurrection. It is more persuasive, surely, given the mingled tone of hope and desperation in Lear's final speeches, that he dies torn between belief and uncertainty—which brings us to the central problem raised by the play's ending. Both those Christian critics who overzealously search for final assurance

[19] This argument can perhaps be traced back to Bradley, *Shakespearean Tragedy*, who says of Lear's illusion: "To us, perhaps, the knowledge that he is deceived may bring a culmination of pain: but if it brings us *only* that ... we are false to Shakespeare.... Lear's last accents and gestures [express] ... an unbearable joy" (p. 291).

of transcendence in the play and those who, opposing the Christian view, see Lear's cruel illusion as somehow negating the redemptive pattern that precedes it, are guilty of misunderstanding the nature of faith. Faith, properly understood, is by its very nature coupled with uncertainty. As philosopher Glenn Hughes eloquently notes:

> As a response to the appeal of a transcendent ground of meaning, the open soul must suffer the vicissitudes of *faith*—of affirming that its own meaning depends upon an intangible, unpossessible, essentially mysterious reality. The difficulties of faith ... are notoriously daunting. Basic to faith is the uncertainty involved in understanding that we cannot understand, in any substantive way, the answers to our most searching questions, [including] ... the mystery of evil and of its longed for resolution.[20]

To this must be added a final point. In the beginning, Lear selfishly demands from Cordelia an unreserved confession of love that is beyond her power to give:

> Sure I shall never marry like my sisters,
> To love my father all. (1.1.105–6)

Later, when they are reunited and led off to prison by Edgar, Lear still clings to that possessive illusion:

> Come, let's away to prison:
> We two alone will sing like birds i' th' cage. (5.3.8–9)

He imagines the two of them, "God's spies", together renouncing the world of pomp and power:

> Upon such sacrifices, my Cordelia,
> The gods themselves throw incense. Have I caught thee?
> (5.3.17, 20–21)

Yet as we have seen, the moral logic of the play demands that Lear be stripped of all such illusions. Ironically, Cordelia must

[20] Glenn Hughes, "Eric Voegelin and Christianity", *The Intercollegiate Review* Fall/Winter 2004, p. 31.

be offered up as a sacrifice upon the figurative altar of tragic necessity, but that necessity does not in itself negate the possibility of transcendent hope. On the contrary, if we say that the play's redemptive pattern is negated by Cordelia's death, then we have implied that her sacrificial love is meaningless, that it points toward no resolution of the mystery of injustice and evil. Such a denial itself implies a standpoint somehow removed from the flux of human uncertainty. Perhaps that confident assumption of the meaninglessness of human suffering is possible from the heights of the ivory tower. Against such arrogance we can only say with Saint Paul: "For now we see through a glass, darkly; but then face to face.... And now abideth faith, hope, charity, these three; but the greatest of these is charity" (1 Cor 13:12–13).

CONTRIBUTORS

James Bemis is an editorial board member and columnist for *California Political Review* and a frequent contributor to the *Saint Austin Review*, *The Wanderer*, and *The Latin Mass Magazine*.

Paul A. Cantor is Clifton Waller Barrett Professor of English at the University of Virginia. He is the author of numerous essays and several books on Shakespeare, including *Shakespeare's Rome: Republic and Empire* and the *Hamlet* volume in the Cambridge Landmarks of World Literature Series.

Robert Carballo, Ph.D. is Professor of English and Comparative Literature at Millersville University of Pennsylvania, where he served for many years as Director of Graduate English studies. He regularly teaches courses in Victorian literature, comparative literature, and drama. His publications include studies on John Henry Newman, Matthew Arnold, and Shakespeare, among others, and have appeared in scholarly journals in the United States, France, England, Puerto Rico, and Hungary.

Scott Crider is an Associate Professor of English and Director of the Writing Program at the University of Dallas. He has published articles on Shakespeare and a textbook, *The Office of Assertion: An Art of Rhetoric for the Academic Essay* (ISI, 2005). He is currently working on a book on Shakespeare and the ethics of rhetoric.

Joseph Pearce is Writer in Residence and Associate Professor of Literature at Ave Maria University in Naples, Florida. He is the author of many books, including literary biographies of Solzhenitsyn, Tolkien, C. S. Lewis, G. K. Chesterton, and Oscar Wilde.

Jack Trotter has a Ph.D. in Medieval and Renaissance Drama from Vanderbilt University. He teaches at Trident College in Charleston, South Carolina, and has written frequently on Shakespeare.

R.V. Young is Professor of English at North Carolina State University. In addition to scholarly books and articles on literature, he has also published in journals such as *Touchstone*, *First Things*, *Crisis*, and *National Review*.